REGENTS CRITICS SERIES

General Editor: Paul A. Olson

BERNARD SHAW'S
NONDRAMATIC LITERARY
CRITICISM

BERNARD SHAW'S NONDRAMATIC LITERARY CRITICISM

Edited by

Stanley Weintraub

UNIVERSITY OF NEBRASKA PRESS • LINCOLN

Regents Critics Series

The Regents Critics Series provides reading texts of significant literary critics in the Western tradition. The series treats criticism as a useful tool: an introduction to the critic's own poetry and prose if he is a poet or novelist, an introduction to other work in his day if he is more judge than creator. Nowhere is criticism regarded as an end in itself but as what it is—a means to the understanding of the language of art as it has existed and been understood in various periods and societies.

Each volume includes a scholarly introduction which describes how the work collected came to be written, and suggests its uses. All texts are edited in the most conservative fashion consonant with the production of a good reading text; and all translated texts observe the dictum that the letter gives life and the spirit kills when a technical or rigorous passage is being put into English. Other types of passages may be more freely treated. Footnoting and other scholarly paraphernalia are restricted to the essential minimum. Such features as a bibliographical check-list or an index are carried where they are appropriate to the work in hand. If a volume is the first collection of the author's critical writing, this is noted in the bibliographical data.

PAUL A. OLSON

University of Nebraska

Contents

Introduction

Bernard Shaw: The Social Critic as Literary Critic

*"For art's sake alone" I would not face the toil of writing a single
sentence.*—Preface to *Man and Superman* (1903)

In a writing career seldom characterized by understatement
Bernard Shaw remained remarkably modest about his contributions
to nondramatic criticism.[1] However little known, his literary criticism stimulated by the printed page rather than by plays and
performances furnishes uniquely Shavian insights into other writers
and writing, and provides the added bonus that it reflects Shaw's
own creative methods and motives.

Literary criticism was at first more a job for Shaw than a joy.
Most of it was done anonymously, when, in his late twenties and
early thirties, he was a book reviewer for the *Pall Mall Gazette*.
Later an enterprising editor would offer him as many guineas for a
single piece under the by-then-famous by-line as he had collected for
many months' work in the defunct *Gazette;* and it would be for a
book that really interested him.

As a body of criticism, whether produced originally for the *New
Statesman* or the *Evening Standard,* as a preface to a publication of
his own or as an introduction to a new edition of someone else's
work, Shaw's criticism remains remarkably consistent, especially
once we pass that early period when he reviewed books less because
he had something he wanted to say about them, or was interested
in using them as platform for saying something cogent, but because
he would be paid for the job. Yet even in that early phase, when
he had improved his fortunes to the point that he had replaced

1. In his Collected Edition, the volume *Pen Portraits and Reviews* included
reprints of some of his literary essays, but—as the title indicates—it put more
emphasis upon memoir-pieces than literary ones.

writing unsalable novels with steady but unguaranteed journalism, and no longer existed on his mother's earnings, he not only wrote honest reviews but often evidenced the direction his later criticism would consistently take.

Shaw's first serious literary criticism even antedated the *Gazette* stint—a response to a lecture on "Caliban upon Setebos" delivered to the Browning Society on April 25, 1884, and printed in the society's *Papers:*

> Shakspere, being a dramatic poet, has never labelled any work of his dramatic; Browning, being essentially undramatic, has called this Caliban poem a dramatic monologue. Now, there is a difference between the faculty of the dramatic poet and that of the epic or descriptive poet, and they are often strangely divided. The epic poet has a theory of the motives and feelings of his characters, and he describes his theory. The dramatic poet, whether he has a theory or not, instinctively puts the character before you acting and speaking as it would do in actual life. The merely epic and descriptive poet cannot do this. Milton had not the dramatic faculty very strongly; Shakspere had. If you compare Browning and Shakspere, you will find the difference coming out strongly. Browning makes Caliban minutely describe his own feelings and analyze his own thoughts. A creature in the brutish condition of Caliban would not be able to do anything of the sort; and here you have an initial absurdity,—an essentially undramatic condition, which shows you at once that what you are reading is no dramatic monologue at all. Shakspere's method is very simple. His Caliban does not reason about God; but he is terrified by a thunderstorm.

This was the dramatic critic and playwright in Shaw, struggling for birth, as much as the literary critic to be. And as would always be the case, there was for his audience, however much he offended their predilections—and these were Browning idolators—the redeeming Shavian wit. "Browning's Caliban," he concluded to the Browningites, "is a savage, with the introspective powers of a Hamlet, and the theology of an evangelical Churchman. I must confess that I cannot conceive an evangelical Churchman possessing the introspective powers of a Hamlet." In a parenthesis following, the transcript noted, "Great laughter."[2]

At about the same time Shaw had become friendly with William Archer, a young man already successful in London journalism and with whom Shaw abortively collaborated on a play he later turned on his own into *Widowers' Houses*. Through Archer he also acquired literary employment, by the end of 1885 having begun reviewing art in the *World* and books in the *Pall Mall Gazette*. Archer had passed on several of his assignments and in unauthorized but effective fashion Shaw quickly proved his ability to the editors. He got the jobs.

Between 1885 and 1888, while he was switching from art critic to music critic, Shaw continued producing anonymous reviews for the *Gazette*, 107 of them reaching print, along with occasional other writings ranging from musical and dramatic criticism to letters, notes, reports, and spoofs, some contributed under transparently pseudonymous by-lines. But few of the books he was assigned were worth the time he spent reviewing them—*"Verona," and other Poems*, by L. Ormiston Chant, a handbook on physiognomy, a biography of a minor Scottish painter, an excruciatingly bad novel by F. Marion Crawford, the memoirs of a forgotten physician. Others, meanwhile, two of them also young Irishmen, wrote reviews of the major writers.

2. Eleven years later Shaw had more to say about Browning's poem, in a review of Max Nordau's book *Degeneration* he wrote for the American magazine *Liberty* and afterwards expanded into *The Sanity of Art:*

Passion is the stream in the engine of all religious and moral systems. In so far as it is malevolent, the religious are malevolent too, and insist on human sacrifices, on hell, wrath, and vengeance. You cannot read Browning's Caliban upon Setebos (Natural Theology in The Island) without admitting that all our religions have been made as Caliban made his, and that the difference between Caliban and Prospero is not that Prospero had killed passion in himself whilst Caliban has yielded to it, but that Prospero is mastered by holier passions than Caliban's. Abstract principles of conduct break down in practice because kindness and truth and justice are not duties founded on abstract principles external to man, but human passions, which have, in their time, conflicted with higher passions as well as with lower ones.

George Moore was reviewing Huysmans and Zola, and an even younger man named Oscar Wilde was being assigned Turgenev, Tolstoy, Dostoevsky, George Sand, William Morris, and Walter Pater. Shaw chafed quietly as long as the income seemed essential, then in September, 1888, wrote in frustration to the literary editor asking for something significant "as relief to the slow murder of the cursed parcels of rubbish with which you blast my prime. Surely it must be dawning on editors at last that any sort of live copy is better than the mechanical literary stuff poured out on ordinary novels and minor poetry. Why condemn me to read things that I can't review— that no artistic conscience could long survive the reviewing of!" And he went on to suggest that the *Gazette* might just as well review "boots, hats, dogcarts and so on" rather than the latest claptrap novel by Miss Braddon. "There ought to be legislation against this sort of thing—on the lines of the Factory Acts." Thus when Shaw had prepared a lecture the year before for one of the many literary, debating, and reading groups in which he was active, his theme truth in fiction, a subject about which he railed in angry-young-critic fashion, he could speak from the painful experience of having read too much of their work, about the "earnest and able young writers [who], when they commit themselves to the maintenance of a wife and family, or to the habits of fashionable society, or to both at once, degenerate first into elegant triflers, and finally into incurable hacks, absolutely without consciences."

By the end of 1888, although he was finished as a regular book critic, he was just at the beginning of real literary criticism. Still, he had already made the most of his few opportunities, doing missionary work for a nonliterary effort by Samuel Butler, *Luck or Cunning?*, and for Thomas Tyler's thesis that Mary Fitton was the Dark Lady in Shakespeare's *Sonnets*. He had also reviewed bad novels by Wilkie Collins and George Moore—yet at least these were substantial writers. And where he could, even in a notice of a minor title, he would use the occasion for a pronouncement about a major figure, praising Anthony Trollope, for example, in a long paragraph in a review in which Trollope's name need not have been produced. "Society has not yet forgiven that excellent novelist," Shaw wrote, "for having worked so many hours a day, like a carpenter or tailor, instead of going periodically mad with inspiration and hewing Barchester Towers at one frenzied stroke out of chaos, that being notoriously the only genuine artistic method. Yet if we except the giants of the craft, he is entitled to rank among English writers as the first sincerely naturalistic novelist of our day. He delivered us from the marvels, senseless accidents, and cat's cradle plots of old romance."

Later, in a self-interview he published to promote one of his own plays, when asked to reveal a bit of the plot Shaw teased that he was a dramatic poet, not a plotmonger. He was consistent in maintaining that a plot was the least important part of a story. Wilkie Collins, he had written in the *Gazette* in 1886, "shackled and crippled his genius" through "procrustean scaffolds" called plots. "The proper framework for a book is its own natural skeleton: if it be born without one, then let it perish as a shapeless abortion." Often, as here, Shakespeare was Shaw's negative example, his plots allegedly deforming his plays; and later in an essay on Dickens, Shaw withheld the admiration he felt for the later novels from the incomplete last work, *The Mystery of Edwin Drood*, in which he saw the baleful plot-focused influence of Dickens's friend Collins. "Novels," he insisted as early as the 1886 review, "are like other works of art: uninteresting just so far as they are machine made."

Criticizing the revered Shakespeare, even more than the beloved Dickens, was a sacrilege likely to place a bumptious young critic in jeopardy, but Shaw had his own ideas about the role of a critic. It did not follow, he held, that the right to criticize Shakespeare involved "the power of writing better plays." An artist had to be criticized on other terms, among those his ability to reach and sustain his personal peak. "A man's work," he maintained as early as the 1887 lecture, "should be for his best audience, even if it be an ideal audience." It was an easy preachment for a young critic, who learned as he earned his bread among theater audiences that even the greatest writers had to find audiences with potboilers who could not be reached by masterpieces. In part Shaw the critic was exhibiting the critic's need for a certain kind of fulfillment he described well in a musical review in 1891—"that although the satisfaction of seeing a simple thing consummately well done is most joyful and soothing after a long and worrying course of complex things imperfectly done, the simple success must not therefore be placed above the complex half success." But a critic, he wrote at about the same time, was a missionary and elucidator, not a judge and executioner. He did not have the power of life or death over a work of art: "Though the east wind seems to kill the consumptive patient, he dies, not of the wind, but of phthisis. On the strong-lunged man it blows in vain."

A critic had a corollary duty as well, as Shaw observed after viewing an elaborately and expensively mounted Christmas pantomime in 1890: "What struck me most was the extraordinary profusion of artistic talent wasted through mere poverty of purpose." In the 1887 lecture he could not comprehend the "metaphysics" of "art for art's sake," for he was convinced that "a man can be the better or [the] worse morally for going to the theatre or reading a book." Because Art was not "outside the sphere of morals," he insisted that "a work of fiction should have a purpose." Yet if the purpose were today's, or tomorrow's, rather than yesterday's, he recognized that there would be consumer resistance. The novelist, he was aware, could set out to write on a different plan than the mere reproduction of convenient bundles of personified virtues and vices. His hero or heroine could be "simply the most highly evolved person in the book; and if his actions be only dictated by sufficiently developed intelligence, self-control, and, above all, foresight, they will appear a series of crimes, and he an unfeeling scoundrel to the less evolved characters, and to the average reader, whilst yet his superiority will be mysteriously evident throughout." It was a theory he had tried out in his novels with conspicuous lack of success, for he had conceived of several of his leading characters as "improved types of humanity." Yet in a number of his best plays—*Caesar* and *Barbara* and *Joan*, for example—Shaw's title figures are embodiments of his ideas about the possibilities of the race. In his last years his views remained unchanged, and in a 1944 "Postscript" to his *Back to Methuselah* preface to mark its publication in the Oxford

World Classics series he defined a world classic as a work which would "try to solve, or at least to formulate, the riddles of creation." But these might take the form of heresies, which he realized would inevitably be resisted; thus he saw high purpose and high art as the difficult twin concomitants of greatness in literature: "Heretical teaching must be made irresistibly attractive by fine art if the heretics are not to starve or burn."

Samuel Butler's *The Way of All Flesh* was a triumph by his standards—a work of art which not only had a purpose but had succeeded in it: "Butler forged his jests into a weapon which smashed the nineteenth century." There were never enough Butlers. In Shaw's *Pall Mall Gazette* days the nineteenth century was still very much alive. "The most dangerous public house in London," he punned in 1887, ". . . is kept by a gentleman named Mudie." Mudie's and Smith's bookstalls and lending libraries still retained their stranglehold on what the English reader read, for their bulk orders—or their withdrawal—meant the difference between profit and loss on most books and had resulted in a publishers' self-censorship which had emotionally and intellectually emasculated fiction. In a letter to the *Gazette* the same year Shaw, describing himself as "a sufferer from that strange brain disease which drives its victims to write long stories that are not true, and to delight in them more than in any other literature," suggested realistically that cheap editions by publishers would do more to break the power of the circulating libraries than impassioned declamations against their monopoly. Referring to their kind of book and its readership Shaw had noted in an anonymous *Gazette* review the year before, "We always have with us men and women who, born after their due time, clamour to have the clock put back, and would, if they might have their way, reinstate flogging, duelling, confiscation of the property of wives, and a dozen other barbarisms which the rest of us have outgrown." It meant, too, Shaw observed at about the same time, that writers could—and often had to—purvey a "No Man's Land of luxuries for which there is nothing to pay, of poignant griefs that do not hurt, thrilling joys that do not satisfy, virtuous aspirations that do not ennoble, and fierce crusades that leave evil

none the weaker, but rather the more prosperous for the advertisement." It meant, too, that even the most courageous writers sometimes had to work at titillation while being less than direct and less
than candid, Shaw paradoxically attacking one of George Moore's
weaker novels, *A Mere Accident*, not for using a rape as his central
incident and evading the crucial scene by having the victim insensible at the moment, but because the incident—so far as it is described
—"is described for its own sake. . . . The objection, in fact, to Mr.
Moore is not that he is realistic, but that he is a romancer who, in
order that he might take liberties, persuades himself that he is a
pathologist."[3]

Pseudopathology was often licensed by Mudie when Zolaesque
honesty would land a publisher (as happened with Henry Vizetelly)
not on Mudie's shelves but in prison. Searching for the success formula of one of the few popular novelists for whom he retained some
grudging admiration, Shaw saw a half-voyeuristic, half-critical view
of society which made the clever Ouida[4] both pander and perceptive
critic. (She wrote of the pleasure-loving society about which people
love to read and which "breeds monsters," in "half-reasoned but
real" terms which imaginatively combined mock sociology and
spurious sex.) The suggestive qualities of books by women novelists
had long been an accepted fact of Victorian literary life, as a *Punch*
cartoon in 1867 had indicated. A man, shopping for a novel at the
counter of a bookshop, inspects one volume he has opened and
announces through his muttonchop whiskers, "Ah! very Clever, I
dare say. But I see it's written by a Lady, and *I* want a book that my

3. Ironically, it was George Moore who was chief enemy of the Mudie
and Smith censorship, prefacing a Zola translation with the declaration, "We
judge a pudding by the eating, and I judge Messrs. Mudie and Smith by
what they have produced; for they . . . are the authors of our fiction." In an
1885 pamphlet, *Literature at Nurse, or Circulating Morals,* Moore had cen-
sured Mudie for hypocrisy, quoting at length from novels he had passed, and
urged the public to withdraw its patronage from libraries which failed to
furnish the books it wanted. Eventually cheap editions, including Moore's,
rather than polemics, defeated the library censorship.
4. Mary Louise de la Ramée (1839–1908).

Daughters may read. Give me Something else!" For the social criticism in fiction Shaw was willing to forgive much, but when he found
insufficiently redeeming social content he was unwilling to forgive
either the sensuality or the artificiality, noting in the *Gazette* that in
some of the works of Ouida and her disciple Marie Corelli there was
not only "an almost rancourous insistence on the corruption of
society," but an artificiality of background ("drop scenery, in short")
and "a partial view of character, resulting from a keen insight into
the erotic impulses without sufficient observation or study of the
rest of life."

Shaw consistently railed against the imposition of a gratuitous
erotic interest into literature on the excuse that the public wanted it,
pointing to the then contemporary examples of Wells's *Time Machine*
and Bellamy's *Looking Backward*, futuristic fictions sapped in intellectual power by the infusion of amorous sentimentality. "The
pleasures of the senses I can sympathize with and share," he declared; "but the substitution of sensuous ecstasy for intellectual
activity and honesty is the very devil . . . for all institutions have in
the long run to live by the nature of things, and not by childish pretendings." He had always been, he confessed ironically in 1900, a
Puritan in his attitude toward Art. "I am as fond of fine music and
a handsome building as Milton was, or Cromwell, or Bunyan; but if
I found that they were becoming the instruments of a systematic
idolatry of sensuousness, I would hold it good statesmanship to blow
every cathedral in the world to pieces with dynamite, organ and all,
without the least heed to the screams of the art critics and cultured
voluptuaries." Still, he found value even in sheer pruriency, which,
in the 1920s, he said he liked "when it was well done. It has never
occurred to me to try to prevent anyone else reading it. You must
let people eat what agrees with them, even if it seems to you to be
garbage." But there was a higher utility for literary obscenity, or
what passes for obscenity at different periods, Shaw being well aware
that works of his at various times had been censored on such
grounds, and that he had been railed at himself from pulpits and
editorial pages for so seemingly harmless a word as *bloody* when first
used in a popular play (in *Pygmalion*). "The nation's morals," he

wrote after an earlier censorship problem, "are like its teeth: the
more decayed they are the more it hurts to touch them."

Self-righteousness about sex and obscenity in literature was such
a symptom, Shaw thought, seeing a "classic quality" in James Joyce,
and although self-confessedly too prudish to use some of Joyce's
words he thought nonetheless that there should be no limit to "blackguardly language. . . . It depends on what people will stand." The
important thing to him about the controversial texture of Joyce's
work was that his exposure of seaminess in Dublin had a moral
value.[5] "You cannot carry out moral sanitation, any more than physical sanitation, without indecent exposures. . . . If a man holds up a
mirror to your nature and shows you that it needs washing—not
whitewashing—it is no use breaking the mirror. Go for soap and
water." There had always been an economic moral in sex for Shaw,
as had been apparent as early as his condemnation of an exploiting
society in *Mrs. Warren's Profession;* and in the 1920s he added that
there would never be "a healthily sexed literature until you have a
healthily sexed people; and that is impossible under Capitalism,
which imposes commercial conditions on marriage as on everything
else." Ideally, he thought, fiction should deal with healthy people
in circumstances which are—for the imagined period—normal, while
the abnormal and the morbid side of life belonged to the newspapers.
But he understood that this was an impossibility as long as the reaction to nineteenth-century censorship and hypocrisy had to run its
course. "I doubt if there is a single excess in modern fiction that
cannot be traced to a suppression in the reign of Queen Victoria.
It is just because Mr. James Joyce was brought up on the reticences
of the heroes and heroines of Sir Walter Scott that he is so embarrassingly communicative as to the indiscretions of his own heroes
and heroines."

Although Shaw refused to subscribe to the first edition of *Ulysses,*
writing the publisher, Sylvia Beach, that no Irishman would pay 150

5. Joyce had written to his prospective publisher of *Dubliners* that the
book, written with "scrupulous meanness," was intended as a "chapter of the
moral history of my country" and a "first step toward the spiritual liberation
of my country."

francs for a book, and his explanation to her, based on his having read parts of the novel in serial form, has often been ascribed as negative, he nevertheless used such phrases about it as "truthful," "hideously real," and "literary genius," and in several thoughtful paragraphs in the autobiographical preface to the first printing of *Immaturity* (1930) referred to Joyce's Dublin as described "with a fidelity so ruthless that the book is hardly bearable." His first mention of Joyce in what could be called literary criticism had occurred even earlier, when he gave one of his rare lectures on literature, this one at the Little Theatre in Dublin in 1918.[6] An account of it survives in the diary of Joseph Holloway, an Abbey Theatre devotee and passionate Irish nationalist whose references to Shaw were almost always hostile:

> Saturday, October 26. . . . I went down to hear Shaw's discourse on "Literature in Ireland" at the little theatre. . . . His discourse was quite Shavian in his findings, and he kept nagging all the while he spoke; he afterwards said he knew he was nagging, but once set going he could not stop. Only those who don't succeed in art or literature make good critics was his opinion; therefore, he was no critic. He didn't read critically. It was only when they went to Paris Irishmen could write, and then he spoke of George Moore's and Joyce's works and their indecencies. He also said that Synge got his local colour in Paris, and that there is nothing Irish about The Playboy. The central idea is that the worship of crime is universal; in fact, the Irish people don't understand it. Then he went on to say that the Irish should be conscripted out of their own country so that they would learn to know what Ireland was really like. He also said they could never get anything until they ceased to have a grievance. Nobody liked people with a grievance; they were generally bores. The men who didn't leave Ireland wouldn't write like Synge. The plays that were written by Irishmen who

6. Reports survive of two other literary lectures during that decade, one on drama at Oxford just before the war, and another on fiction to a Fabian summer school session during the war.

never travelled were generally those that lacked poetic outlook and were sordid and abusive in character. . . . Shaw is always stimulating and entertaining and never dull. He mixed all he said with a very nimble wit, and his words came ever ready to his lips. He speaks excellently well always, and his delivery is clear and telling!

While Shaw will never be celebrated for his Joyce criticism, or his appreciation of Irish writers in general, he remains one of the better commentators on Dickens, who, along with Bunyan, Butler, and (yes!) Shakespeare, was one of his major English literary heroes. But to Shaw there was a lesser and a greater Dickens, the former being the portrayer of great comic characters before he developed a social conscience. He made the point in a 1906 letter to G. K. Chesterton, and elaborated on it in memorable prefaces to new editions of *Great Expectations* (1937) and *Hard Times* (1912). One paragraph to Chesterton sums it up:

> I find that Dickens is at his greatest after the social awakening which produced Hard Times. Little Dorrit is an enormous work. The change is partly the disillusion produced by the unveiling of capitalist civilization, but partly also Dickens's discovery of the gulf between himself as a man of genius and the public. That he did not realize this early is shown by the fact that he found out his wife before he married her as much too small for the job, and yet plumbed the difference so inadequately that he married her thinking he could go through with it. When the situation became intolerable, he must have faced the fact that there was something more than "incompatibilities" between him and the average man and woman. Little Dorrit is written, like all the later books, frankly and somewhat sadly, *de haut en bas*. In them Dickens recognizes that quite everyday men are as grotesque as Bunsby. Sparkler, one of the most extravagant of all his gargoyles, is an untouched photograph almost. Wegg and Riderhood are sinister and terrifying because they are simply real, which Squeers and Sikes are not.

Shaw also had theory for Chesterton to explain what both saw as a shift in tone between the two parts of *David Copperfield*. It is a convincing hypothesis:

> There is a curious contrast between Dickens's sentimental indiscretions concerning his marriage and his sorrows and quarrels, and his impenetrable reserve about himself as displayed in his published correspondence. He writes to his family about waiters, about hotels, about screeching tumblers of hot brandy and water, and about the seasick man in the next berth, but never one really intimate word, never a real confession of his soul. David Copperfield is a failure as an autobiography because when he comes to deal with the grown-up David, you find that he has not the slightest intention of telling you the truth—or indeed anything—about himself. Even the child David is more remarkable for the reserves than for the revelations: he falls back on fiction at every turn. Clennam and Pip are the real autobiographies.

For the text of *Great Expectations*, to which Shaw furnished his famous preface, he supplied as well the original, and perhaps more artistic, ending to the novel, which Dickens had discarded in favor of the false sentimentality Victorian readers craved. Shaw understood that both conclusions were wistful and that both provided the hero with some consolation, but in this first restoration of the original ending in a modern edition of the novel Shaw wanted readers to see not only how the story might have turned out for Pip and Estella, but how ending a novel was a problem Dickens regularly had to face in the context of popular taste. In *Dombey and Son*, Shaw observed, Dickens had been planning an ending which would include the "degeneration and ruin" of Walter Gay, but instead Walter unexpectedly returns to marry Florence Dombey, providing "a manufactured ending to save a painful one." Similarly, he saw Mr. Pickwick turn from butt to hero of *Pickwick Papers* as Dickens studied reader reaction to the serial parts; and he found that *Martin Chuzzlewit* "begins as a study in selfishness and ends nowhere." Even in *Our*

Mutual Friend, one of the peaks in the canon to Shaw, the dustman Boffin's apparent corruption by wealth[7] is only a benevolent pretense to satisfy middle-class morality. The happy endings, including the one in the intense and bitter *Our Mutual Friend*, are in Shaw's view "consolations" which become "unnecessary and even irritating" as, under Dickens's own tutelage, "our minds grow stronger and sterner."

"Trollope and Thackeray could see Chesney Wold," Shaw wrote of *Hard Times*; "but Dickens could see through it." It is the writer in maturity who, to Shaw, capsulized for Victorian fiction the preachments of Carlyle, Marx, Ruskin, and Morris "that it is not our disorder but our order that is horrible." Thus while never losing sight of the compromises which Dickens, even in his later, greater novels felt forced to make, Shaw emphasized the social critic and revolutionary that had emerged from Dickens's dissection of his world and his conversion during the 1850s to a sense of "social sin." "Marx knew he was a revolutionist," Shaw wrote, "whilst Dickens had not the faintest suspicion of that part of his calling. . . . Little Dorrit is a more seditious book than Das Kapital. All over Europe men and women are in prison for pamphlets and speeches which are to Little Dorrit as red pepper to dynamite." But Dickens would not have understood, whatever his sense of social outrage. He was hardly a systematic thinker, and as J. B. Priestley put it, while Shaw wanted to abolish the poor and replace them with sensible people, Dickens only wanted to make the poor happy. Shaw's embrace of Dickens as humorist and satirist was genuine, but his vision of the novelist would have embarrassed Dickens. In the words of George Ford, in *Dickens and His Readers* (1965), "his hug is hugely affectionate but so powerful that the object of his affections is squeezed out of shape."

Even in viewing the nineteenth-century romantic poets Shaw used a moral perspective. Shelley, he thought, had first been seen as a moral monster, but by the end of the century critics were attempting

7. Noddy Boffin, the dustman who inherits a fortune from the miserly dust-removal contractor Harmon, and is immediately beset by selfish merchants, begging relatives, and rapacious charities, is a clear precursor of Shaw's Alfred Doolittle in *Pygmalion*.

to find in him a latter-day sanctity by stressing the beauty of his lyrics and shunting aside his major poetic statements as indiscretions. The approach was one Shaw found repellent, emphasizing that Shelley's longer poems, like his political and philosophical writings, were serious and carefully thought out in their moral position, something Shaw found seldom to be so with English poets, up to and including the contemporary great name, Tennyson. If Shelley was a sinner, he declared, "he was a hardened sinner, and a deliberate one." Surprisingly, Shaw managed, in a convincing tour de force of critical imagination, to also find a radical social critic in Keats, in whom he saw more than a writer of lovely lyrics. "It often happens," he observed, "that a prophet-poet begins as a literary poet, the prophet instinctively training himself by literary exercises for his future work." But Keats, Shaw regretted, did not live long enough to effect the transition, although he "achieved the very curious feat of writing one poem of which it may be said that if Karl Marx can be imagined as writing a poem instead of a treatise on Capital, he would have written Isabella." [8] Few indictments of capitalistic exploitation of, and profiteering upon, human misery seemed to him more forcible than several stanzas of Keats beginning

> With her two brothers this fair lady dwelt
>   Enrichéd from ancestral merchandise;
> And for them many a weary hand did swelt
>   In torchéd mines and noisy factories. . . .

"Nothing could be more literary than the wording . . . ," Shaw wrote. "But it contains all the Factory Commission Reports that Marx read, and that Keats did not read because they were not yet written in his time. And so Keats is among the prophets with Shelley, and, had he lived, would no doubt have come down from Hyperions and

8. Yet Shaw also saw in Keats something rare among "lyrical genius of the first order," the quality of "geniality," generally missing from artists who took themselves and their work seriously. Keats "could not only carry his splendid burthen of genius, but swing it round, toss it up and catch it again, and whistle a tune as he strode along."

Endymions to tin tacks as a very full-blooded modern revolutionist."

On rare occasions Shaw searched almost in vain for a moral focus in a writer he intended to praise, writing a centenary piece on Poe partly because he had accepted a commission to do it, and partly because he genuinely enjoyed Poe as a lyric poet. There were only two writers then in the American pantheon, he thought, Poe and Whitman. (He would add Twain later, but the novelist was still alive.) At a time when even the best other American writers were philistines, Poe to Shaw was a natural aristocrat, a writer of "exquisitely refined" poetry that was magical in its beauty. But Poe was also great because he was in his writings (and here Shaw found his theme) "independent of sex, of patriotism, of fighting, of sentimentality, snobbery, gluttony, and all the rest of the vulgar stock-in-trade of his profession. This is what gives him his superb distinction."

With some strain Shaw had found a negative approach to explain his affection for Poe. It was what Poe did *not* resort to in subject matter that justified him. Elsewhere Shaw would continue to maintain that "the main thing in determining the artistic quality of a book is not the opinions it propagates, but the fact that the writer has opinions. . . . I cannot be a belletrist. No doubt I must recognize, as even the Ancient Mariner did, that I must tell my story entertainingly if I am to hold the wedding guest spellbound in spite of the siren sounds of the loud bassoon. . . . But a true original style is never achieved for its own sake. . . . Effectiveness of assertion is the Alpha and Omega of style. He who has nothing to assert has no style and can have none." The style, if powerful enough, would survive the assertion, he thought, pointing for evidence to ancient and medieval art and music as well as literature. Further, he thought, the assertion could reasonably be reinterpreted or even misinterpreted by critics, who had as much right to their insights as the artist did to his original creation; for the creator when inspired was working beyond himself, and when only churning out copy was beneath serious criticism.

Writing that aspired to the name of literature, Shaw insisted, and would insist to the end, "is not a keyhole for people with starved affections to peep through at the banquets of the body." Poe, to his credit, he said, did not seek that end. "Life cannot give you what he gives you except through fine art."[9] What the highest literary art should provide Shaw had explained in 1895, in a condemnatory review of Max Nordau's *Degeneration*—a book, which, paradoxically, attacked the art-for-art's-sake school with which Shaw found little sympathy. Shaw's point of view never changed, no matter what he wrote, over the remaining fifty-five years of his life:

> The claim of art to our respect must stand or fall with the validity of its pretension to cultivate and refine our senses and faculties until seeing, hearing, feeling, smelling, and tasting become highly conscious and critical acts with us, protesting vehemently against ugliness, noise, discordant speech, frowzy clothing, and re-breathed air, and taking keen interest and pleasure in beauty, in music, and in nature, besides making us insist, as necessary for comfort and decency, on clean, wholesome, handsome fabrics to wear, and utensils of fine material and elegant workmanship to handle. Further, art should refine our sense of character and conduct, of justice and sympathy, greatly heightening our self-knowledge, self-control, precision of action, and considerateness, and making us intolerant of baseness, cruelty, injustice, and intellectual superficiality or vulgarity. The worthy artist or craftsman is he who serves the physical and moral senses by feeding them with pictures, musical compositions, pleasant houses and gardens, good clothes and fine implements, poems, fictions, essays, and dramas which call the heightened senses and ennobled faculties into pleasurable activity. The great artist is he who goes a step beyond the demand, and, by supplying works of a higher beauty and a higher interest than have yet been perceived, succeeds after a brief struggle with its strangeness, in adding this fresh extension of sense to the heritage of the race.

Although Shaw's artist-philosopher could be a poet with a pur-

9. As Shaw put it in his Ruskin lecture, "You may aim at making a man cultured and religious, but you must feed him first.... Unless you build on that, all your [cultural and social] superstructure will be rotten."

pose, he was more likely a writer of prose, and at his highest very likely a playwright like Sophocles or Shakespeare or a polemicist with an inherent sense of drama on the order of Bunyan. Poetry to Shaw was often "prosaic fabric disguised as poetry by the arts of versification"; and no man knew better than Milton, he wrote in his essay on Keats, that "prose has a music of its own, and that many pensters write verses because their ears are not good enough to enable them to write readable prose." Blank verse in particular failed to earn his awe. It was "so childishly easy and expeditious" that it explained Shakespeare's "copious output" to him, and inspired his parody of Elizabethan blank verse, the farce *The Admirable Bashville* (1902), poetasted from his jejune novel *Cashel Byron's Profession* (1882) in a week, he claimed, when a prose version would have taken him a month.

Having discovered early that the novel was not his forte, but that he could write crisp dialogue, Shaw naturally saw the novel as a lesser form of the writer's art than the drama, attacking with delight Arnold Bennett's thesis in *The Author's Craft* (1914) that "a play is easier to write than a novel." (Bennett, Shaw diplomatically did not mention, was a failed playwright.) One simplistic reason Bennett had given for his elevation of the novel over the play is "that a play is shorter than a novel," leaving Shaw to quote Pascal's statement, "Excuse the length of my letter. I had no time to write a short one." And Shaw followed up his barb by rewriting the "Lay on, Macduff" scene from *Macbeth* "as a chapter in a novel in the style of my friends Bennett and Galsworthy when they are too lazy to write plays." That sort of writing, Shaw concluded, he could produce "by the hundred thousand words on my head" or even "make a typewriter attachment that would do it." But in truth he denigrated no literary genre. "Fine art of any sort is either easy or impossible."

For Shaw the art of criticism, especially when it came to music and theater, was easy; but his purely literary criticism, once he no longer had to produce it, was irregular in appearance and often uninspired. At its best it was intellectualy agile, complementary to the philosophical biases of his plays, and a joy to read. Pillaged from the prefaces, looted from the lectures, or extricated from his journalism, his major statements on writers and writing have a life of their own.

A Note on the Text

Earlier writings have been edited into conformity with Shaw's later style, which was characterized by the elimination of italics and quotation marks in titles, omission of most apostrophes in contractions, and of some hyphens in compound words. Peculiarities and inconsistencies of spelling (including variant spellings of Shakespeare) have been retained.

In any other place where the text has been tampered with for reasons not specified above, an editor's note explains the alteration. Editorial deletions are indicated by three asterisks (* * *).

Some of Shaw's critical writings have been reprinted before, in his Collected Edition volume *Pen Portraits and Reviews* (London, 1931), long out of print. Even that volume contained more personality sketches than criticism, and lacked the early journalistic reviews, the literary parts of the famous prefaces, the Dickens essays and the Ruskin lecture, as well as other literary criticism included here. "Ruskin's Politics" was reprinted in *Platform and Pulpit,* ed. Dan H. Laurence (London and New York, 1961). Each essay or extract in the current volume is identified by its first appearance in print or its manuscript location.

STANLEY WEINTRAUB

Pennsylvania State University

I. THE ANGRY YOUNG CRITIC

Fiction and Truth

A lecture Shaw prepared for delivery in April, 1887, when he was thirty, "Fiction and Truth" was not published in his lifetime. It is reproduced here as edited from the holograph manuscript in the British Museum Shaw Archive. At the time of the lecture Shaw was writing anonymous book reviews for the Pall Mall Gazette *and had already written five disappointing novels. Ironically, considering his comments, on May 14, 1887, he began a sixth novel, which he worked at less than halfheartedly and finally abandoned in January, 1888. The fragment remained unpublished until 1958.*

The common saying that Truth is stranger than Fiction, implying that Fiction is not Truth, raises the question whether a writer of Fiction is anything better than a mere liar. His business is to persuade people that things have happened which never really did happen, and that persons have existed who never actually did exist. He tells us of crimes, shipwrecks, fights, fires, and love affairs of which humanity is guiltless. What is more important, he invents a morality of these things, and, by repeated fictitious instances, creates a public opinion that it is indecent in a young man not to be athletic, violent, and quarrelsome, or in a young woman to survive a disappointment in love, or in anybody to doubt that love affairs are, beyond all other mundane matters, the highest, holiest, and most exclusively worthy of our deepest consideration. The extent to which this fictitious morality influences conduct was felt by Larochefoucauld[1] when he said that very few people would fall in love if they had never read anything about it. If he were alive now, when everybody is taught to read, and when stacks of fiction are on every stationer's

1. François de La Rochefoucauld (1613–1680) was France's greatest maxim writer (*Maxims*, 1665), and a profound influence upon Shaw's appendix to *Man and Superman* (1903), "Maxims for Revolutionists."

counter to be retailed in pennyworths to readers of all classes, he might say the same of many crimes and follies even more serious than falling in love. Many of our worst habits are acquired in an imaginary world, created by Frankensteins whose only excuse is that they are not intelligent enough to be conscious of their ignorance and insincerity. Every man wishes to act like the hero of a novel: every woman like the heroine. If the average novel-hero is an idle gentleman and an egotistical snob when he is not plunging into the Thames after drowning women, or opportunely knocking down rude villains:—if the average heroine is influenced by amativeness and nothing else from end to end of her adventures, all young people who do not conform to these types will be ashamed of their virtues, and will conscientiously struggle to suppress them. When they have succeeded, bad novels will have made a bad nation. Then, cries the Bismarckian statesman, let us suppress bad novels. Let us have a censor. But if the censor be not himself infected with the novelistic morality, he will be dislodged by public opinion as either righteous overmuch, or else outrageous and disreputable in his views. If, on the other hand, his morals are novelistic, he will suppress, not the bad novels, but the good ones, because he is corrupt: he thinks the novelistic novel good and the naturalistic novel bad; and thence, in the upshot, the fictitious morality will receive official sanction and gain greater authority than ever. We have a practical example of this in the influence of our official licenser of plays,[2] under whose arbitrary rule only two sorts of play are certain of toleration—Drury Lane melodramas and Criterion farcical comedies, respectively the most absurd and the most indecent forms of composition for the stage known to us.

Obviously then, Fiction cannot be moralized by a Censor. Nor can it be wholly forbidden, since the popular craving for it is unappeas-

2. Until September, 1968, for more than three centuries one royal appointee had despotic power to decide what plays could be publicly performed in theaters in England. As censor, the Lord Chamberlain could order an offending word, line, or scene striken from a script or ban a play altogether by refusing to license it. Shaw, who had three of his own plays so interdicted, the first of them *Mrs. Warren's Profession* (1893), fought against the censorship all his life.

able. Neither can it be outlawed by withholding copyright from authors of Fiction, since that, in our existing individualistic social arrangements, would make them absolutely dependent for their remuneration on instantaneous success, or what are called "advance sheets," a state of things which would make the largest circulation in the world the normal standard in literary fiction. The only real remedy is the purification of the source of fiction. For, if bad novels make, as we have seen that they can make, a bad nation, the question remains, what makes bad novels? Clearly, a bad nation: Thus we have got the nation corrupting fiction, and fiction reacting on the nation to make it more corrupt. At the center of this vicious circle, we find the root of all evil—bad economic conditions. In this country, for example, the economic conditions under which we live have resulted in the association of dignity, refinement, education, wealth and power, with idleness and luxury. Idleness with luxury must result *from* dishonesty, and must result *in* sensuality. Dishonesty and sensuality with wealth and power mean tyranny and rapacity. Tyranny and rapacity mean cruel and brutalizing oppression. The brutalization of the oppressed must cause the contrast between the condition of the oppressor and the victim to breed contempt in the one and envy in the other rather than a desire for justice in both. Refinement and education make the oppressor recoil from a confession of his dishonesty, sensuality, tyranny, rapacity, cruelty and contempt. The struggling pride of humanity in his victim recoils no less from acknowledging that it stoops to bear oppression and to envy the oppressor. This twofold recoil produces a general hypocrisy of the most searching kind, under the influence of which everyone dreads the truth, and agrees to stigmatize all efforts to expose it as indecent. Hence springs up a false morality which seeks to establish dignity, refinement, education, social importance, wealth, power and magnificence, on a hidden foundation of idleness, dishonesty, sensuality, hypocrisy, tyranny, rapacity, cruelty, and scorn. When the novelist comes to build his imaginary castle, he builds on the same foundation, but adds heroism, beauty, romance, and above all, possibility of exquisite happiness to the superstructure, thereby making it more beautiful to the ignorant, and more monstrous to the initiated. Exceptionally, the novelist himself is one of the initiated, and attempts to lay bare the rotten foundation, and to shew what villainous imitations of the genuine articles are the heroism, beauty, romance, and so on. In that case, he is denounced as a person whose filthy mind degrades every subject of his consciousness. Witness M. Zola, whose novels, because the truth is in them, have been declared unfit for reading and are very largely read on that account. Now M. Zola, if he is to write novels at all, and not to fill them with lies, must either write as he does, or describe life as it used to be in New England villages in the days when life there, if comparatively barbarous, was reasonably honest. But this alternative is neither possible nor right; for those villages no longer exist; he has no firsthand knowledge of them; and the apologists of the society which he wishes to expose and have reconstructed, would proceed to assume that modern Paris is simply a New England village on a large scale, and that in both places righteousness was equally sure of its reward and sin of its punishment. So M. Zola honestly sticks to his infamy; and his infamy sticks to him. The majority of novelists naturally prefer to adopt the manners and tone of good society, which are thus spread from Mayfair through South Kensington, through Belgravia and Paddington, through Bayswater and Bloomsbury, through Brixton and Holloway, and so outward from the poisoned heart until even the New Cut [of readers] is corrupted, and the human brutes who are the refuse of our civilization and who are too dull even to despair, begin to feel the stirring of the potential snob within. If the snob would only shew some sign of the stirring of the potential righteous man within *him*, all might yet be well: the stream of fiction might flow from a pure source, and clean the national mind as effectively as it now fouls it. But in the meantime, I can assure you that the most dangerous public house in London is at the corner of Oxford St, and is kept by a gentleman named Mudie.[3] So much by way of exordium: perhaps I had better get on now to the beginning of my paper.

It is probable that nearly every person in this room has written a novel, or at least begun one. Those who have not, believe that they

3. See the Editor's Introduction for details about Mudie.

could if they set about it. Has not somebody said that every man has one good novel in him? The remark is so acceptable, and yet so shallow, that I think it must have proceeded from the Autocrat of the Breakfast Table. He might just as sensibly have said that every dog has one good novel in him, since it is true that if the events in the life of an average dog occurred to a good novelist, they would no doubt serve him as material for a good novel. But the dog's experience is limited to such events as it can observe and interpret; and its powers of observation and interpretation are so much smaller than a man's, that after a life of the wildest adventure it would have less experience to write novels about than a boy of ten. The great novelist surpasses the ordinary man, not in the eventfulness of his life, but in his capacity for experience. Otherwise Sir Walter Raleigh would have been a greater writer than Shakspere: and any metropolitan police inspector than Raleigh. All that can be admitted in the direction of the one good novel is, that were every man to write a true autobiography, the first crop of such volumes would be not only valuable as a collection of scientific documents, but might quite conceivably contain chapters far more thrilling than any in our popular romances. But a man would have to write many books in order to qualify himself for a branch of fiction so extraordinarily difficult as autobiography! Autobiography requires all the qualifications of the novelist and more besides. To know the truth about oneself; to know how to tell it with the pen; to know how much is worth telling; to dare to tell it!—all this implies power and practice which not one novelist in a thousand possesses. Even the few who might reasonably make the attempt would sit down to their work rather with a desperate hope of betraying the truth in spite of themselves than of succeeding in directly telling it. So that the modified statement that every man has one good autobiography in him is even further from the truth than the original one about one good novel.

We now seem to have arrived at the familiar conclusion that novelists are born, not made. This is true; but do not for a moment suppose that they are born ready-made. What is born is the raw material of the novelist, not the finished product. To begin, the mere art of expression *by words alone* is very difficult. Conversation would be impossible to most people if it depended wholly on words.

If you write down in a book the words "The cat is on the table,"
you will leave the reader completely in the dark as to what table,
whose table, whether there is valuable china, or cream, or a pet bird
on the table—in short, whether it matters two straws whether the
cat is on the table or not. When you use the same words in conversation to draw attention to an actual occurrence, the person you
address already knows, or can see for himself at a glance, all about
the cat and the table; and so your statement, bald as it was, becomes
highly significant. Even at that advantage, consider how difficult
mere conversation is between parties who have no stock of previous
knowledge in common! When you are introduced to a stranger, your
first care is to find a subject common to your experience and his—
or hers. The only subject certain to fulfill that condition is the
weather. When that is exhausted, you try whether there is not some
family which both visit, some person whom both dislike, some play
which both have witnessed, or book that both have read. Shakspere is generally to be depended on among people of literary tastes.
But if Shakspere fails, and the stranger does not move in your set,
and is not a playgoer, then there is nothing for it but to exchange
opinions concerning the surrounding objects, and get away from one
another as soon as possible. Now imagine yourself bound to utter a
hundred thousand words for the entertainment of an utter stranger,
invisible, dumb, separated from you by hundreds of miles of tele-
phone wire, knowing nothing about you or your antecedents, and
with the weather and Shakespeare strictly barred. That is what a novelist has to do; and if you think that he can do it artistically the first
time he tries—or the second—or the third, you are most prodigiously
mistaken. Charles Dickens, the most gifted novelist of our time,
began novel-writing when he was 24. He did not reach his first great
novel, Little Dorrit until he was 44; and in that twenty years' apprenticeship he had produced ten large books which, if measured in
the popular way, by their power of making readers laugh and cry,
would rank as masterpieces of fiction.

I am aware that the conception of skilled authorship as a result of
study and practice conflicts with the common notion of a literary man
as a person subject to attacks of what is called inspiration, during
which stories dart into his brain ready-expressed in words which he

has only to transcribe as fast as he can gallop. A little practical experience of composition is the best remedy for this illusion. When you take up the pen in search of ideas, you may find them plentiful or sparse, according to your natural fertility; but you will not find them coherently arranged in book form, and, what is more, only a small percentage of them will be worth using. A cheap and fast writer will use forty per cent of them. A thorough workman will hesitate to use five and thus the better the work is the longer it takes. When the ideas are selected, they have to be arranged; and when they are arranged, they have to be expressed—a process which consists of a laborious search for the right words, and in which the success of the writer will be proportionate to his knowledge, first, of what he himself means; and, second, of what all the various words in the language mean. When an author is too lazy or deficient in intelligence to thresh out his ideas, and to word them carefully, he produces that sort of easy writing which is called hard reading, because that which is left undone by the author must be supplied by the reader before he can arrive at a complete understanding of the matter in hand. Thus, if the complete expression of a synthesis costs 20 units of force; if the author does only 5, the reader will have to do 15; but if the author does the 15 the reader will only have to do 5. Unfortunately for the author, the more he does, the less he gets credit for. The clearer he makes himself, the easier and more spontaneous does his work seem to the reader, who argues that because the matter comes easily to him it must have come much more easily to a clever fellow like the author. When a highly gifted author does his very best, and is not only accurate and logical, but helpfully suggestive and familiar into the bargain, he is as likely as not to be regarded as a literary cheap Jack whose work costs him next to no trouble. Well-meaning people, intending to flatter, insult him by telling him that he has the pen of a ready writer, and by asking him to dash off a bright little article for their philanthropic magazine, or a paper about some amusing subject as it will only take him half an hour. The half hour usually means half a week or more; and the unfortunate author, reckoned up on the half-hour hypothesis, is put down as lazy because he does not dash off ten articles a day; unwilling to oblige because he does not keep his friends' unremunerative magazines and newspapers supplied with gratuitous articles; full of ready cash because he must be making twice as much as his prosperous colleagues who dont write half so easily; and stingy because, though so rich, he is always pretending to be at his wits' end to make up his rent or the price of a necessary pair of boots. These tricks, with their temptations to scamping, are those of the art of literary expression in all departments. As part of the applied economics of the subject they explain why journalism, or the art of scamping your work so as to make it last exactly a day or a week, according to whether you write for the St. James's Gazette or the Spectator, is so much more remunerative immediately and pecuniarily than solid literature; and how it is that earnest and able young writers, when they commit themselves to the maintenance of a wife and family, or to the habits of fashionable society, or to both at once, degenerate first into elegant triflers, and finally into incurable hacks, absolutely without consciences. Also why, in fiction, authors who could write one good novel a year, write three bad ones instead. There are, however, men who will suffer anything rather than do their work badly. They are scarce, and by no means invariably men of noble ideals or amiable personalities. Beethoven did his very best regardless of money. Balzac made his books as perfect as he could, although he had to pay for proof correction out of his own pocket. But your Tom Sayerses and Fred Archers, by exactly the same determination to excel in their art at any cost, attain just such a rare eminence in a world of ruffians and blackguards, as Beethoven and Balzac in a world of poets and romancers. Therefore it is not safe to contend that this incorruptible devotion is one of the highest developments of mind, not even to deny that it may be a survival of the brute in us; since the sacrifices it entails are often out of all proportion to the value they add to the work. All that can be said is that it exists; and so it comes about that the one good novel is occasionally produced instead of the three more lucrative bad ones. And it is from these good novels that we may see how misleading is the vulgar conception of the inspired or ready-made and finished artist.

Fortunately, the advance of education is destroying the superstitions that surround the art of writing. A man who has written a book is no longer regarded as an extraordinary person except when he goes away for a holiday to some unsophisticated village. A necessary result is that authors no longer give themselves the airs that were once tolerated. The young writer of today has some justification for regarding his senior who dates from the age of Bulwer Lytton and Disraeli as an obsolete humbug. Those of a later and more enlightened, yet still remote generation, retain sufficient of the Mumbo-Jumbo tradition to wrap themselves up in their togas rather more majestically than modern manners encourage. Coming still nearer to our own day, one finds at certain literary clubs a comparatively faint and quite harmless, but still perceptible disposition to assume a certain degree of what is called "side" towards the unliterary mob. But the modern spirit is to allow the author's special privilege of making a fool of himself to fall into entire disuse; and at present there is a fair proportion of writers who are fully aware that the baker and candlestick maker are as worthy members of society as even a critic, much less an author. A great improvement in the quality of literary workmanship has accompanied this rationalizing of the author's position. It is true that much of our literature is so bad that it is difficult to believe that it could compare favorably with anything earthly. Nevertheless at our worst we are better off in this respect than our grandfathers. Our poorest books and papers are read by a class which, fifty years ago, could not read, and was therefore not written for; and so, bad as they are, they are better than nothing. The Edinburgh Review in its palmy days consisted largely of articles which no shilling magazine would accept nowadays. What were called slashing reviews were considered creditable to the writer: "slashing" meaning malicious, coarse, pedantic, drunken, ignorant, brutal—anything, in short, that was likely to hurt. Such work is recognized today as unskillful and unmannerly. Authors do not get much justice or mercy from reviewers now; but only very old-fashioned editors any longer consider them fair game for open insolence and derision.

It must not be forgotten that writers of good fiction, like all artists who take their art seriously, never quite escape from their apprenticeship until they die or retire from their profession. Their education only ends with their activity. The progress made by the greatest

artists during their careers is always so remarkable that no intelligent
critic could mistake their early work for their late, or either for that
of their middle period. Beethoven's ninth symphony is out of sight
of his first. Raphael's cartoons for the Sistine tapestry seem a whole
epoch ahead of his Sposalizio. Shakspere's maddest admirer could
never have hoped for Lear or the Winter's Tale from the author of
Love's Labours Lost or the Two Gentlemen of Verona. The difference between the Dickens who wrote Pickwick and the Dickens who
wrote Great Expectations is analagous to the difference between a
funny street boy and Schopenhauer. Let me say in passing that the
early work is always considered better than the later by the author's
contemporaries. Nowadays, however, no artist need start so far back
as Dickens or Shakspere. In Shakspere's case there is for this the
obvious reason that we are three centuries ahead of him. Dickens
was nearer our own time; but he started as an uneducated man.
I do not mean, of course, that he was an illiterate man. He could
read and write, and had no doubt been taught a little history and
geography, the simpler operations in arithmetic, a book or two of
Euclid, some Latin grammar and shorthand. He had done much
desultory reading and had been through works by such great writers
as Shakspere, Bunyan, Swift, and Goldsmith; but he had not a
student's knowledge of them, though he had his own peculiar insight
to certain sides of them. This was enough to put him on a level as
to acquirements with most of his readers. But he was not educated
in the sense in which de Quincey and George Eliot were educated.
No equally gifted man was ever less of an artist and philosopher
than he was in 1835 when, in his 23rd year, he wrote the Sketches
by Boz in a fashion which Bulwer Lytton or Macaulay would have
been ashamed of in their teens. He had a shabby genteel knowledge
of society, a Londoner's knowledge of outdoor incident, and a reporter's knowledge of public life, besides his genius, which enabled
him to succeed easily in spite of the inadequacy of the rest of the
equipment. The inadequacy was there nevertheless; and it was
the ground of the academic criticism of Dickens as "no gentleman"
which persisted long after his great progress made it ridiculous. But
at first he seems to have regarded all social phenomena as fortuitous
and unconnected; he had neither knowledge of science nor science

of knowledge, no philosophy of history, no system of ethics, no grounding of economics, no suspicion of the theories that were behind the abuses he attacked, much less of the social conditions behind the theories; and the gentlemen who were provided with secondhand academic articles of this description despised him accordingly. Much of the abuse he got from them was richly deserved. If his early narrative style could be decomposed so as to separate the workmanship from the fun, and to shade off the reflected felicity of the dialogue, the result would shock his most devoted admirers. His female characters were either purely ridiculous, like Mrs. Nickleby; or awkwardly botched, like Rose Maylie, Madeline Bray, Emma Haredale and the rest; or else, like Mrs. Lupin and Dolly Varden, served up to the reader like the gross feasts of turkey and sausage, pudding, and brandy-and-water which goaded M. Taine[4] to describe him as imbued with the spirit of the English Christmas. Little Nell is of course nothing but a sort of literary onion, to make you cry. The Pecksniff girls shew traces of growing knowledge of female character; but the poor little fool Dora, in David Copperfield, was his first distinct success in that department. That was in 1850, in his 8th book, and in his 38th year. Up to that date, and indeed for a few years later, no critic of wide and deep culture could have read Dickens without occasionally being offended and annoyed by his shortcomings. I by no means pretend that all the critics who condemned Dickens are to be defended on this ground; for the more he improved the less many of them liked him; but I do affirm that his most popular books justified many of the complaints they were met with. His last four completed novels form the only part of his work which placed him above all his contemporaries as a master of fiction. Whether he would have matured sooner had he graduated in the university instead of in the streets may be doubted. Thackeray was a university man; but, as he did not work there, he was fully as ignorant as Dickens when he left it; and he took away into the bargain a class feeling which Dickens escaped. In the slang of our day it might be said that one of these eminent novelists started as a cad; the other as a snob; and that the cad proved the better equipped

4. Hippolyte Adolphe Taine (1828–1893), French literary critic and historian.

of the two. In their lack of education proper they were on equal terms. I think they were both the worse for it; and that they blundered and failed in many points to the end of their careers for want of the mental training which de Quincey and George Eliot enjoyed. It will hardly be asserted that George Eliot, as a fictionist, was as gifted as either Dickens or Thackeray. But it will also hardly be denied that parts of her works put parts of theirs to shame in point of intelligence, wise tolerance, and quality of workmanship. She often shewed herself a scientific thinker and a trained sympathiser, where they were only shrewd guessers and vehement partisans.

Whilst harping on this education aspect of my subject, I had better warn you against inferring that the best-educated writer, other qualifications being assumed equal, will write the pleasantest novel. The reader's education must be taken into account; and the uneducated novel reader will always find the educated writer passionless, abstract, mechanical, unfeeling, and even inhuman and selfish. An educated writer is a disillusioned person with a cultivated taste for truth and reality. An uneducated reader is consoled and sustained by illusions, and shrinks from the light like an owl. Surrounded by the unknown, he is superstitious, trusts to luck, and thinks the uniformity and sure prevision of science deadly, because it steadily eliminates luck and kills the excitement of uncertainty. Being to himself the centre of the universe, he cherishes a vain sense of unique individuality, which science offends by *classifying* him. He feels that knowledge is trying to rob him of the romance of ignorance, just as it robbed the savages of the spirits with which the savage imagination peopled the woods, streams, and clouds. The unknown is his realm of romance; and he does not suspect that it is only through knowledge that he can become fully conscious of its vastness. Education takes the Family Herald from him and gives him Faust instead; and as the Family Herald is a world of delightful visions for him, and Faust a dry, heavy, tedious, oppressive, and three fourths absolutely unintelligible piece of task work, he protests against the exchange, to him wholly unprofitable. The aversion to science is extended from books to their authors. We are all familiar with the popular verdict on Goethe, the most highly educated of the great fictionists. He was cold; he was selfish; he was callous; he was unsympathetic and exclusive. Just so we hear complaints of George Eliot having talent but no genius, lacking feeling, being a soulless pedant, and the like. This is an inevitable result of evolution. I have no doubt that if the tigers and monkeys were to express their opinion of mankind, they would vote us cold, passionless, calculating, and mysteriously dreadful. The Celtic peasant, who, when a member of his family dies, weeps, hires men to howl with him, and finally exhausts his grief in a drunken orgie, would be scouted as a callous monster if he acted like the self-controlled, sober, tearless ladies and gentlemen of our acquaintance. Even the gentleman wears crape on his hat and writes on paper with a black rim, the width of which is always in inverse ratio to his education. The people who are fairly abreast of the century, and who of course no more wear black hatbands or write on black rimmed paper than they hold drunken wakes, are still very generally stigmatized as brutal and indecent, so that many of them comply with the custom for the sake of a quiet life. In Lord Lytton's Coming Race,[5] he represents an ordinary man —a mining engineer—of our own time straying by accident into a subterranean country inhabited by a race several centuries ahead of us in evolution. He meets a man of that race, and though there is nothing grotesque or frightful about him, the mere facial expression of superhumanly passionless and serene wisdom scares the unfortunate engineer almost out of his wits. And though he stays in that country for some time, and is kindly used there, he never gets used to these comparatively godlike people, nor ever overcomes his instinctive dread of them. The mistrust and aversion excited by Goethe and George Eliot are part of the same conflict between the highly evolved men and those who are still comparatively savage. An artificial variety of that conflict is produced in our society by the association of educated people with the uneducated. This application of the theory of evolution introduces something like scientific method into the modern novel. Formerly the hero of a novel was a lay figure

5. An 1871 romance by Bulwer-Lytton, set in a utopia in which there is neither war nor crime nor poverty nor inequality. Shaw's description of the novel suggests that he was later much indebted to it for futuristic elements of his highly evolved race in the fourth and fifth plays of his *Back to Methuselah* tetralogy (1921), *The Tragedy of an Elderly Gentleman* and *As Far as Thought Can Reach*.

with a bundle of virtues arbitrarily tacked to him. Another lay figure with a bundle of vices was the villain. Nowadays the novelist can set to work on a different plan. His hero is simply the most highly evolved person in the book; and if his actions be only dictated by a sufficiently developed intelligence, self-control, and, above all, foresight, they will appear a series of crimes, and he an unfeeling scoundrel, to the less evolved characters, and the average reader, whilst yet his superiority will be mysteriously evident throughout.

There is a class of readers in this country consisting of uneducated young ladies, too sensible to care for tales of crime and mystery, too ignorant to share the view of life taken by educated authors, and too lazy to do anything except read novels. Of such are the admirers and heroines of Miss Rhoda Broughton,[6] who is, after Shakspere and one or two others, my favorite fictionist. She was the first to give us sincere pictures of the girls who drift to womanhood with some obsolete schooling and no training whatever, and whose minds have been fed on a stimulating but not strengthening hotch potch of Dickens, Miss Braddon,[7] Mark Twain, Miss Ellen Terry, and Family Herald, and the daily papers. She has shewn us these neglected children of easygoing, preoccupied, or foolish parents in their most attractive guise, amiable, quickwitted, full of fun, and perfectly well disposed, yet wasting their time, missing the chances, failing in their duties, and eventually suffering the doom of the unfit. I am not sure that Miss Broughton's young lady readers all drew the proper moral,—I am not even sure that Miss Broughton quite understood it herself at first; but her great and deserved success proved how much her work needed doing, and how truthfully she had done it.

All this stress on education raises the question—How much should a competent novelist know? Well, everything. A perfect set of perfect novels ought to be everything our grandmothers believed the

6. Rhoda Broughton (1840–1920) began her career as a writer of audacious light novels. Since the audacity remained unchanged over half a century it later lost its shocking content.

7. Mary Elizabeth Braddon (1837–1915) not only wrote poetry and plays, and edited such popular Victorian magazines as *Temple Bar* and *Belgravia*, but turned out eighty cheaply sensational novels, including the immensely popular *Lady Audley's Secret*.

Bible to be—except true as an actual record of the past. That however is an unattainable ideal. It is simple enough to say to a novelist:
Learn everything; and when you know it, stick to naturalism, and
write every word as if you were on your oath in a witness box. Let
your subject be some important social relation, and let your book
demonstrate a theorem concerning it, or at least give a clear statement of the problem it presents to the sociologist. This, however, requires the novelist to be God Omniscient, if not God Almighty. It
is a counsel of perfection; but it is not therefore useless. A counsel
of perfection is the great desideratum in all branches of conduct—
to be striven towards if never attained. The novelist must do his best.

In thus prescribing a scientific and moral character for works of
fiction, I cannot avoid compromising my credit for artistic feeling
in the eyes of those reactionists who declare that moral considerations
are outside the sphere of art; that the sole function of the artist is
to please; that art should be pursued for its own sake. At this hour
in the evening I think I may dismiss those who assert that moral
considerations are outside any sphere of human activity as—to put
it politely—inconsiderate persons. And if I be told that the sole
function of the artist is to please, I shall ask—to please whom? The
same fiction will not please a schoolgirl and a foxhunter, a Tory
and a Radical, General Booth and Mr Bradlaugh.[8] Even if it be
confined to certain matters—love affairs, for instance—to which
schoolgirls, foxhunters, Radicals, Tories, General Booth and Mr
Bradlaugh are all susceptible, the same treatment of them will not
please educated and uneducated, frivolous and serious readers
equally. Since, then, you must choose; and since your choice cannot

8. William Bramwell Booth (1829–1912) was founder and chief officer of
the Salvation Army, which had begun from his Christian Mission in London's
Whitechapel District in 1865.

Charles Bradlaugh (1833–1901), the most notorious freethinker of the
century, and a magnetic platform orator, was the first avowed atheist to be
elected to Parliament (1880). His refusal to be sworn in on a religious oath,
and subsequent debates on religious freedom in the House of Commons,
ended in 1886 (after he was reelected five times, each election after his seat
had been declared vacant) with his being permitted to engage in what
everyone understood to be the empty and hypocritical ceremony of taking
the usual oath.

be pronounced morally indifferent except by a reasoning which would make all conduct morally indifferent; you are bound to appeal to the very highest wisdom you can reach. When moral considerations have determined (1) the choice of subject, (2) the light in which it needs to be put, and (3) the class of readers to be addressed, then the novelist's own vanity and interest will urge him to make himself as pleasant as he can. Omit the moral considerations, and the same vanity and interest will make an artist of the vilest of panders.

It is perhaps worth adding that circumstances may arise in which a writer may think it well to write a fiction for the instruction of an audience to whose level he must descend in order to make his work intelligible to them. Swift, for instance, wrote a fictitious last speech and confession of a condemned criminal for circulation among thieves and prostitutes. Naturally he did not write it in the style of a paper on ethics to be read to the Philosophical Society. He wrote down to the thieves' level, but to their highest—not to their lowest level. With what shocking success he could have done the latter if he had chosen to, some of his less conscientious leaflets prove. But a man's best work should be for his best audience, even if it be an ideal audience. Indeed the very best work of all is that written for posterity. Unfortunately a writer thus untimely great, if he is not also a man of property, must starve unless he wastes a good deal of his energy on lower work. As to practising art for art's sake, I cannot see my way through the metaphysics of that. It implies acting without motive or aim—blindly obeying an instinctive impulse —letting oneself go as the savage does when, exhilarated by the fire-water of civilization, he tomahawks the nearest human skull. This is tomahawking for tomahawking's sake; but surely it would be better to intelligently choose your victim—better still, perhaps, to go home quietly and not meddle with your tomahawk until you have a tree to cut down, or some other object—useful, but extraneous to the pure art of tomahawking. I do not deny that savages may have occasionally benefited themselves or society at large by bringing down at hazard a troublesome relative or a whiskey seller; and I do not deny either that very entertaining works of art have been hit off by utterly reckless artists. But I demur to the general validity of a speculative policy founded on such instances; and I

contend that unless you are in so rude a phase of intellectual culture
as to be unable to see how a man can be the better or worse morally
for going to the theatre or reading a book, you must admit that the
production of works of fiction is conditioned by morality. And when
you admit that, you must, in view of the fact that a book may touch
thousands of people who could not be reached by any act or spoken
word of the author, and that of these thousands many would be
young people with their minds in a highly plastic state, you can
hardly refuse to admit further that the consequences of writing
wrongly are likely to be far graver than those of speaking or acting
wrongly. If, after that, you still contend that art is outside the sphere
of morals, it becomes a question whether your relatives are justified
in leaving you at large.

Finally, in contending that a work of fiction should have a purpose, as the phrase goes, I must beg for a reasonable interpretation.
I do not mean that it should have only one purpose, or that the
achievement of some novel beauty of sound and grace of expression
should not have its due weight and place among the other purposes.
Nor do I by any means claim that all purposes can be suitably furth-
ered by works of fiction. If a reformer were to ask me whether the
removal of the bars and bolts on the Bedford Estate[9] might not be

9. The dukes of Bedford were among the great ground landlords in
London. Early in the nineteenth century they had permitted the architect
Thomas Cubitt to begin building homes within the estate in a style and
quality superior to anything previously available on the speculative market.
There had long been dwellings within the estate, these protected from public
access since 1759 by gates and bars which remained through that century and
into the next the visible symbol of ground landlord power. Returns made in
1866 listed twenty-nine in the parish of St. Pancras alone, closing streets—
most of them on the Bedford estate—to all vehicles from 11 P.M. to 7 A.M.
and causing inconvenience, traffic problems, and great resentment. Among
the outraged, as these remarks make clear, was G.B.S. Despite vigorous opposition from the landlords and their tenants, in which the duke of Bedford
played a prominent part, Parliament was finally prevailed upon several years
later, in 1890, to authorize the London County Council to remove four gates
in St. Pancras. Three of them—in Torrington Place, Gordon Street, and
Upper Woburn Place—were on the Bedford estate. "The motion of thanks
to the St. Pancras Vestry for rendering Gower Street open for ever," the
Times reported (April 27, 1893), "was carried with loud cheers."

effected by a novel, I should recommend him to try direct agitation instead. If he were to suggest the same method of helping to reform the Lunacy Laws, I should not object; but I should perhaps remind him that fiction is not evidence; and that if a novel is to further a purpose, the purpose must in return further the novel. Therefore, I would say, first catch your novelist; and then see that he gets hold of proved facts to work upon. If the great Drink curse were proposed as a subject, I should point out that much good has already been done in that way, but that personally I should incline towards a measure outlawing distillers and licensed victuallers, and offering facilities for dynamite experiments on their premises by temperance societies. If a novelist were to ask my opinion of Socialism as matter for a new work, I should perhaps refer him to existing novels on the subject, and ask him whether he thought the public would stand much more of that sort of thing. But in each case I should add that there are finer purposes which concern us all today, and will concern posterity when antiquaries will be disputing over the site of the Bedford bars; when the term Lunacy Laws will be supposed to have applied to our whole statute book; when alcohol will be used only as any other dangerous poison is; and when nineteenth-century individualism will be commemorated in the histories of the period as the final phase of cannibalism. The novels which had no further purpose than the achievement of this will then be dead as the Reform pamphlets of 1830. Hamlet and Faust will live longer, though of these too the human race will someday be well rid; for there is an end to the tether even of Shakspere. For the present, I also am at the end of my tether; and so I leave the matter to your discussion.

Add. MS 50702, pp. 219–246, British Museum.

II. NOVELISTS

A New Novel of Wilkie Collins

A review of Collins's The Evil Genius *(1885).*

Is it too much to hope that Mr Wilkie Collins may be remembered as the best really able novelist who shackled and crippled his genius, and worried his admirers almost into giving up reading him, by systematically cumbering his stories with what are called "plots"? The perverse ingenuity with which he devises these Procrustean scaffolds cannot excuse the cruelty with which he stretches or chops the children of his imagination to fit them. The proper framework for a book is its own natural skeleton: if it be born without one, then let it perish as a shapeless abortion: no external apparatus of splints and crutches will make it presentable. Shakspeare has set us a bad example in this matter. He unfortunately suffered himself to be persuaded by custom and prejudice that plots were necessary; and as he was far too great a man to be capable of inventing them, he stole them. His sin soon found him out. The stolen plots forced him to deform his plays by uncharacteristic actions, inconsistencies, anachronisms, digressions, wordy trivialities, impertinent messengers, tedious journeys, and uninteresting letters, to which, after all, nobody attended; for we find the bard, by the mouth of Hamlet, complaining that the clowns made the pit laugh whilst the serious actors were wearying it by "some necessary question of the play." Would we had such clowns now! Shakspeare was not wiser than the whole world. His irritation at having taken a great deal of trouble for nothing was quite natural; but the pit and the clowns were right and he was wrong. The wise readers skip all explanations in novels: the wise playgoer, during the exposition of the drama, sleeps if alone, or, if companioned, discusses Home Rule. It is a mistake to suppose that the public cannot accept a situation without knowing exactly what has led to it. The *flâneurs* who stop to witness a street fight do not find the spectacle a whit less enjoyable and instructive because they do not happen to know the antecedents of the combatants or the particulars of their feud. The fight's the thing.

Mr Wilkie Collins's plots, unlike Shakspeare's, are honestly come by. He makes them for himself with travail and heavy sorrow, hardly disguising his sense of the respect and gratitude we owe him in return. To so conscientious a workman no honest person will deny respect. But gratitude is out of the question: enough that we try to forgive him! Perhaps Mr Wilkie Collins innocently believes that it is in average human nature to like his cryptograms, his deciphering experts, his lawyers, his letters, his extracts from diaries, his agony-column advertisements, his detectives, his telegrams, and his complicated railway and hotel arrangements. If so, he errs: these things are only tolerable for the sake of the stories they all but strangle. In The Evil Genius we have hardly one volume of human life and character to two volumes of plot. We bear with this because we cannot help ourselves, just as we submit to take our milk two-thirds water. Would the milkman but leave us the milk and water in separate jugs, we should willingly pay the same price and throw the water away. Fain would we take in Mr Wilkie Collins's plot and his story in separate covers; but, like the milkman, he insists on mixing them and then denying our analysis.

The Evil Genius begins well with an amusing jury discussing a criminal case, and with the most entertaining loves of Mrs Westerfield and James Beljames. The story of the neglected child who escapes from drudgery in a sordid school to happiness in a refined home, and then is driven by her unlucky star to wreck that home, is full of interest. The two scenes which form the dramatic climax of this part of the narrative are especially effective. But the plot soon begins to close in and crush the life out of the book. A marionette lawyer enters; and Mr Wilkie Collins strives desperately to make him seem alive. Characteristics supposed to be inherited from a French ancestry are tacked on to him. His appetite for truffles is enlarged upon. His mechanical plottering is relieved at five-minute intervals by a jerk at the wires, which makes the poor puppet start spasmodically. In vain! there is no life in his gambols: he is only there to advise every one to carry on the plot, and to supply missing links by letters to his wife such as no male creature ever yet did or will write. He is clumsily abetted by a certain Captain Bennydeck (there is but one novelist alive who could have perpetrated such a name), a sanctimonious bore, who makes an infirm bid for the dignity of hero late in the book, and is eventually, like a virtuous but ineffectual politician, kicked upstairs into the odour of philanthropy, and left with an off chance of marrying the disgraced governess. The mother-in-law, Mrs Presty, though she too is used chiefly to engineer the plot, has some independent merits. The child Kitty is delightful: the brightest pages in the book are those which record her doings and sayings. The dialogue, as usual in a Wilkie Collins novel, is sometimes natural and expressive; sometimes a mere string of terse statements, having no purpose except to advance or explain the plot incubus, and no humanity or interest except as examples of the author's mannerisms. On the whole, novels are like other works of art: uninteresting just so far as they are machine made.

Pall Mall Gazette, September 18, 1886.

Mr. George Moore's New Novel

A review of George Moore's A Mere Accident *(1887)*.

It is customary to say of such books as Mr George Moore's that they are not *virginibus puerisque*. Yet the lasses and lads are the very people who read them—if they ever do read them—without being any the worse. Those who have been allowed the run of the library in their childhood know by experience that in young hands Tom Jones is as innocent as The Pilgrim's Progress, and that Mademoiselle de Maupin is unreadably dull to little bookworms whose choice of literature is still subject to the parental censorship. As to people old enough to insist on choosing for themselves, they are under no compulsion to read Mr Moore's novels; and as his licence is now notorious, and his method not in the least insidious, it is only necessary, each time he publishes a book, to indicate plainly how far he has gone in it. Our readers can then decide for themselves whether the book is to be widely read or not; for Mr Moore's existence as a novelist depends wholly on the general reader, and not on the particular reviewer.

The "mere accident" which gives the novel now in question its name is this. A young lady, a clergyman's daughter, about to be happily married, is overtaken on a lonely road by a tramp and outraged. Next day she goes mad, throws herself from a window, and dies. In describing this "realistically," Mr Moore has not done his worst: by making the victim insensible, he has contrived to avoid the most painful moment of his narrative. From his point of view this is perhaps a sacrifice of principle—a flinching from his duty. From the point of view of the British public, it will be welcomed as a commendable reticence that might have been carried further, even to the point of not writing the book. For there is no moral. The incident is described for its own sake. It has no consequences or antecedents to recommend it; and unless Mr Moore wished to bring home to us in a startling way the danger of allowing young ladies to go out without an escort, he must stoop to be classed with the vulgar novelists who depend for their effects on the mere sensation stirred up by any appalling crime or abnormal occurrence. In their school, the taste of the sensationalist author determines the particular crime selected; and Mr Moore's ready preference for a rape is explained by the opportunity it affords him for one of his favourite sham clinical lectures on morbid sexual conditions. Let it be freely admitted that these discourses would, if truly realistic, have a scientific value sufficient to fortify Mr Moore against prudish criticism. But as they are realistic only as symptoms of the condition of Mr Moore's own imagination, which hardly deserves a set of volumes all to itself, they have no more claim on our forbearance than the gratuitously romantic passages in a shilling shocker. The objection, in fact, to Mr Moore is not that he is realistic, but that he is a romancer who, in order that he may take liberties, persuades himself that he is a pathologist. Now, whilst there are people who like to take liberties, and other people who like to submit to them, they will be taken, and, within the due limits of personal freedom, must not be interfered with; but pray let us have no hypocritical pretence that they are disinterested researches in psychology or sociology. They are not even an acceptable protest against the evil of obscurantism; for their effect is really to reinforce it. The remedy for obscurantism is responsible scientific instruction, and not licentious fiction.

The workmanship of A Mere Accident can be most conveniently considered by calling a truce—a temporary truce—with Mr Moore on the subject of his moral accountability. It has often been urged upon him that "fine writing" is his weak point. He evidently thinks it just the reverse; and he is right. To appeal to the intelligence, and lead it to convictions which become a permanent spring of emotion, is all very well for writers who can do it; but Mr Moore's business is to strike the fancy and rouse the imagination with pictures and rhythms. Accordingly he first "gets up" the needful Sussex scenery as if he were commissioned to write a guide book, and then he describes it thus:—

> The country is as flat as a smooth sea. Chanctonbury Ring
> stands up like a mighty cliff on a northern shore: its crown of
> trees is grim. The abrupt ascents of Toddington Mount bear
> away to the left, and tide-like the fields flow up into the great
> gulf between.

That is not the landscape style of Bunyan, or Cobbett, or George
Borrow; but it is the style of styles to serve Mr Moore's turn; and
he sticks to it wisely, and does it well. But when, inspired by Mr
Walter Pater, he applies the same method to mediaeval Latin, and
and pours out the result in twenty-page doses, the critic, detecting
"cram," winks, and—unless he skips—even sleeps. Nor, despite his
interest in the doctrine of heredity, is he disposed to admit the term
"psychical investigation" as appropriate to a long explanation of the
hero's temperament, in which "direct mingling of perfect health
with spinal weakness had germinated into a marked yearning for
the heroic ages—for the supernatural as contrasted with the meanness of the routine of existence." Pretentious fustian of this kind
abounds in the book; but the persons of the story are none the less
shrewdly sketched; for Mr Moore, within his range, is no bad
observer. It is a range peopled by drunkards and vagabonds, by the
"average sensual man," the half-educated, the morbidly adolescent,
the provincial and ignorant gentry—in short, the unfit and inade-
quate for all noble parts in life. Among them there is not stuff
enough to make a successful costermonger. Since they have their
place among the many failures of our civilization, they must have
their limner and chronicler. Only, one would fain meet some handsome and wholesome fellow-creature among them, if only as a
standard to measure the shortcoming of the others. Here is Mr
Moore's own description of his hero: —

> To the superficial, therefore, John Norton will appear but
> the incarnation of egotism and priggishness; but those who see
> deeper will have recognized that he is one who has suffered
> bitterly, as bitterly as the outcast who lies dead in his rags
> beneath the light of the policeman's lantern.

A couple of hundred pages or so of pseudo-psychological analysis of this gentleman's emotions will reconcile most readers to his sufferings. As to the young lady with "the delicate plenitudes of the bent neck bound with white cambric," in the author's most characteristic style, it need only be said that what there is natural of her is evidently drawn from an Irish model, and that it is not her fault that Mr Moore did not find a better use for her.

Pall Mall Gazette, July 19, 1887.

Ouida's Latest Novel

A review of Ouida's Othmar *(1885).*

Othmar is a sequel to Princess Napraxine. Good news, this, for all who have not had enough of that gifted lady. And, indeed, when one considers Nadine Napraxine's celestial beauty, the Lubbockian[1] extent of her reading, her exquisite taste in painting, her "profound and scientific knowledge of the tone art," her silvern speech adorned with choice expressions culled from the French language, her untold wealth and her pedigree co-extensive with history, it is difficult to conceive that she could pall on any reasonable reader. And yet, such is the insatiable discontent of man, that he cavils even at this phoenix—actually yawns and skips when the loftiest phases of her philosophy are in full exposition. The fact is that Nadine repeats herself to an extent surprising in a woman of her prodigious and mercilessly exercised power of analyzing the smaller human weaknesses. And though she propounds problems of life and mind with a careless spontaneity that would have taken the late Mr George Lewes's[2] breath away, she does not do so, like him, with any intention of contributing to their solution but rather as unanswerable conundrums—impassable obstacles that make no thoroughfares of the courses of conversation, and confound her interlocutors. When she discusses art with a fashionable portrait painter, she silences him—shuts him up, in fact—by asking "Do you think Michel

1. Sir John Lubbock (1834–1913), a banker and M.P., was also an eclectic and prodigious author, producing such books as *The Origin of Civilisation* (1870), *On the Origin and Metamorphoses of Insects* (1874), *On the Senses, Instincts and Intelligence of Animals* (1888), and such lists as the "Hundred Best Books" and the "Pleasures of Life."
2. George Henry Lewes (1817–1878), lifelong companion of Mary Ann Evans (George Eliot), was a drama critic and biographer of Goethe as well as author of such formidable works as *The Biographical History of Philosophy* (1846), *Physiology of Common Life* (1859), and *Problems of Life and Mind* (1873–1879).

Angelo could have endured to dwell in Cromwell-road?" She then
addresses the abashed hireling as "my poor court poodle," and leaves
him to his reflections, which possibly turn on the manners of the
aristocracy, and on whether Michel Angelo could have afforded
to live in the Cromwell-road, even if he had made up his mind to
endure the architecture there. On the whole, Nadine Napraxine
hardly does herself justice in casual conversation, although even her
husband (her second husband, to whom she has been married for
several years) gives her plenty of opportunities. He is no commonplace paterfamilias. Where another man would have nothing more
interesting to say than, "Naddy, dear; I shall want my breakfast
early to-morrow morning," Othmar says, "Our minds are all finite,
alas!"&c. The lamentable truth is that Nadine is an impostor whose
conversational equipment is a precarious power of allusion gained
by her from the references to art, letters, and philosophy, which
she has come across in much desultory reading, chiefly of novels and
periodicals. Her platitudes and impertinences might be pardoned
to smart seventeen, or even to sweet and twenty; but in the mouth
of a matron of thirty-two they are intolerable.

It must be admitted that the authoress, when she takes up the
parable, delivers herself so much in the manner of her heroine as
to suggest that the stream of Nadine's utterances "meanders level
with its fount," as Robert Montgomery puts it; and that Ouida's
attainments are only as genuine, and her culture and scholarship
as profound and exact, as those of the Princess Napraxine. To
prove her deficiency has been the easy task of many a swashing
review. Probably no writer has ever been caught and exposed in the
act of writing on subjects without knowing much about them so
often as Ouida. Into this Othmar, for instance, she introduces an
Anarchist, and quite wantonly mentions that "his prophet was Karl
Marx," which is as sensible as it would have been to introduce an
English Radical whose prophet was Lord Salisbury. Karl Marx
might more easily have been left out. But the fatality which drives
the burglar to sack a mansion and yet to leave behind him a foot-
print, or a bloodstain, or a visiting card of some sort for the police
to find, pursues Ouida, and drives her to betray herself when she

tries to invent observation and learning. The musicians discover that she does not know a fugue from a fandango; collectors wink at her extensive display of bric-a-brac; schoolboys laugh at her cricket matches; and murderers probably chuckle over her ideas of homicide. To which one may conceive her condescending to reply, "All very well, gentlemen; but when you have done pointing out my little technical errors, how will you proceed to account for my popularity?"

It can only be accounted for by the perfect sincerity of Ouida's view of the society she describes. She is true to herself and to the facts as she sees them. Though her share of the optimistic illusions of humanity tempt her from within, and Mrs Grundy threaten her from without, she insists on the naked truth concerning the hordes of wealthy vagabonds who spend their lives unprofitably roving through Western Europe in pursuit of pleasure. She perceives that the society they form breeds monsters—that it is impervious to all healthy emotions and interests, and responsive only to coarse stimulation of its lower instincts. A noble nature, enlisted in it by the accident of birth, and rebelling against it, is a capital tragic theme. Graft some pure romance on this by providing a beautiful and heroic child of nature for the rebellious plutocrat to fall in love with; and eke out the whole by shoddy philosophical reflections and criticisms of imaginary works of art spuriously labelled with the names of real artists; add copious descriptions, repeated *ad-libitum*, and you have the typical Ouida novel, diffuse, over-loaded with worthless mock sociology, perceptibly tainted by a pervasion of the sexual impulses, egotistical and tiresome, and yet imaginative, full of vivid and glowing pictures, and not without a considerable moral stiffening of enthusiasm—half-reasoned but real—for truth and simplicity, and of protest against social evils which is not the less vehement because certain emotional and material aspects of it have a fascination which the writer has not wholly escaped.

Pall Mall Gazette, January 25, 1886.

Ouida's Successor

A review of Marie Corelli's Thelma *(1887).*

Marie Corelli, imagining a new heaven and a new earth, and throwing them passionately in the teeth of an obstinate reality that will not conform to them, must greatly stir the hearts and fire the fancies of her younger readers. Her latest heroine, Thelma, comes from the land of the midnight sun. Thelma's father, a worthy descendant of the sea kings, repudiates modern civilization and worships Odin. A baronet arrives in a steam yacht; marries the Norse maiden; and bears her off to "the land of Mockery," known to cabmen as the four-mile radius. The point of the story lies in the intense superiority of Thelma to the frivolous units of London society. Now, far be it from any reasonable critic to justify the West-end ways which Thelma found so weary, or to exalt that race-in-the-wrong-direction after Pleasure which ends in a pessimistic conviction that Pleasure is a mirage, and life not worth living. But the ground of Thelma's alleged superiority to her London circle turns out to be her barbarous superstitions, ignorance, and prejudice. London wives shocked her. "Her character," we are told, "moulded on grand and simple lines of duty, saw the laws of Nature in their true light, and accepted them without question. It seemed to her quite clear that man was the superior, woman the inferior, creature; and she could not understand the possibility of any wife not rendering instant and implicit obedience to her husband, even in trifles." Let us, for the sake of illustration, apply these grand and simple lines of duty to a particular case. Man is superior to woman; therefore any man is superior to any woman; therefore Mr E. M. Langworthy is superior to Florence Nightingale, Mrs Josephine Butler, the Queen, or any other female; therefore his wife is bound to render him instant and implicit obedience even in trifles. Thelma's pity for the fine ladies who knew better than this, was no more grand or dutiful than is the pity which

Mr Cody's Indians possibly feel for us when we go to Earl's Court to wonder at them.[1]

Thelma, disgusted at finding men of science "trying to upset each other's theories," attributed this necessary incident of progress and research to "mean jealousies" and "miserable heartburnings." She also "invited two lady authoresses of note to meet at one of her at-homes; welcomed both the masculine-looking ladies with a radiant smile; and introduced them, saying gently" (and, it must be added, most impertinently), " 'You will be pleased to know each other.' " As it happened, they were not pleased; and Thelma's "simple Norse beliefs in the purity and gentleness of womanhood were startled and outraged," as they were later on by "the platform women, unnatural products of an unnatural age." How if the "platform women" were to retort by inviting the "Mudie women" to meet their audiences face to face, and submit their criticisms of society to the prompt and stern discipline of public discussion? If Marie Corelli may write her opinions, why may not other women speak theirs?

These indignant misunderstandings, which prompted the vile phrase "a society novel" on the title-page of Thelma, need not, how-ever, be taken too seriously. Their ignorance, their audacity, even the groundless assumption of superiority in them, are so amusingly sincere and well intended that they are never insufferable. Their author evidently feels that she is fearlessly fighting the good fight; and though she has the vaguest notions of what the good fight is about, and is youthfully deficient in charity and spiritual modesty, most of her blows fall on people who, for one misdeed or another, deserve them. As a romancer, she lacks nothing but originality; and she fails in that because she is more learned in operas, poems, and tales than in the realities of the living world, for which she has far too little sympathy. Her maiden in white, singing at the spinning-wheel, is borrowed from M Gounod; and her Odin worshipper

1. E. M. Langworthy was a minor Victorian social reformer. Josephine Elizabeth Butler (1828–1906) was a crusader for equal educational and economic opportunities for women, and for reform of laws relating to marriage and prostitution. William Frederick Cody (1846–1917), better known as Buffalo Bill, scout and buffalo hunter, afterwards a Wild West carnival entrepeneur.

meeting the Walkyrie comes from the "Nibelungen Lied," and was probably impressed on her by the scene between Siegmund and Brynhild in Wagner's Die Walküre. Still, these things are not tiresome as stale denunciations of society papers and footmen's calves are. And it must be acknowledged that she transfigures even her own shortcomings by the glamour of her ardent and vivid imagination, recklessly furnishing her air castles with all that is costly, magnificent, and voluptuous; peopling them with heroes, vikings, and sun maidens; surrounding them with landscapes of tropical glow or Alpine majesty; suffusing them with the warmth and radiance of splendid days; hiding them in the gloom and terror of dreadful nights; and, in short, playing prodigal in that No Man's Land of luxuries for which there is nothing to pay, of poignant griefs that do not hurt, thrilling joys that do not satisfy, virtuous aspirations that do not ennoble, and fierce crusades that leave evil none the weaker, but rather the more prosperous for the advertisement.

Pall Mall Gazette, June 29, 1887.

Marie Corelli

A review of Marie Corelli's Vendetta! *(1886).*

Last spring there appeared in these columns a notice of an audacious novel entitled A Romance of Two Worlds. The writer of that
notice, a gentleman of whose judgment the present reviewer enter-
tains a favourable opinion, declared in conclusion, "It is impossible
for a sober critic to quite approve of the author's rush into print;
but it may perhaps be admitted that 'Marie Corelli' might do worse
than rush again, so much less wearisome is she than many more exact
philosophers." "Marie Corelli" has accordingly rushed again, quite
as impetuously as before, and with the advantage of the experience
gained in her former attempt. The impression then made by her
vivid imagination, her extraordinary ardour, and her facility in description and declamation, is confirmed and reinforced by a most
prodigal display of them all in her new work. Its plot, though extremely sensational, contains no surprises for the reader, whose interest depends rather on a clear prevision of what is coming. Therefore
a sketch of it will in no way discount the effect of Vendetta on
those who may read it hereafter. Count Fabio Romani tells us how
he died of cholera at Naples in 1882; how he was buried; how he
revived, burst his coffin, found a vast treasure concealed in his family
vault, and disinterred himself and it; how he went home to find his
widow in the arms of his bosom friend, not for the first time; and
how, seized with a diabolical jealousy, he planned and carried out
a revenge in which the most merciful incidents were the murders
which completed it. Count Fabio is a gentleman as the devil is said
to be one: his appetite for evil is so intense that vulgar vices and
littlenesses are tasteless to him. He has a conscience too: for its sake
he assumes death to be the just punishment of adultery, and so
persuades himself that he is but a sword in the hand of God. Thus,
in order that the murder he desires to commit may pass for an

execution, he becomes, by his own appointment, legislator, judge, prosecutor, jury, witness, counsel on both sides, and hangman. Unfair as the trial is, there is no doubt as to the guilt of the culprit. She is by nature incapable of being a respectable woman and honest wife. What should be done with such a person? "She must die: else she'll betray more men," says Othello. "Ce n'est pas la femme, ce n'est même pas une femme; elle n'est pas dans la conception divine, elle est purement animale; c'est la guenon du pays de Nod, c'est la femelle de Caïn; tue la," says M Alexandre Dumas. Count Fabio agrees, but goes further. As his daughter is in heaven, he insists that his wife shall go elsewhere; and as to the method of killing her, he describes as "the best" that which "shall inflict the longest, the cruellest agony upon those by whom honour is wronged." His contempt for the British divorce court may be imagined. Our simple rule of not marrying such women, or, if we marry them unawares, untying the knot and quitting them, seems as sordid to him as his wounded vanity and lust for vengeance seem puerile to us. His opinions will nevertheless find friends in England. We have always with us men and women who, born after their due time, clamour to have the clock put back, and would, if they might have their way, reinstate flogging, duelling, confiscation of the property of wives, and a dozen other barbarisms which the rest of us have outgrown. These belated people gain for a time the support of enthusiastic young geniuses overtaking them on the way to maturity. It is possible that the author of Vendetta may be such a passer-by; for we are not told whether Count Fabio is offered as an example or as a warning. If the former, then the book must be intended to do for London what L'Homme-Femme was intended to do for Paris. In that case, nothing that is said here in recognition of Marie Corelli's success as a romancer must be taken as implying the smallest concession to the "tue-la" doctrine. If we cannot let the loose women severely alone—if we must make a heroine of her, let us confine her to farcial comedy as the form of art that flatters her least. Her pet notion that the vulgarity of her emotional instability is redeemed by some sort of tragic interest, is only nourished by the Fabio Romani regimen of pistols and daggers. The prosaic methods of Sir James Hannen[1] are far healthier for her and for us.

To compare Marie Corelli to Ouida may seem an equivocal compliment; but the association is inevitable, so much alike are they in many striking points. There is more freshness and fire in the younger writer; her men are far manlier and her women more real; she is guiltless of Ouida's terrible repetitions; and her culture is not wholly fictitious. But the resemblance is strong for all that. In the Corelli as in the Ouida novel we find an almost rancorous insistence on the corruption of modern society; a taste for artificial splendour indoors and for blue skies or moonlit seas without (drop scenery, in short); romantic Southern servants, peasants, or sailors whose impossible little conversations serve for padding; and a partial view of character, resulting from a keen insight into the erotic impulses without sufficient observation or study of the rest of life. The author of Vendetta appears to have some advantage of the author of Tricotrin both in intelligence and conscientiousness; but her probation is not yet ended. Her imagination, if scientifically trained, will make her: if let run wild, it will mar her. The latter course is the easier, and probably the more lucrative. It is the path or inspiration, which is popularly supposed to be the breath of genius. But Marie Corelli's renunciation in her new work of the supernatural quackery which disqualified A Romance of Two Worlds, raised some hope that she is becoming aware that inspiration is never right save by an improbable accident; and that genius consists chiefly of the power of detecting inspiration's errors, although much current novel-writing is nothing more than recording them in black and white.

One detail in Count Fabio's narrative needs transposition. When he issues from his tomb, he disguises himself as a coral-fisher before returning home. But the motive for disguise does not exist until he arrives there and discovers his wife's treachery. If a report that Mr Gladstone had lost his coat while bathing in the Tegernsee, and had thereupon hurried to a slop shop and purchased a coalheaver's costume to return home in, were to appear in to-morrow's newspa-

1. Sir James Hannen (1821–1894) was a well-known barrister and later judge (in Shaw's time) of the probate and divorce court.

per, we should be either incredulous or alarmed for the great statesman's sanity. Count Fabio is represented as acting no less unreason-
ably without a word of explanation. It is a small improbability
among many great ones; but it sticks in the throat for all that. The
consumer of fiction, though not a very dainty feeder, strains at the
gnat in spite of the complaisance with which he bolts the camel.

Pall Mall Gazette, September 11, 1886.

Hard Times

An introduction to Dickens's novel Hard Times *(1854).*

John Ruskin once declared Hard Times Dickens's best novel. It is worth while asking why Ruskin thought this, because he would have been the first to admit that the habit of placing works of art in competition with one another, and wrangling as to which is the best, is the habit of the sportsman, not of the enlightened judge of art. Let us take it that what Ruskin meant was that Hard Times was one of his special favorites among Dickens's books. Was this the caprice of fancy? or is there any rational explanation of the preference? I think there is.

Hard Times is the first fruit of that very interesting occurrence which our religious sects call, sometimes conversion, sometimes being saved, sometimes attaining to conviction of sin. Now the great conversions of the XIX century were not convictions of individual, but of social sin. The first half of the XIX century considered itself the greatest of all the centuries. The second discovered that it was the wickedest of all the centuries. The first half despised and pitied the Middle Ages as barbarous, cruel, superstitious, ignorant. The second half saw no hope for mankind except in the recovery of the faith, the art, the humanity of the Middle Ages. In Macaulay's History of England, the world is so happy, so progressive, so firmly set in the right path, that the author cannot mention even the National Debt without proclaiming that the deeper the country goes into debt, the more it prospers. In Morris's News from Nowhere there is nothing left of all the institutions that Macaulay glorified except an old building, so ugly that it is used only as a manure market, that was once the British House of Parliament. Hard Times was written in 1854, just at the turn of the half century; and in it we see Dickens with his eyes newly open and his conscience newly stricken by the discovery of the real state of England. In the book that went im-

mediately before, Bleak House, he was still denouncing evils and
ridiculing absurdities that were mere symptoms of the anarchy that
followed the industrial revolution of the XVIII and XIX centuries,
and the conquest of political power by Commercialism in 1832. In
Bleak House Dickens knows nothing of the industrial revolution:
he imagines that what is wrong is that when a dispute arises over
the division of the plunder of the nation, the Court of Chancery,
instead of settling the dispute cheaply and promptly, beggars the
disputants and pockets both their shares. His description of our
party system, with its Coodle, Doodle, Foodle, etc., has never been
surpassed for accuracy and for penetration of superficial pretence.
But he had not dug down to the bed rock of the imposture. His
portrait of the ironmaster who visits Sir Leicester Dedlock, and
who is so solidly superior to him, might have been drawn by
Macaulay: there is not a touch of Bounderby in it. His horrible and
not untruthful portraits of the brickmakers whose abject and
battered wives call them "master," and his picture of the now
vanished slum between Drury Lane and Catherine Street which he
calls Tom All Alone's, suggest (save in the one case of the outcast
Jo, who is, like Oliver Twist, a child, and therefore outside the
old self-help panacea of Dickens's time) nothing but individual
delinquencies, local plaguespots, negligent authorities.

In Hard Times you will find all this changed. Coketown, which
you can see to-day for yourself in all its grime in the Potteries (the
real name of it is Hanley in Staffordshire on the London and North
Western Railway),[1] is not, like Tom All Alone's, a patch of slum
in a fine city, easily cleared away, as Tom's actually was about fifty
years after Dickens called attention to it. Coketown is the whole
place; and its rich manufacturers are proud of its dirt, and declare
that they like to see the sun blacked out with smoke, because it
means that the furnaces are busy and money is being made; whilst

1. Hanley was one of the "Five Towns" (there were actually six) in the
Potteries District of the Midlands afterwards merged into Stoke on Trent.
It was the setting of George Moore's landmark of naturalistic fiction, *A
Mummer's Wife* (1884), and later (as part of the Five Towns) of a number
of Arnold Bennett's novels, including *An Old Wives' Tale* (1908).

its poor factory hands have never known any other sort of town, and are as content with it as a rat is with a hole. Mr Rouncewell, the pillar of society who snubs Sir Leicester with such dignity, has become Mr Bounderby, the self-made humbug. The Chancery suitors who are driving themselves mad by hanging about the Courts in the hope of getting a judgment in their favor instead of trying to earn an honest living, are replaced by factory operatives who toil miserably and incessantly only to see the streams of fold they set flowing slip through their fingers into the pockets of men who revile and oppress them.

Clearly this is not the Dickens who burlesqued the old song of the Fine Old English Gentleman, and saw in the evils he attacked only the sins and wickednesses and follies of a great civilization. This is Karl Marx, Carlyle, Ruskin, Morris, Carpenter, rising up against civilization itself as against a disease, and declaring that it is not our disorder but our order that is horrible; that it is not our criminals but our magnates that are robbing and murdering us; and that it is not merely Tom All Alone's that must be demolished and abolished, pulled down, rooted up, and made for ever impossible so that nothing shall remain of it but History's record of its infamy, but our entire social system. For that was how men felt, and how some of them spoke, in the early days of the Great Conversion which pro-duced, first, such books as the Latter Day Pamphlets of Carlyle, Dickens's Hard Times, and the tracts and sociological novels of the Christian Socialists, and later on the Socialist movement which has now spread all over the world, and which has succeeded in con-vincing even those who most abhor the name of Socialism that the condition of the civilized world is deplorable, and that the remedy is far beyond the means of individual righteousness. In short, whereas formerly men said to the victim of society who ventured to complain, "Go and reform yourself before you pretend to reform Society," it now has to admit that until Society is reformed, no man can reform himself except in the most insignificantly small ways. He may cease picking your pocket of half crowns; but he cannot cease taking a quarter of a million a year from the community for nothing at one end of the scale, or living under conditions in which

health, decency, and gentleness are impossible at the other, if he
happens to be born to such a lot.

You must therefore resign yourself, if you are reading Dickens's
books in the order in which they were written, to bid adieu now
to the light-hearted and only occasionally indignant Dickens of the
earlier books, and get such entertainment as you can from him now
that the occasional indignation has spread and deepened into a
passionate revolt against the whole industrial order of the modern
world. Here you will find no more villains and heroes, but only
oppressors and victims, oppressing and suffering in spite of themselves, driven by a huge machinery which grinds to pieces the people
it should nourish and ennoble, and having for its directors the basest
and most foolish of us instead of the noblest and most farsighted.

Many readers find the change disappointing. Others find Dickens
worth reading almost for the first time. The increase in strength
and intensity is enormous: the power that indicts a nation so terribly
is much more impressive than that which ridicules individuals. But
it cannot be said that there is an increase of simple pleasure for the
reader, though the books are not therefore less attractive. One cannot
say that it is pleasanter to look at a battle than at a merry-go-round;
but there can be no question which draws the larger crowd.

To describe the change in the readers' feelings more precisely,
one may say that it is impossible to enjoy Gradgrind or Bounderby
as one enjoys Pecksniff or the Artful Dodger or Mrs Gamp or
Micawber or Dick Swiveller, because these earlier characters have
nothing to do with us except to amuse us. We neither hate nor fear
them. We do not expect ever to meet them, and should not be in
the least afraid of them if we did. England is not full of Micawbers
and Swivellers. They are not our fathers, our schoolmasters, our
employers, our tyrants. We do not read novels to escape from them
and forget them: quite the contrary. But England is full of Bounder-
bys and Podsnaps and Gradgrinds; and we are all to a quite appalling extent in their power. We either hate and fear them or else we
are them, and resent being held up to odium by a novelist. We have
only to turn to the article on Dickens in the current edition of the
Encyclopedia Britannica to find how desperately our able critics

still exalt all Dickens's early stories about individuals whilst ignoring or belittling such masterpieces as Hard Times, Little Dorrit, Our Mutual Friend, and even Bleak House (because of Sir Leicester Dedlock), for their mercilessly faithful and penetrating exposures of English social, industrial, and political life; to see how hard Dickens hits the conscience of the governing class; and how loth we still are to confess, not that we are so wicked (for of that we are rather proud), but so ridiculous, so futile, so incapable of making our country really prosperous. The Old Curiosity Shop was written to amuse you, entertain you, touch you; and it succeeded. Hard Times was written to make you uncomfortable; and it will make you uncomfortable (and serve you right) though it will perhaps interest you more, and certainly leave a deeper scar on you, than any two of its forerunners.

At the same time you need not fear to find Dickens losing his good humor and sense of fun and becoming serious in Mr Gradgrind's way. On the contrary, Dickens in this book casts off, and casts off for ever, all restraint on his wild sense of humor. He had always been inclined to break loose: there are passages in the speeches of Mrs Nickleby and Pecksniff which are impossible as well as funny. But now it is no longer a question of passages: here he begins at last to exercise quite recklessly his power of presenting a character to you in the most fantastic and outrageous terms, putting into its mouth from one end of the book to the other hardly one word which could conceivably be uttered by any sane human being, and yet leaving you with an unmistakable and exactly truthful portrait of a character that you recognize at once as not only real but typical. Nobody ever talked, or ever will talk, as Silas Wegg talks to Boffin and Mr Venus, or as Mr Venus reports Pleasant Riderhood to have talked, or as Rogue Riderhood talks, or as John Chivery talks. They utter rhapsodies of nonesense conceived in an ecstasy of mirth. And this begins in Hard Times. Jack Bunsby in Dombey and Son is absurd: the oracles he delivers are very nearly impossible, and yet not quite impossible. But Mrs Sparsit in this book, though Rembrandt could not have drawn a certain type of real woman more precisely to the life, is grotesque from begin-

ning to end in her way of expressing herself. Her nature, her tricks
of manner, her way of taking Mr Bounderby's marriage, her instinct
for hunting down Louisa and Mrs Pegler, are drawn with an
unerring hand; and she says nothing that is out of character. But
no clown gone suddenly mad in a very mad harlequinade could
express all these truths in more extravagantly ridiculous speeches.
Dickens's business in life has become too serious for troubling over
the small change of verisimilitude, and denying himself and his
readers the indulgence of his humor in inessentials. He even calls
the schoolmaster McChoakumchild, which is almost an insult to the
serious reader. And it was so afterwards to the end of his life. There
are moments when he imperils the whole effect of his character
drawing by some overpoweringly comic sally. For instance, happen-
ing in Hard Times to describe Mr Bounderby as drumming on his
hat as if it were a tambourine, which is quite correct and natural,
he presently says that "Mr Bounderby put his tambourine on his
head, like an oriental dancer." Which similitude is so unexpectedly
and excruciatingly funny that it is almost impossible to feel duly
angry with the odious Bounderby afterwards.

This disregard of naturalness in speech is extraordinarily entertaining in the comic method; but it must be admitted that it is not
only not entertaining, but sometimes hardly bearable when it does
not make us laugh. There are two persons in Hard Times, Louisa
Gradgrind and Cissy Jupe, who are serious throughout. Louisa
is a figure of poetic tragedy; and there is no question of naturalness
in her case: she speaks from beginning to end as an inspired
prophetess, conscious of her own doom and finally bearing to her
father the judgment of Providence on his blind conceit. If you once
consent to overlook her marriage, which is none the less an act of
prostitution because she does it to obtain advantages for her brother
and not for herself, there is nothing in the solemn poetry of her
deadly speech that jars. But Cissy is nothing if not natural; and
though Cissy is as true to nature in her character as Mrs Sparsit,
she "speaks like a book" in the most intolerable sense of the words.
In her interview with Mr James Harthouse, her unconscious courage
and simplicity, and his hopeless defeat by them, are quite natural

and right; and the contrast between the humble girl of the people and the smart sarcastic man of the world whom she so completely vanquishes is excellently dramatic; but Dickens has allowed himself to be carried away by the scene into a ridiculous substitution of his own most literary and least colloquial style for any language that could conceivably be credited to Cissy.

> MR HARTHOUSE: the only reparation that remains with you is to leave her immediately and finally. I am quite sure that you can mitigate in no other way the wrong and harm you have done. I am quite sure that it is the only compensation you have left it in your power to make. I do not say that it is much, or that it is enough; but it is something, and it is necessary. Therefore, though without any other authority than I have given you, and even without the knowledge of any other person than yourself and myself, I ask you to depart from this place to-night, under an obligation never to return to it.

This is the language of a Lord Chief Justice, not of the dunce of an elementary school in the Potteries.

But this is only a surface failure, just as the extravagances of Mrs Sparsit are only surface extravagances. There is, however, one real failure in the book. Slackbridge, the trade union organizer, is a mere figment of the middle-class imagination. No such man would be listened to by a meeting of English factory hands. Not that such meetings are less susceptible to humbug than meetings of any other class. Not that trade union organizers, worn out by the terribly wearisome and trying work of going from place to place repeating the same commonplaces and trying to "stoke up" meetings to enthusiasm with them, are less apt than other politicians to end as windbags, and sometimes to depend on stimulants to pull them through their work. Not, in short, that the trade union platform is any less humbug-ridden than the platforms of our more highly placed political parties. But even at their worst trade union organizers are not a bit like Slackbridge. Note, too, that Dickens mentions that there was a chairman at the meeting (as if that were rather surprising), and that this chairman makes no attempt to preserve the usual order of public meeting, but allows speakers to address the assembly and interrupt one another in an entirely disorderly way. All this is pure middle-class ignorance. It is much as if a tramp were to write a description of millionaires smoking large cigars in church, with their wives in low-necked dresses and diamonds. We cannot say that Dickens did not know the working classes, because he knew humanity too well to be ignorant of any class. But this sort of knowledge is as compatible with ignorance of class manners and customs as with ignorance of foreign languages. Dickens knew certain classes of working folk very well: domestic servants, village artisans, and employees of petty tradesmen for example. But of the segregated factory populations of our purely industrial towns he knew no more than an observant professional man can pick up on a flying visit to Manchester.

It is especially important to notice that Dickens expressly says in this book that the workers were wrong to organize themselves in trade unions, thereby endorsing what was perhaps the only practical mistake of the Gradgrind school that really mattered much. And having thus thoughtlessly adopted, or at least repeated, this error, long since exploded, of the philosophic Radical school from which he started, he turns his back frankly on Democracy, and adopts the idealized Toryism of Carlyle and Ruskin, in which the aristocracy are the masters and superiors of the people, and also the servants of the people and of God. Here is a significant passage.

> "Now perhaps," said Mr. Bounderby, "you will let the gentleman know how you would set this muddle (as you are so fond of calling it) to rights."
>
> "I donno, sir. I canna be expecten to't. Tis not me as should be looken to for that, sir. Tis they as is put ower me, and ower aw the rest of us. What do they tak upon themseln, sir, if not to do it?"

And to this Dickens sticks for the rest of his life. In Our Mutual Friend he appeals again and again to the governing classes, asking them with every device of reproach, invective, sarcasm, and ridicule of which he is master, what they have to say to this or that evil which it is their professed business to amend or avoid. Nowhere does he appeal to the working classes to take their fate into their own hands and try the democratic plan.

Another phrase used by Stephen Blackpool in this remarkable fifth chapter is important. "Nor yet lettin alone will never do it." It is Dickens's express repudiation of *laissez-faire*.

There is nothing more in the book that needs any glossary, except, perhaps, the strange figure of the Victorian "swell," Mr James Harthouse. His pose has gone out of fashion. Here and there you may still see a man—even a youth—with a single eyeglass, an elaborately bored and weary air, and a little stock of cynicisms and indifferentisms contrasting oddly with a mortal anxiety about his clothes. All he needs is a pair of Dundreary whiskers, like the officers in Desanges' military pictures, to be a fair imitation of Mr James Harthouse. But he is not in the fashion: he is an eccentric, as Whistler was an eccentric, as Max Beerbohm and the neo-dandies of the *fin de siècle* were eccentrics. It is now the fashion to be energetic, to hustle as American millionaires are supposed (rather erroneously) to hustle. But the soul of the swell is still unchanged. He has changed his name again and again, become a Masher, a Toff, a Johnny and what not; but fundamentally he remains what he always was, an Idler, and therefore a man bound to find some trick of thought and speech that reduces the world to a thing as empty and purposeless and hopeless as himself. Mr Harthouse reappears, more seriously and kindly taken, as Eugene Wrayburn and Mortimer Lightwood in Our Mutual Friend. He reappears as a club in The Finches of the Grove of Great Expectations. He will reappear in all his essentials in fact and in fiction until he is at last shamed or coerced into honest industry and becomes not only unintelligible but inconceivable.

Note, finally, that in this book Dickens proclaims that marriages are not made in heaven, and that those which are not confirmed there, should be dissolved.

Introduction to *Hard Times*, by Charles Dickens (London: 1912).

Great Expectations

An introduction to Dickens's novel Great Expectations *(1860-1861)*.

Great Expectations is the last of the three full-length stories written by Dickens in the form of an autobiography. Of the three, Bleak House, as the autobiography of Miss Esther Summerson, is naturally the least personal; for Esther is not only a woman but a maddening prig, though we are forced to admit that such paragons exist and are perhaps worthy of the reverent admiration with which Dickens regarded them. Ruling her out, we have David Copperfield and Great Expectations. David was, for a time at least, Dickens's favorite child, perhaps because he had used him to express the bitterness of that episode in his own experience which had wounded his boyish self-respect most deeply. For Dickens, in spite of his exuberance, was a deeply reserved man: the exuberance was imagination and acting (his imagination was ceaseless, and his outward life a feat of acting from beginning to end); and we shall never know whether in that immensely broadened outlook and knowledge of the world which began with Hard Times and Little Dorrit, and left all his earlier works behind, he may not have come to see that making his living by sticking labels on blacking bottles and rubbing shoulders with boys who were not gentlemen, was as little shameful as being the genteel apprentice in the office of Mr Spenlow, or the shorthand writer recording the unending twaddle of the House of Commons and its overflow of electioneering bunk on the hustings of all the Eatanswills in the country.

That there was a tragic change in his valuations can be shewn by contrasting Micawber with William Dorrit. Beside Dorrit Micawber suddenly becomes a mere marionette pantaloon with a funny bag of tricks which he repeats until we can bear no more of him, and Dorrit a ruthless study of what snobbish gentility can make of reasonably decent human material. Now turn to Great Expectations,

49

and, comparing David Copperfield with Pip, believe, if you can, that there was no revision of his estimate of the favorite child David as a work of art and even as a vehicle of experience. The adult David fades into what stage managers call a walking gentleman. The reappearance of Mr Dickens in the character of a blacksmith's boy may be regarded as an apology to Mealy Potatoes.

Dickens did in fact know that Great Expectations was his most compactly perfect book. In all other books, there are episodes of wild extravagance, extraordinarily funny if they catch you at the right age, but recklessly grotesque as nature studies. Even in Little Dorrit, Dickens's masterpiece among many masterpieces, it is impossible to believe that the perfectly authentic Mr Pancks really stopped the equally authentic Mr Casby in a crowded street in London and cut his hair; and though Mr F's aunt is a first-rate clinical study of senile deficiency in a shrewd old woman, her collisions with Arthur Clennam are too funny to be taken seriously. We cannot say of Casby, Pancks, and the aunt, as we can say of Sam Weller, that such people never existed; for most of us have met their counterparts in real life; but we can say that Dickens's sense of fun ran away with him over them. If we have absolutely no fun in us we may even state gravely that there has been a lapse from the artistic integrity of the tragic picture of English society which is the subject of Little Dorrit.

In Great Expectations we have Wopsle and Trabb's boy; but they have their part and purpose in the story and do not overstep the immodesty of nature. It is hardly decent to compare Mr F's aunt with Miss Havisham; but as contrasted studies of madwomen they make you shudder at the thought of what Dickens might have made of Miss Havisham if he had seen her as a comic personage. For life is no laughing matter in Great Expectations: the book is all-of-one piece and consistently truthful as none of the other books are, not even the compact Tale of Two Cities, which is pure sentimental melodrama from beginning to end, and shockingly wanting in any philosophy of history in its view of the French Revolution.

Dickens never regarded himself as a revolutionist, though he certainly was one. His contempt for the House of Commons, founded on his experience as an exclusively parliamentary reporter, never wavered from the account of the Eatanswill election and of Nicholas Nickleby's interview with Pugstyles to the Veneering election in Our Mutual Friend, his last book. (Edwin Drood is only a gesture by a man three quarters dead.) And this was not mere satire, of which there had been plenty. Dickens was the first writer to perceive and state definitely that the House of Commons, working on the Party system, is an extraordinarily efficient device for dissipating all our reforming energy and ability in Party debate and, when anything urgently needs to be done, finding out "how not to do it". It took very little time to get an ineffective Factory Act. It took fifty years to make it effective, though the labor conditions in the factories and mines were horrible. After Dickens's death, it took thirty years to pass an Irish Home Rule Bill, which was promptly repudiated by the military plutocracy, leaving the question to be settled by a competition in slaughter and house burning, just as it would have been between two tribes of savages. Liberty under our British parliamentary routine means slavery for nine tenths of the people, and slave exploitation or parasitic idolatory and snobbery for the rest. Parliament men—one cannot call them statesmen—and even historians, keep declaring that the British parliamentary system is one of the greatest blessings British political genius has given to the world; and the world, swallowing the tale, has set up pseudo-republican imitations of it all over Europe and America, always with the same result: political students outside Parliament exposing the most frightful social evils and prescribing their remedies, and Parliament ignoring them as long as possible and then engulfing their disciples and changing them from reformers into partisans with time for nothing but keeping their party in power or opposing the Government, rightly or wrongly ("it is the duty of the Opposition to oppose") as the case might be. In the middle of the nineteenth century Dickens saw this and said it. He had to be ignored, as he would not stand for Parliament and be paralyzed.

Europe is learning from hard experience what it would not learn from Dickens. The Fascist and Communist revolutions which have swept the great parliamentary sham into the dustbin after its production of a monstrous war, made no mention of Dickens; but on the parliamentary point he was as much their prophet as Marx was the economic prophet of the Soviets. Yet a recent reactionist against Dickens worship declares that he "never went ahead of his public". He should re-read Little Dorrit.

Marx and Dickens were contemporaries living in the same city and pursuing the same profession of literature; yet they seem to us like creatures of a different species living in different worlds. Dickens, if he had ever become conscious of Karl Marx, would have been classed with him as a revolutionist. The difference between a revolutionist and what Marx called a bourgeois is that the bourgeois regards the existing social order as the permanent and natural order of human society, needing reforms now and then and here and there, but essentially good and sane and right and respectable and proper and everlasting. To the revolutionist it is transitory, mistaken, dishonest, unhappy, pathological: a social disease to be cured, not to be endured. We have only to compare Thackeray and Trollope with Dickens to perceive this contrast. Thackeray reviled the dominant classes with a savagery which would have been unchivalrous in Dickens: he often denied even the common good qualities and accomplishments of ladies and gentlemen, making them mean, illiterate, profligate, ignorant, sycophantic to an inhuman degree, whilst Dickens, even when making his aristocrats politically and socially ridiculous and futile, liked making real gentlemen of them. Trollope, who regarded Thackeray as his master and exemplar, had none of his venom, and has left us a far better balanced and more truthful picture of Victorian well-off society, never consciously whitewashing it, though allowing it its full complement of black sheep of both sexes. But Trollope's politics were those of the country house and the hunting field just as were Thackeray's. Accordingly, Thackeray and Trollope were received and approved by fashionable society with complete confidence. Dickens, though able to fascinate all classes, was never so received or approved except by the goodnatured or stupid ladies and gentlemen who were incapable of criticizing anyone who could make them laugh and cry. The rest said that Dickens could not describe a gentleman and called Little Dorrit twaddle. And the reason was that in his books the west-end heaven appears as a fool's paradise that must pass away instead of being an indispensable preparatory school for the New Jerusalem. Our leading encyclopedia still tells us that Dickens had "no knowledge of country gentlemen". It would be nearer the mark to say that Dickens knew all that really mattered to the world about Sir Leicester Dedlock, and that Trollope knew nothing that really mattered about him. Trollope and Thackeray could see Chesney Wold; but Dickens could see through it. Sir Leicester was no joke to Dickens. He was deeply concerned about him, and understood how revolutions begin with burning the chateaux.

The difference between Marx and Dickens was that Marx knew that he was a revolutionist whilst Dickens had not the faintest suspicion of that part of his calling. Compare the young Dickens looking for a job in a lawyer's office and teaching himself shorthand to escape from his office stool to the reporters' gallery, with the young Trotsky, the young Lenin, quite deliberately facing disreputable poverty, and adopting revolution as their profession with every alternative of bourgeois security and respectability much more fully open to them than to Dickens.

And this brings us to Dickens's position as a member of the educated and cultured classes who had neither education nor culture. This was fortunate for him and for the world, as he escaped the public school and university routine which complicates cultural Philistinism with the mentality of a Red Indian brave. Better no schooling at all than the schooling of Rudyard Kipling and Winston Churchill. But there are homes in which a mentally acquisitive boy can make contact with the fine arts. I myself learnt nothing at school, but gained in my home an extensive and highly educational knowledge of music. I had access to illustrated books on painting which sent me to the National Gallery; so that I was able to support myself as a critic of music and painting as Dickens supported himself by shorthand. I devoured books on science and on the religious controversies of the day. It is in this way, and not in our public schools and universities, that such genuine spontaneous culture as there is in England is kept alive.

Now the Dickenses seem to have been complete barbarians. Dickens mentions the delight with which he discovered in an attic a heap of eighteenth-century novels. But Smollett was a grosser barbarian than Dickens himself; and Don Quixote and the Arabian Nights, though they gave the cue to his eager imagination, left him quite in the dark as to the philosophy and art of his day. To him a philosopher, an intellectual, was a figure of fun. Count Smorltork is born of a street Arab's derision: Dickens did not even know that the Count's method of acquiring Chinese metaphysics by studying metaphysics and China and "combining the information" was not only sensible and correct, but the only possible method. To Dickens as to most Victorian Englishmen metaphysics were ridiculous, useless, unpractical, and the mark of a fool. He was musical enough to have a repertory of popular ballads which he sang all over the house to keep his voice in order; and he made Tom Pinch play the organ in church as an amiable accomplishment; but I cannot remember hearing that he ever went to a classical concert, or even knew of the existence of such entertainments. The articles on the National Gallery in All the Year Round, though extremely funny in their descriptions of The Apotheosis of William the Silent (the title alone would make a cat laugh), and on some profane points sensible enough, are those of a complete Philistine. One cannot say that he disliked all painters in the face of his friendship with Maclise and Clarkson Stanfield; but it was not a cultural friendship: Stanfield was a scene painter who appealed to that English love of landscape which is so often confused with a love of art; and Maclise was a pictorial anecdotist who presented scenes from Shakespear's plays exactly as they were presented on the stage. When Dickens introduced in his stories a character whom he intensely disliked he chose an artistic profession for him. Henry Gowan in Little Dorrit is a painter, Pecksniff is an architect. Harold Skimpole is a musician. There is real hatred in his treatment of them.

Now far be it for me to imply that they are false to nature. Artists are often detestable human beings; and the famous Anti-Scrape, officially The Society for the Protection of Ancient Buildings, was founded by William Morris and his friends to protect ancient build-

ings from architects. What is more, the ultra-artistic sets, the pre-
Raphaelites and the aesthetes grouped round Rossetti and Morris
and Ruskin, were all Dickens worshippers who made a sort of cult
of Trabb's boy and would have regarded me as a traitor if they
had read what I am now writing. They knew better than anyone
else that Leigh Hunt deserved all he got as Harold Skimpole, that
Gowan's shallow sort of painting is a nuisance, and that architecture
was just the right profession for a parasite on Salisbury Cathedral
like Pecksniff. But all their Dickensian enthusiasm, and all the truth
to life of Dickens's portraiture, cannot extenuate the fact that the
cultural side of art was as little known to Dickens as it is possible
for a thing so public to remain to a man so apprehensive. You may
read the novels of Dickens from beginning to end without ever
learning that he lived through a period of fierce revivals and revolutionary movements in art, in philosophy, in sociology, in religion:
in short, in culture. Dean Inge's remark that "the number of great
subjects in which Dickens took no interest whatever is amazing" hits
the nail exactly on the head. As to finding such a person as Karl
Marx among his characters, one would as soon look for a nautilus
in a nursery.

Yet Little Dorrit is a more seditious book than Das Kapital. All
over Europe men and women are in prison for pamphlets and
speeches which are to Little Dorrit as red pepper to dynamite.
Fortunately for social evolution Governments never know where
to strike. Barnacle and Stiltstalking were far too conceited to recognize their own portraits. Parliament, wearing its leaders out in a
few years by the ceaseless drudgery of finding out how not to do it,
and smothering it in talk, left members and ministers no time to
read the Coodle-Doodle discussions in Sir Leicester Dedlock's draw-
ingroom. As to the Circumlocution Office, well, perhaps the staffs,
owing their posts to patronage and regarding them as sinecures,
were a bit too insolent to the public, and would be none the worse
for a little chaff from a funny fellow like Dickens; but in their ineffi-
ciency as a public service was actually a good thing, as it provided
a standing object lesson in the superiority of private enterprise. Mr
Sparkler was not offended: he struck to his sinecure and never read

anything. Little Dorrit and Das Kapital were the same to him: they never entered his world; and to him that world was the whole world. Thackeray coveted a sinecure.

The mass of Dickens readers, finding his politicians too funny to be credible, continued to idolize Coodle and Doodle as great statesmen, and made no distinction between John Stuart Mill at the India Office and Mr Sparkler. In fact the picture was not only too funny to be credible: it was too truthful to be credible. But the fun was no fun to Dickens: the truth was too bitter. When you laugh at Jack Bunsby, or at The Orfling when the handle of her corkscrew came off and smote her on the chin, you have no doubt that Dickens is laughing with you like a street boy, despite Bunsby's tragic end. But whilst you laugh at Sparkler or young Barnacle, Dickens is in deadly earnest: he means that both of them must go into the dustbin if England is to survive.

And still Dickens never saw himself as a revolutionist. It never occurred to him to found a Red International, as Marx did, nor even to join one out of the dozens of political reform societies that were about him. He was an English gentleman of the professional class, who would not allow his daughter to go on the stage because it was not respectable. He knew so little about revolutionists that when Mazzini called on him and sent in his card, Dickens, much puzzled, concluded that the unknown foreign gentleman wanted money, and very kindly sent him down a sovereign to get rid of him. He discovered for himself all the grievances he exposed, and had no sense of belonging to a movement, nor any desire to combine with others who shared his subversive views. To educate his children religiously and historically he wrote a Child's History of England which had not even the excuse of being childish, and a paraphrase of the gospel biography which is only a belittling of it for little children. He had much better have left the history to Little Arthur[1] and Mrs Markham[2] and Goldsmith, and taken into account the

1. "Little Arthur" was the pseudonym of Lady Maria Calcott (1785–1842), who published Little Arthur's History of England (in eight volumes) in 1835.
2. "Mrs. Markham" was the pseudonym of Mrs. Elizabeth Penrose

extraordinary educational value of the Authorized Version as a work of literary art. He probably thought as seldom of himself as a literary artist as of himself as a revolutionist; and he had his share in the revolt against the supernatural pretensions of the Bible which was to end in the vogue of Agnosticism and the pontificate of Darwin. It blinded that generation to the artistic importance of the fact that at a moment when all the literary energy in England was in full eruption, when Shakespear was just dead and Milton just born, a picked body of scholars undertook the task of translating into English what they believed to be the words of God himself. Under the strain of that conviction they surpassed all their normal powers, transfiguring the original texts into literary masterpieces of a splendor that no merely mortal writers can ever again hope to achieve. But the nineteenth century either did not dare think of the Bible in that way, it being fetish, or else it was in such furious reaction against the fetishism that it would not allow the so-called Holy Scriptures even an artistic merit. At all events Dickens thought his Little Nell style better for his children than the English of King James's inspired scribes. He took them (for a time at least) to churches of the Unitarian persuasion, where they could be both sceptical and respectable; but it is hard to say what Dickens believed or did not believe metaphysically or metapolitically, though he left us in no doubt as to his opinion of the Lords, the Commons, and the ante-Crimean Civil Service.

On the positive side he had nothing to say. Marxism and Darwinism came too late for him. He might have been a Comtist—perhaps ought to have been a Comtist, but was not. He was an independent Dickensian, a sort of unphilosophic Radical, with a complete disbelief in government by the people and an equally complete hostility to government in any other interest than theirs. He exposed many abuses and called passionately on the rulers of the people to remedy them; but he never called on the people to do such skilled work for themselves. He would as soon have thought of calling on them to write their own novels.

(1730–1837), who wrote popular schoolbook histories of England (1823) and France (1828).

Meanwhile he overloaded himself and his unfortunate wife with such a host of children that he was forced to work himself to death prematurely to provide for them and for the well-to-do life he led. The reading public cannot bear to think of its pet authors as struggling with the economic pressures that often conflict so cruelly with the urge of genius. This pressure was harder on Dickens than on many poorer men. He had a solid bourgeois conscience which made it impossible for him to let wife and children starve whilst he followed the path of destiny. Marx let his wife go crazy with prolonged poverty whilst he wrote a book which changed the mind of the world. But then Marx had been comfortably brought up and thoroughly educated in the German manner. Dickens knew far too much of the horrors of impecuniosity to put his wife through what his mother had gone through, or have his children pasting labels on blacking bottles. He had to please his public or lapse into that sort of poverty. Under such circumstances the domestic conscience inevitably pushes the artistic conscience into the second place. We shall never know how much of Dickens's cheery optimism belied his real outlook on life. He went his own way far enough to make it clear that when he was not infectiously laughing he was a melancholy fellow. Arthur Clennam is one of the Dismal Jemmies of literature. For any gaiety of heart we have to turn to the impossible Dick Swiveller, who, by the way, was intended to be a revoltingly coarse fortune hunter, and still appears in that character in the single scene which precedes his sudden appeal to Dickens's sense of fun, and consequent transformation into a highly entertaining and entirely fantastic clown. This was a genuine conversion and not a concession to public taste; but the case of Walter Gay in Dombey and Son, whose high spirits were planned as a prelude to his degeneration and ruin, is a flagrant case of a manufactured happy ending to save a painful one. Martin Chuzzlewit begins as a study in selfishness and ends nowhere. Mr Boffin, corrupted by riches, gets discharged without a stain on his character by explaining that he was only pretending for benevolent purposes, but leaves us with a feeling that some of his pretences were highly suspicious. Jarndyce, a violently good man, keeps on doing generous things, yet ends by practising a stupidly cruel and indelicate deception on Esther Summerson for the sake of giving her a pleasant melodramatic surprise. I will not go so far as to say that Dickens's novels are full of melancholy intentions which he shrank from carrying through to their unhappy conclusions; but he gave us no vitally happy heroes and heroines after Pickwick (begun, like Don Quixote, as a contemptible butt). Their happy endings are manufactured to make the books pleasant. Nobody who has endured the novels of our twentieth-century emancipated women, enormously cleverer and better informed than the novels of Dickens, and ruthlessly calculated to leave their readers hopelessly discouraged and miserable, will quarrel with Dickens for speeding his parting guests with happy faces by turning from the world of destiny to the world of imaginary good luck; but as our minds grow stronger and sterner some of his consolations become unnecessary and even irritating. And it happens that it is with just such a consolation that Great Expectations ends.

It did not always end so. In the Clarion of May 16, 1902, the late Hugh Mann, known to Clarion readers as Slender, quoted a different ending as the original, and raised the question whether an author has any right to commit what the editor (Mr Robert Blatchford) had called "literary infanticide" by discarding his inspired version of a story and substituting a changeling under external pressure. In 1918 Forster's Life of Dickens was edited by Mr J. W. T. Ley. In a footnote on pages 737–8 is quoted Dickens's letter to Forster declaring "I have no doubt the story will be more acceptable for the alteration". The alteration was urged on him by Bulwer Lytton. Forster then goes on to say "This turned out to be the case; but the first ending nevertheless seems to me more consistent with the drift as well as the natural working out of the tale; and for this reason it is preserved in a note". The note tallies with the Clarion version.

Then I butted in and muddled matters by declaring that in my childhood I had read Great Expectations in its first form in All the Year Round, and that it was so much better that if ever I edited the book I should unhesitatingly restore the original ending. The result of this was a demand for such an edition, met by the Limited Editions Club of New York with an announcement of the present work.

Now the real editing has been done by Mr William Maxwell of Edinburgh, head of a famous firm of printers there; and when he referred to All the Year Round for the alleged original ending which had made such an impression on my infant mind, he found that I had been romancing; for the ending there was the Bulwer Lytton ending just as it stands today. He might thereupon very well have dismissed the original ending as a fancy of mine (as in fact it was) had it not been for the letter from Dickens to Forster about the change, the recorded protest of Dickens's son, and the actual text of the first ending given by Forster and in The Clarion, all of which Mr Maxwell tracked down after examining the original manuscript of the book and finding that it too had the changed ending. Yet the proofs read by Bulwer Lytton, which, one would suppose, must have followed the manuscript, contained the original ending. Why did Dickens attach so much importance to the change that he altered the manuscript after the printer had finished with it?

The answer, I think, is that the second ending, though psychologically wrong, is artistically much more congruous than the original. The scene, the hour, the atmosphere are beautifully touching and exactly right. Only at the end of the very last line did Dickens allow himself to say that between Pip and Estella there was "no shadow of parting". If I ever indulge in the luxury of a copy of Great Expectations made all for myself, Pip shall end by saying "Since that parting I have been able to think of her without the old unhappiness; but I have never tried to see her again, and I know I never shall". That would be the perfect ending.

But it would not have satisfied Bulwer Lytton. In his day there was a convention called a happy ending. It did not mean a happy ending: it meant that the lovers were married in the last chapter. Byron complained that "romances paint at full length people's wooings but only gives a bust of marriages". Early in the present century the late St John Hankin published a volume entitled Three Plays with Happy Endings. In none of them did the lovers marry: they all had very happy escapes. That made us more critical of happiness and of marriage, and incidentally made us less tolerant of the convention that a marriage between Pip and Estella had any prospect of happiness for either of them, or indeed was not the most unhappy ending that could possibly be devised.

The discarded ending was, in fact, the true happy ending; and when the text of it was recovered by Mr Maxwell there was no further obstacle to the publication of the Club's edition exactly as promised. Its atmosphere is a change which only the English climate could produce from the melancholy marshes where Magwitch starved and shivered in the winter dusk, with the guns of the horrible prison hulks booming their sullen hue and cry in the distance, to Piccadilly in spring. And the Shropshire doctor seems almost unbearably eupeptic in the procession of morbid or unhappy or dislikeable creatures who make the book so tragic. In fact, this ending is too happy if we may assume that Bentley Drummle had really thrashed the malicious complex out of Estella, and been himself well hammered by the doctor, who, being able to thrash both of them, was capable of living happily for ever after even with Estella. It is quite a healthy ending and a possible one; but it somehow does not belong to the tale. And the other ending belongs to the tale, but falsifies it at the last moment. I really think my own ending is the right one because I recollected it so in spite of that fatal phrase, and a child's wisdom is to be respected; but as Dickens is the final authority I am afraid the Bulwer Lytton version must stand for all editions beyond this very special one.

Note, by the way, that the passing carriage in the Piccadilly ending was unconsciously borrowed from A Day's Ride: A Life's Romance, the novel by Charles Lever which was so unpopular that Dickens had to write Great Expectations to replace it in All the Year Round. But in Lever's story it is the man who stops the carriage, only to be cut dead by the lady. That also, was the happiest possible ending both for Potts and Katinka, though the humiliation of Potts makes it painful for the moment. Lever was shewing Dickens the way; and Dickens instinctively took it until Lytton moidered[3] him by fears for its effect on the sales.

Estella is a curious addition to the gallery of unamiable women painted by Dickens. In my youth it was commonly said that Dickens

3. *Moidered:* bewildered, distracted.

could not draw women. The people who said this were thinking of Agnes Wickfield and Esther Summerson, of Little Dorrit and Florence Dombey, and thinking of them as ridiculous idealizations of their sex. Gissing stopped that by asking whether shrews like Mrs Raddle, Mrs Macstinger, Mrs Gargery, featherheads like Mrs Nickleby and Flora Finching, warped spinsters like Rosa Dartle and Miss Wade, were not masterpieces of woman drawing. And they are all unamiable. But for Betsy Trotwood, who is a very lovable fairy godmother and yet a genuine nature study, and an old dear like Mrs Boffin, one would be tempted to ask whether Dickens had ever in his life met an amiable female. The transformation of Dora into Flora is diabolical, but frightfully true to nature. Of course Dickens with his imagination could invent amiable women by the dozen; but somehow he could not or would not bring them to life as he brought the others. We doubt whether he ever knew a little Dorrit; but Fanny Dorrit is from the life unmistakably. So is Estella. She is a much more elaborate study than Fanny, and, I should guess, a recent one.

Dickens, when he let himself go in Great Expectations, was separated from his wife and free to make more intimate acquaintances with women than a domesticated man can. I know nothing of his adventures in this phase of his career, though I daresay a good deal of it will be dug out by the little sect of anti-Dickensites whose fanaticism has been provoked by the Dickens Fellowships, and threatens to become as pathological as Bacon-Shakespear. It is not necessary to suggest a love affair;[4] for Dickens could get from a passing glance a hint which he could expand into a full-grown character. Estella is a born tormentor. She torments Pip all through for the fun of it; and in the little we hear of her intercourse with others there is no suggestion of a moment of kindness: in fact her tormenting of Pip is almost affectionate in contrast to the cold disdain of her

4. But there was a love affair, with Ellen Ternan, a young actress, whom Dickens secretly maintained from 1863 until his death in 1870. Dickens's later women, from Estella on, have a greater sexual reality than his previous feminine characters, and apparently owe something to Ellen Ternan. Dickens's will even begins with a bequest to her.

attitude towards the people who were not worth tormenting. It is not surprising that the unfortunate Bentley Drummle, whom she marries in the stupidity of sheer perversity, is obliged to defend himself from her clever malice with his fists: a consolation to us for Pip's broken heart, but not altogether a credible one; for the real Estellas can usually intimidate the real Bentley Drummles. At all events the final sugary suggestion of Estella redeemed by Bentley's thrashings and waste of her money, and living happily with Pip for ever after, provoked even Dickens's eldest son to rebel against it, most justly. And yet Pip never loses his sense of "the indescribable majesty and indescribable charm" of her beauty. She still forces us to accept her as a superior creature who never learnt how to live in the real vulgar world. That is entirely true to nature.

Save for the last words the story is the most perfect of Dickens's works. In it he does not muddle himself with the ridiculous plots that appear like vestiges of the stone age in many of his books, from Oliver Twist to the end. The story is built round a single and simple catastrophe: the revelation to Pip of the source of his great expectations. There is, it is true, a trace of the old plot superstition in Estella turning out to be Magwitch's daughter; but it provides a touchingly happy ending for that heroic Warmint. Who could have the heart to grudge it to him?

As our social conscience expands and makes the intense class snobbery of the nineteenth century seem less natural to us, the tragedy of Great Expectations will lose some of its appeal. I have already wondered whether Dickens himself ever came to see that his agonizing sensitiveness about the blacking bottles and his resentment of his mother's opposition to his escape from them was not too snobbish to deserve all the sympathy he claimed for it. Compare the case of Mr H. G. Wells, who is our twentieth century Dickens. Mr Wells hated being a draper's assistant as much as Dickens hated being a warehouse boy; but he is not in the least ashamed of it, and never blamed his mother for regarding it as the summit of her ambition for him. Fate having imposed on that engaging cricketer Mr Wells's father an incongruous means of livelihood in the shape of a small shop, shopkeeping did not present itself to the young Wells as be-

neath him, whereas to the genteel Dickens being a warehouse boy
was an unbearable comedown. Still, I cannot help speculating on
whether if Dickens had not killed himself prematurely to pile up
money for that excessive family of his, he might not have reached
a stage at which he could have got as much fun out of the blacking
bottles as Mr Wells has got out of his abhorred draper's counter.

Dickens never reached that stage; and there is no prevision of
it in Great Expectations, in which he never raises the question why
Pip should refuse Magwitch's endowment and shrink from him
with such inhuman loathing. Magwitch no doubt was a Warmint
from the point of view of the genteel Dickens family and even from
his own; but Victor Hugo would have made him a magnificent hero,
another Valjean. Inspired by an altogether noble fixed idea, he had
lifted himself out of his rut of crime, and honestly made a fortune
for the child who had fed him when he was starving. If Pip had no
objection to be a parasite instead of an honest blacksmith, at least he
had a better claim to be a parasite on Magwitch's earnings than, as
he imagined, on Miss Havisham's property. It is curious that this
should not have occurred to Dickens; for nothing could exceed the
bitterness of his exposure of the futility of Pip's parasitism. If all
that came of spunging on Miss Havisham (as Pip thought) was the
privilege of being one of the Finches of the Grove, he need not have
felt his dependence on Magwitch to be incompatible with his entirely baseless self-respect. But Pip—and I am afraid Pip must be
to this extent identified with Dickens—could not see Magwitch
as an animal of the same species as himself or Miss Havisham. His
feeling is true to the nature of snobbery; but his creator says no word
in criticism of that ephemeral limitation.

The basic truth of the situation is that Pip, like his creator, has
no culture and no religion. Joe Gargery, when Pip tells a monstrous
string of lies about Miss Havisham, advises him to say a repentant
word about it in his prayers; but Pip never prays; and church means
nothing to him but Mr Wopsle's orotundity. In this he resembles
David Copperfield, who has gentility but neither culture nor religion. Pip's world is therefore a very melancholy place, and his conduct, good or bad, always helpless. This is why Dickens worked

against so black a background after he was roused from his ignorant middle class cheery optimism by Carlyle. When he lost his belief in bourgeois society and with it his lightness of heart he had neither an economic Utopia nor a credible religion to hitch on to. His world becomes a world of great expectations cruelly disappointed. Mr Wells's world is a world of greater and greater expectations continually being fulfilled. That is a huge improvement. Dickens never had time to form a philosophy or define a faith; and his later and greater books are saddened by the evil that is done under the sun; but at least he preserved his intellectual innocence sufficiently to escape the dismal pseudo-scientific fatalism that was descending on the world in his latter days, founded on the preposterous error as to causation in which the future is determined by the present, which has been determined by the past. Mere accident apart, the true dynamic causation is always the incessant irresistible attraction of the evolutionary future.

Preface to the Limited Editions Club edition of *Great Expectations*, by Charles Dickens (London, 1937).

Samuel Butler

*Two critiques of Samuel Butler, based upon reviews of the Festing
Jones and Gilbert Cannan biographies.*

THE NEW LIFE REVIEWED

In the great tradition of British criticism a book to review is an
occasion to improve. Even if it were not so, the life of Samuel
Butler would be an irresistible temptation to any writer with an
ounce of homily in him. It is a staggering object-lesson in the
villainy (no milder expression is adequate) of our conventional
clergyman schoolmaster education, and of the family and class life
to which it belongs.

Mr Festing Jones's memoir, though one of the most complete ever
written, is nevertheless not quite complete. Butler told the story
of his childhood so frightfully well in his novel, The Way of All
Flesh, that Mr Festing Jones has recognized the hopelessness of
attempting to do that work again and do it better. It cannot be
done better: The Way of All Flesh is one of the summits of human
achievement in that kind; and there is nothing for it but to require
from the reader of the memoir as a preliminary qualification that
he shall read the autobiography in the novel. Indeed a good deal
of Mr Jones's memoir will be only half intelligible to anyone who
has not already come to know Butler's parents as the detestable
Theobald and his Christina, whose very names proclaim that they
had made their gods as hateful to their son as themselves. Butler
is the only man known to history who has immortalized and actually
endeared himself by parricide and matricide long drawn out. He
slew the good name (and it was such a very good name!) of his
father and mother so reasonably, so wittily, so humorously, and even
in a ghastly way so charitably, that he convinced us that he was
engaged in an execution and not in a murder.

66

But the moral of this memoir is that not even genius can come through such an education as Butler's with its mind unwounded and unlamed. It was his genius, always breaking through to the truth, that revealed to him, whilst he was still a boy, that this devoted father to whom he could never be too grateful, and this pious angel mother in whose watchful care he was so fortunate, were at best a pair of pitiably perverted and intimidated nobodies, and that he hated them, feared them, and despised them with all his soul. Unfortunately the matter could not stop there. Butler was naturally affectionate to the point of being gulled by heartless people with ridiculous ease. As a child he had sought for affection at home, only to have his feelings practised on by his mother to wheedle confidences from him and have him beaten by his father, who trained him exactly as if he were a performing animal, except that he did not teach him anything amusing. But the child went on assuming that he loved his dear parents, and that they were all happy together in their domestic affection, spotless respectability, and unchallenged social precedence. When he realized how he had been duped and how he had duped himself, he reacted to the opposite extreme with such violence that he set up as a rule in the art of life that the stupidest and most mischievous of mistakes is to force yourself or humbug yourself into liking things that are really repugnant or uninteresting to you. Accordingly, all through this memoir we find Butler "hating," on principle, everything that was not immediately congenial and easy to him at the very first taste. He "hated" Plato, Euripides, Dante, Raphael, Bach, Mozart, Beethoven, Blake, Rossetti, Tennyson, Browning, Wagner, Ibsen, and in fact everyone who did not appeal to his palate instantly as a lollypop appeals to the palate of a child. The exception was Handel, because he had learned to like Handel's music in the days of his childish illusion; but I suspect that if he had never heard Handel's music until after he had set up his rule he would have denounced him as a sanctimonius drum major, and classed him as one of The Seven Humbugs of Christendom.

It is true that these repeated denunciations of great men as impostors and humbugs are made with a tart humor which betrays a subconscious sense of their folly, and saves Butler from being classed as a vulgar nil-admirerist; but the trick is none the less tiresome and even sinister, because it is plain that Butler did seriously narrow his mind and paralyse his critical powers by refusing to take any trouble to find out what our greatest teachers were driving at, or to face the drudgery of learning their peculiar idiom. For a man with his love of music to begin with gavottes and minuets and never get any further (for that is what it came to) was monstrous. I risk his rising from the grave to smite me when I add, as I must, that he never said a word about Handel worth reading; he liked the hailstones running along the ground and the sheep going astray, every one to his own way; but Handel could hardly have said more to him on that than "Thank you for nothing." It is flatly impossible to believe that a man who could see no greatness in Bach was really admiring what is great in Handel, however sincerely he may have relished Handel's more popular vein.

Then, again, Butler's public manners were atrocious. Privately, he was most courteous, most considerate, if anything too delicate in his conscientiousness. But if he did not like a man's public opinion and work, or the man did not like his: in a word, if he did not feel perfectly happy with him, he treated him as a moral delinquent, derided him, insulted him, and even cut him in the street. In other words, he behaved exactly as his father would have behaved if his father had had courage and wit as well as thoroughly bad civic manners. In the war of cliques which never ceases in London, he heaped scorn on the Darwin clique, and not only resented the shallow snobbery which led it to underrate him, and to persuade Darwin himself that it was beneath his dignity to clear up a very simple misunderstanding which had led Butler quite naturally to accuse him of controversial foul play, but retaliated in kind. For there was inevitably a Butler clique as well as a Darwin clique. Butler's bite was so powerful that he may be said to have been a clique in himself in so far as he acted in the clique spirit; but with Miss Savage, Festing Jones, Gogin, Pauli, not to mention Emery Walker, Sydney Cockerell,[1] and the steadily growing outer

1. Eliza Savage, a lame ex-governess who was one of the few people with

ring of Butlerites of whom I was one, he was by no means alone
contra mundum. As the best brains were always with Butler,
Darwin, a simple-souled naturalist with no comprehension of the
abyss of moral horror that separated his little speciality of Natural
Selection from Butler's comprehensive philosophic conception of
Evolution, may be pardoned for his foolish estimate of Butler as
"a clever unscrupulous man," and for countenancing the belittling
of him by Huxley and Romanes that now seems so ridiculous. They
really did not know any better. But in the selfsame spirit, without
the selfsame excuse, Butler and his clique belittled poor Grant Allen,
one of the most amiably helpful men that ever lived, and one, moreover, who recognized Butler as a man of genius, and declared that
he "bore its signet on his brow." Butler, with unconscious but
colossal arrogance, simply damned his impudence, denying that
there was any such thing as genius, and heaping scorn on Allen
because he was not at once ready to declare that Butler was right
about evolution, and Darwin a disingenuous sciolist. Miss Savage,
pretending to forget Allen's name, wrote of him as Allen Grant;
and Mr Festing Jones leaves the readers of his memoir to infer that
he was an unamiable and rather contemptible man. All the more
annoying this because Grant Allen had the same grievance as
Butler: he could not live by his serious scientific work, and had
to write novels and stories to keep himself and his family alive.

The truth is, we all did that sort of thing in those days; and we
are doing it still. Nine-tenths of English criticism today is either
log-rolling or bad manners; and at the root of the evil are pure
snobbery, bigotry, and intolerance. I will not say that Butler was as
bad as his father, because, with his greater powers and opportunities,

---

whom Butler felt he could exchange confidences and offer his manuscripts for
appraisal; Festing Jones, a Butler crony and his first memoirist; Charles
Gogin, an artist friend and Butler traveling companion; Charles Paine Pauli,
a journalist friend whom Butler financially assisted for years only to discover
after Pauli's death that he had been sponged upon needlessly; Emery Walker,
an associate of William Morris in the Kelmscott Press; Sydney Cockerell,
with Walker, a Butler neighbor in his later years in Cilfford's Inn, later
director of the Fitzwilliam Museum, Cambridge.

he was very much worse. Ardent Butlerite as I am, I cannot deny that Butler brought a great deal of his unpopularity on himself by his country parsonage unsociability and evangelical bigotry. One does not get rid of that bigotry by merely discarding the Resurrection and making pious people laugh against their wills with such sallies as "Resist God and He will flee from you," or "Jesus: with all Thy faults I love Thee still." Bigotry in a parson is at least not unexpected, and not unnatural if he is in earnest about the 39 articles; but in a rampant anticlerical like Butler it tempts us to say that as he brought so much of the worst of the Church with him when he came out of it he might as well have stayed in it to please his father.

Still, when all is said that can be said against Butler, the fact remains that when he was important he was so vitally important, and when he was witty he was so pregnantly witty, that we are forced to extend an unlimited indulgence to his weaknesses, and finally to embrace them as attractions. His excessive and touchy self-consciousness; his childish belief that everything that happened to him, no matter how common and trivial, was interesting enough to be not only recorded for the sake of an authentic human document but sold to the public as *belles lettres;* his country parsonage conviction that foreigners with their quaint languages, and working-class people with their ungentlemanlike and unladylike dialects, were funny creatures whose sayings were to be quoted like those of clever children; his patronizing and petting of his favorites and his snubbing and cutting of his aversions: all these, with his petulant and perverse self-limitation and old-bachelorism, would have damned fifty ordinary men; yet they were so effectually redeemed by belonging to Butler, and in fact being Butler, that it never occurs to Mr Festing Jones to conceal, extenuate, or apologize for them.

Those to whom Butler was a stranger did not forgive him so easily. Take, for example, his Alps and Sanctuaries. We have to read it today not only for the promise and beauty of its title, but for the sake of the titbits it contains: in short, because it is by Butler. But barring those titbits it is surely the silliest book ever written by a clever man. Its placid descriptions of itineraries compared to which the voyages of a motor-bus from Charing Cross to Hyde Park Corner are chapters of romance, and its promiscuous quotations from Handel, in which elegiac passages which might conceivably have been recalled by the beauty of an Italian valley are not distinguished from toccata stuff that reeks of the keyboard and of nothing else, explain only too fully why the book was refused by the publisher who had rashly commissioned it, and why its first sale did not reach 500 copies. No Butlerite was surprised or offended when, buying a later book with a title[2] which suggested a pious pilgrimage, he had suddenly sprung on him a most irreverent onslaught on Sir Benjamin Layard,[3] whose only offense was that he was a bigwig, and that to Butler a bigwig meant merely a silk-stockinged calf to fix his teeth in; but Butlerites were few and strangers many; and strangers could not be expected to know that when you bought a book by Butler you never got what you paid for. True, you got something better; but then you did not want something better. A bookseller who responded to an order for La Vie Parisienne by sending The Methodist Times might establish a reputation as a humorist, but he would hardly make a fortune in his business.

There were other ways in which Butler did not live up to his professions. In Erewhon he would have been tried for the serious offense of gullibility, and very severely punished. The Pauli case would have put him quite beyond the pale of Erewhonian sympathy. And Pauli would have been knighted for gulling Butler so successfully. It is all very well to call Butler's forbearance to Pauli delicacy; but in any other man we should call it moral cowardice. I am not sure that it was not something worse. The rectory-born lust for patronage and charity was in Butler's blood: he had absolutely no conscience as to how he demoralized other people provided he could make them his pensioners. If Pauli, infamously pocketing his pension of £200 a year under pretence of penury when he was

2. *Ex Voto* (1888), about Varallo-Sesia, a sequel to *Alps and Sanctuaries* (1881).

3. Butler's onslaught was upon Sir Austen Henry (not Benjamin) Layard's writings about Varallo.

making £900 as a barrister and a mendicant whilst Butler was on
the verge of bankruptcy, had avowed and asserted his independence,
I verily believe Butler would have quarrelled with him at once. As
it was, when death revealed the fraud, Butler's only regret was that
Pauli was not alive to be forgiven. In that Butler was his father
all over. Well might he make his prototype Ernest, in The Way of
All Flesh, put his children out to nurse with a bargee on the ground
that, if he kept them with him, an inexorable heredity would force
him to treat them as badly as his father had treated him.

If these things are not firmly said about Butler, his example will
corrupt the world. From idiotic underestimate and neglect of him
we are already turning to deify him, in spite of his own warnings,
as one who could do no wrong. The reviews of Mr Jones's memoirs
are as shameless in this matter as the memoir itself. Mr Jones has,
on principle, concealed nothing. He even gives the name of the
witty and amiable French mistress whom Butler patronized incog-
nito very faithfully but very cautiously for sixteen years, at the end
of which he ventured to tell her who he was and where he lived,
and admitted her to his circle (one gathers) for the four more years
which elapsed before her death. Twenty years ago such a revelation
might have pilloried Butler. Today we steadily refuse to overhear
Mr Jones's communication. It is, by the way, a great pity that
Butler did not carry out his intention of dealing with the question
of marriage as he had dealt with evolution. His reiteration of the
not very respectable old proverb that it is cheaper to buy the milk
than to keep the cow did not, in spite of the French lady, do Butler
justice, being obviously a relic of that shallow Hedonism which
seemed to the mid-century Victorians to follow logically when they
discovered that the book of Genesis is not a scientific account of the
origin of species, and that the accounts given by the evangelists of
the Resurrection do not tally so exactly as the depositions of police
witnesses in Sinn Fein prosecutions. Instead of concluding that
these things were not of the real substance of religion, and that it
did not matter one straw to that real substance whether they
believed or disbelieved this or that tradition or parable that had
become connected with it, they still went on assuming that it

mattered so tremendously that they could not get rid of the crudest and most utterly irrelevant miracle story without bringing down the whole ethical structure of religion with a crash. Those were the days when an army officer of my acquaintance said to me gravely, "I know for a fact that the rector's son behaved disgracefully with the housemaid; and you may tell me after that that the Bible is true if you like, but I shall not believe it." The alternative to believing silly things about God seemed to be blank materialist Hedonist atheism. Yet Rousseau had said a hundred years before, "Get rid of your miracles, and the whole world will fall at the feet of Christ." And there you have it. As Butler's education consisted in concealing Rousseau's religious discoveries from him, he imagined that he had lost his faith when he had only lost his superstitions, and that in getting rid of the miracles he had got rid of Christ, of God, of The Church, and of any obligations to pursue anything but his own pleasure. It was in this phase that he nicknamed his father Theobald and his mother Christina, and perhaps decided to buy his milk instead of keeping a cow. His mind was too powerful to be imposed on in that way for long: but it need not have been imposed on for five seconds if his University had treated Voltaire and Rousseau as classics and seers, instead of as "infidels." It was at Shrewsbury School and Cambridge that Canon Butler had been taught to pretend to his son that his mother was killed by Erewhon. That is, his public school and university education had inculcated an ignorance more dense and dangerous than the ignorance of an illiterate ploughman. How silly it all seems now, except perhaps to the hundreds of Canon Butlers still corrupting their sons in our parsonages, and probably beating them if they catch them reading Butler— Butler! who stood for the very roots of religion when Darwin was "banishing mind from the universe"!

I cannot judge whether Mr Festing Jones's exhaustive and very cleverly documented memoir is going to be one of the great British biographies or not. It interests me throughout; but then I knew Butler and many of the other persons with whom the two volumes deal. For strangers, possibly, the death of Miss Savage at the end of the first volume will make it hard for the second to be equally amusing. She was a most entertaining woman who had caught Butler's comedy style so well, and even assimilated his art of life so congenially, that but for her alert feminine touch Butler might be suspected of inventing her letters. Her stories and jokes are all first-rate. Butler is not at his brightest in his remorse for having been occupied with his own affairs instead of with hers: his affectionate feeling that he had treated her badly was, as he would probably have admitted if some robust person had taxed him with it, priggish and childish.

Besides, Butler's bolt is shot in the first volume. In the second he is no longer the great moralist of Erewhon and the forerunner of the present blessed reaction towards Creative Evolution, but a dryasdust dilettante fussing about Tabachetti and Gaudenzio di Ferrara, Shakespear's Sonnets, and the authoress of the Odyssey. His shot about the Odyssey got home. All the pedants thought the attribution of the Odyssey to a woman monstrously improbable and paradoxical only because the Odyssey had always been thoughtlessly attributed to a man; but the moment the question was raised it became, to those who were really familiar with the two epics, not only probable but almost obvious that Butler had hit on the true secret of the radical and irreconcilable difference between the Odyssey and the Iliad. It was equally clear that he was right in his opinion that the first batch of Shakespear's Sonnets was the work of a very young man. But who cared, outside the literary fancy? To the mass of people whose very souls' salvation depended on whether Erewhom and Life and Habit were sound or unsound it mattered not a dump who wrote the Odyssey, or whether Shakespear was 17 or 70 when he wrote the sonnets to Mr W. H. And though Raphael's stocks were down heavily and Michael Angelo's not what they had been, yet the stocks of Tabachetti and Gaudenzio di Ferrara, whose works are not visible to us in England, were not sufficiently up to induce anyone to exchange. His other heroes, Giovanni Bellini and Handel, were very far from being overlooked or needing his assistance in any way, unless, indeed, he had struck a blow at the horrible festivals at which the scattered wheezings and roarings and screamings of four thousand Crystal Palace holiday-makers were making Handel's oratorios ridiculous. He missed that chance of a hook hit at the white chokers. He had nothing new to say about his two pets: he was only a Don Quixote with two Dulcineas. Meanwhile the intellectual and artistic world to which he was appealing was intensely interested in two new giants: Richard Wagner and Henrik Ibsen, the latter carrying on young Butler's battle against old Butler's ideals most mightily. And what had Butler to say about them? "Ibsen may be, and I dare say is, a very wonderful man, but what little I know of him repels me, and, what is worse, bores me." After not only saying this, but actually writing it, could Butler pretend that the worst we can conceive of his father the Canon or his grandfather the headmaster-Bishop in the way of dull arrogance, insolence, snobbery, pomposity, Podsnappery, ignorance half genuine, half wilful and malicious, were not squared and cubed in their gifted son and grandson? And again, "Carlyle is for me too much like Wagner, of whom Rossini said that he has *des beaux moments mais des mauvais quarts d'heure* —my French is not to be trusted." Were we to be expected to listen to a man who had nothing better than that to say about the composer of The Ring twenty years after the super-Homeric music epic had been given to the world? Surely we were entitled to reply that if Butler was too gross a Philistine or too insular an ignoramus to be civil to Wagner, he might at least have been just to Rossini, who, with unexpected and touching greatness of character, earnestly repudiated the silly anti-Wagner gibes attributed to him, and said to Wagner himself—Wagner being then the worst-reviled musician in Europe, and Rossini classed as the greatest—that if it had been possible for serious music to exist in the Italian opera houses, he might have done something; for "*j'avais du talent.*" How disgraceful Butler's sneer appears in the light of such sublime self-judgment! No doubt Butler did not know of it; but he could have found it out in less time than it cost him to learn Shakespear's Sonnets by heart. He could at least have held his tongue and concealed his ignorance and spite, which, please observe, was not provoked spite, but sheer gratuitous insular spite for spite's sake. His own experience should have warned him. Why did nobody say this to him, and produce that conviction of sin to which he was certainly accessible? Mr Festing Jones, a serious and remarkable musician, must have known that when Butler went on like this he was talking and writing vulgar and uppish nonsense. Perhaps he did venture occasionally; but he is too loyal a biographer to tell us about it.

Nothing more is needed to explain why Butler made no headway with his books about art and literature, and his records of his globe trottings. He accounted for it himself by saying that failure, like success, is cumulative, and that therefore it was inevitable that the longer he lived the less successful he should be. But the truth is that he spent the first half of his life saying all that he had to say that was important, and the second half dabbling in painting and music, and recording the thrills of "a week in lovely Lucerne" (much as the sisters he derided might have done), without getting beyond mediocrity in painting and slavish imitation in music, or gaining knowledge and sense of proportion in criticism. It is really appalling to learn that this man of genius, having received the very best education our most expensive and select institutions could give him, and having withal a strong natural taste for music and literature, turned from Bayreuth in mere ignorant contempt, and yet made every Christmas a pious pilgrimage to the Surrey pantomime, and wrote an anxiously careful account of its crude buffooneries to his musician friend. Is it to be wondered at that when an investment in house property obliged him to engage a man of the people as his clerk, this recruit, Mr Alfred Emery Cathie, had to constitute himself his valet, his nurse, his keeper, and his Prime Minister and Executive all in one, and to treat him as the grown-up child his education had left him? Alfred is the real hero of the second volume, simply as a good-natured sensible Englishman who had been fortunate enough to escape the public schools and the university. To Butler he was a phenomenon, to be quoted with patronizing amazement and admiration whenever he exploded a piece of common sense in the Clifford's Inn lunatic asylum. What Butler was to Alfred (except a great man) will never be known. Probably a rare good old sort, quite cracked, and utterly incapable of taking care of himself. Butler was at least not ungrateful.

Throughout this later period we see Butler cramped and worried when he was poor, spoilt when he was rich, and all the time uneasy because he knew that there was something wrong, and yet could not quite find himself out, though his genius was always flashing through the fog and illuminating those wonderful notebooks, with their queer strings of over-rated trivialities, profound reflections, witty comments, humorous parables, and family jokes and gibes to please Gogin and Jones or annoy the Butlers.

Now why, it may be asked, do I, who said, and said truly, that Butler was "in his own department the greatest English writer of the latter half of the nineteenth century," now attack him in his grave by thus ruthlessly insisting on his failings? Well, I do so precisely because I want to carry on his work of demonstrating the falsehood and imposture of our "secondary education" and the mischief of treating children as wild beasts to be tamed and broken instead of as human beings to be let develop. Butler held up his father to ridicule and infamy, and exclaimed, "This is what your public school, your university, your Church, made of him." But the world replied, "Oh, yes: that is all very well; but your father was a rotter and a weakling: all public school and university men are not like him." Now if, as is at last possible with this ruthlessly faithful memoir of him in our hands, we can say, "This is what your public school and your university and your country parsonage made, not of a rotter and a weakling, but of a man of genius who was all his life fiercely on his guard against their influence," then we can go one better than Butler, and make his ghost cry "Splendid! Dont spare me. Rub it in; and more power to your elbow!"

For we must not deceive ourselves. England is still governed from Langar Rectory, from Shrewsbury School, from Cambridge, with their annexes of the Stock Exchange and the solicitors' offices; and even if the human products of these institutions were all geniuses, they would finally wreck any modern civilized country after maintaining themselves according to their own notions at the cost of the squalor and slavery of four-fifths of its inhabitants. Unless we plough up the moral foundations of these places and sow them with salt, we are lost. That is the moral of the great Butler biography.

GILBERT CANNAN ON SAMUEL BUTLER

In choosing Mr Gilbert Cannan to write on Butler for his critical series, Mr Martin Secker has shewn either luck or cunning; for the book has style and wit, and does its work in a highly readable manner up to the point at which Butler must be left to speak for himself. Its presentation of Butler as a Character with an engaging literary talent and a racy vein of eccentric humor is complete and elegant. It does not present Butler as a man of genius, because Mr Cannan does not consider Butler a man of genius. I do. And I may as well explain the difference.

A man of genius is not a man who can do more things, or who knows more things, than ordinary men: there has never been a man of genius yet who has not been surpassed in both respects in his own generation by quite a large number of hopeless fools. He is simply a man who sees the importance of things. Otherwise every schoolmaster would be greater than Christ. Mr Cannan says that the nearest in spirit to Butler of any man of his time was W. S. Gilbert. This is a staggering statement, because on Butler's plane one does not think of Gilbert; and when we are reminded of him there we feel that Butler mattered enormously more than Gilbert, who in such a comparison seems not to have mattered at all. Yet, on reflection, one has to admit that they have something in common. The particular vein of wit which leads some men to take familiar and unquestioned propositions and turn them inside out so neatly as to convince you that they are just as presentable one way as the other, or even that the sides so unexpectedly and quaintly turned out are the right sides, is one in which Butler and Gilbert were natural adepts. But Gilbert never saw anything in the operation but a funny trick. He deliberately separated its exercise from his serious work, and took it off as a man takes off his hat in church when he attempted serious drama. Whenever Butler performed it he presently realized that the seeming trick was an inspired revelation. His very hoaxes were truths which Providence tempted him to entertain for fun until they made themselves indispensable. "Every jest is an earnest in the womb of time." That womb was incarnated in Butler's head, not in Gilbert's. Butler saw the importance of what he had hit on, and developed it into a message for his age. Gilbert saw it as a quip and left it at that: he could hardly develop a string of quips as far as a second act without petering out. Gilbert was a belittler: he jeered at old women like a street boy with a bad mother. Butler tore off the mask and tripped up the cothurnus of many a pretentious pigmy, thereby postponing public recognition of him until the PPs of his generation had died or doddered out; but he was a man of heroic admirations, whereas the people whom Gilbert admired have yet to be discovered. Mr Cannan himself points out appreciatively that Butler made a Sybil of Mrs Jupp, which may in the books of the recording angel balance his making a booby of Sir Benjamin Layard. There is stuff enough in Trial by Jury and The Pirates of Penzance to set up an Ibsen in his business; but Gilbert, though he could penetrate to the facts, and saw the fun of their incongruity with the glamor through which most of us see them, could not see their importance. Thus Butler forged his jests into a weapon which smashed the nineteenth century, whilst Gilbert only made it laugh. No two men could have been more widely disparate in the scope of their spirit, though their specific humor reacted to the stimulus of human folly in the same manner. Gilbert with the word Chesterton added can turn things inside out and write amusing phrases as well as Gilbert; but he does it to high purpose. Oscar Wilde at his best knew that his gift was divine in its nature. In this they both stood far nearer to Butler than Gilbert did. Gilbert, in short, is an excellent illustration of how useless Butler's specific turn of humor would have been to him had he not been a man of genius; and in this capacity only has he the right to appear in a book about Butler.

Butler's great achievement was his perception, after six weeks of hasty triumph in Darwin's deathblow to the old Paleyan assumption that any organ perfectly adapted to its function must be the work of a designer, of the unspeakable horror of the mindless purposeless world presented to us by Natural Selection. Even with Butler's guidance those of us who are not geniuses hardly see that yet; and we babble about Nietzsche and Treitschke with Darwin's name written all over the Prussian struggle for the survival of the fittest. Mr Cannan, exquisitely appreciative of Butler as a British Worthy, and enamored of Mrs Jupp (who is, by the way, a reincarnation of Mrs Quickly), does not see it in the least, and thereby wholly misses Butler's greatness, being indeed rather ignominiously driven at the end, in spite of the evidence of the earlier chapters to which Butler has stimulated him, to deliver a half-hearted verdict of Spoiled Artist, and Failure, and to dismiss Butler's great vision as the effect of the terror inspired in the ex-evangelical by Darwin, "the greatest figure of the time." Here the word Figure seems well chosen to avoid calling Darwin the greatest man of his time (he *was* the greatest naturalist of his time, and a very amiable person to boot) ; but the phrase may be a mere *cliché;* for Mr Cannan does not follow up the distinction it implies. "It became a passion with Butler," he continues, "to tell others not to be afraid; and this passion, as fear died down, was congealed into an obsession which is responsible for the tiresome reiteration of the evolution books." This is a settler. Mr Cannan has grasped neither the point at issue nor its importance. That is why he fails to see how Butler was a great man, and invents a silly-clever explanation of his quarrel with Darwin. Nothing that I have read in Butler, or gathered from his conversation, conveys the very faintest suggestion of terror or of the "who's afraid" attitude. On the contrary, he was distinguished by his derisive insensibility to the awe which conventional and pious reputations inspire; and as to Darwin, though it was considered very wicked in Butler's time to countenance Darwin in any way, Butler's attitude towards him was one of strenuous championship until he foresaw how the Darwinians, in their revolt against crude Bible worship, would empty the baby out with the bath and degrade the whole conception of Evolution by leveling it down to Natural Selection, which, though a potent method of adaptation, is not true Evolution at all. As a young man, Butler said, in Life and Habit, that Darwin had "banished mind from the Universe." As an old man, he said the same thing to me in private conversation with an intensity that flatly violated his advice to all of us to hold convictions lightly and cultivate Laodiceanism. Until Mr Cannan grasps the importance of that simple statement through an intuition that the difference between Butler's view of the universe and the Darwinian view of it as a product of Natural Selection is the difference between heaven and hell, he will not begin to imagine what Butler's life was about, though he may write very pleasantly and wittily about Butler's talents and accomplishments and foibles. Nor will he appreciate the grimly humorous satisfaction with which Butler on that occasion added, "My grandfather quarrelled with Darwin's grandfather; my father quarrelled with Darwin's father; I quarrelled with Darwin; and my only regret in not having a son is that he cannot quarrel with Darwin's son."

But Mr Cannan's book is the better in some respects for leaving Butler's message to be taken from Butler himself, especially as it will send people to Butler instead of scaring them off, as mere paraphrases of great writers do. To write a book about a man who has written books about himself is an impertinence which only an irresistible charm of manner can carry off. The unpardonable way of doing it, and the commonest, is to undertake to tell the public what a writer has already told them himself, and to tell it worse or tell it all wrong. Mr Cannan has not committed this outrage. Indeed he interferes too little: for instance, he says not a word of Butler's epoch-making suggestion that poverty and ugliness should be attacked as crimes instead of petted and coddled like diseases. He just allows his mind to play round Butler, and thus makes him the attractive occasion of a book rather than its subject. Here are some samples of his play. "Butler could never respect Darwin when he found humor lacking in The Origin of Species. That was really the beginning and the end of Darwin's offence; and because of it Butler at last could not take anything Charles Darwin said or did seriously." Now this, though quite wrong—for Butler was the only contemporary of Darwin who took him really seriously—is much better than saying that Butler was terrified by Darwin; and it is amusing, anyhow. Again, "In Butler's world there is no freedom except freedom from humbug. He knows nothing of the proud insistence that volition shall proceed contaminated by desire. His view was that volition was in all probability contaminated by the interests of ancestors and posterity, and that there was no help for it." This is better still. And such literary frivolities as "I cannot believe in Butler's God, simply because he does not write about his God with style," have the merits of frivolity; for frivolity has merits: for instance, it is often pleasant. Besides, the laugh here is with Butler, who had the supreme sort of style that never smells of the lamp, and therefore seems to the kerosene stylist to be no style at all. I do not offer these quotations as at bottom more relevant to Butler than to Boccaccio; but a writer who can go on so is readable on his own account, Butler or no Butler; and if the samples encourage my readers to try the whole book, they can judge for themselves its stupendous demerits as a criticism of Butler the Great as distinguished from Butler the Character.

I am disposed to reproach Mr Cannan a little for saying in effect that Butler was no use except as a literary artist, and then giving him away to the so-called scientific people because he was an artist. If Mr Cannan chooses to allow himself to be humbugged by these ridiculous distinctions, he might at least give his own side the benefit of them. But he would do still better if he would revise his book in the light of a serious consultation with himself as to whether he really believes that a naturalist is always, and a thinker never, a man of science; and if so, why? Butler told us a great deal about life and habit, luck and cunning, that nobody had ever told us before, having an extraordinary talent for observing and interpreting both. Darwin told us a great deal about pigeons and worms that nobody had ever told us before, having a remarkable turn for watching pigeons and worms. Why is Darwin classed as a man of science and Butler as an artist of no science? Leonardo da Vinci remarked that the sun did not go round the earth. Galileo made the same remark. Why did nobody believe Leonardo or regard him

as a man of science; and why does everybody applaud Galileo as
the great scientific discoverer of the fact that it is the earth that
goes round the sun? Does anyone seriously suggest that these Galileos
and Harveys and Darwins had greater minds than Leonardo or
Goethe or Kant or Butler or any of the great artists and philosophers who have grasped the importance of science and applied their
wits to its problems? Even Weismann, who was so much more
speculative than Darwin that he developed Darwinism into an extravagant lunacy, and made some brilliant hits in the process, describes
how the "discovery" of the cellular structure of living organisms
was anticipated fully by a pure mystic whose very name nobody can
recollect without referring to Weismann's History of Evolution.
Why should Mr Cannan do less justice to the scientific importance
of poets and prophets than a naturalist like Weismann?

The real distinction between the two classes is clear enough. The
so-called discoverers have been the collectors of evidence and the
demonstrators (by put-up jobs called experiments) of facts and
forces already divined by men with brains enough not to be wholly
dependent on material demonstration. St Thomas, with Christ staring him in the face, refused to believe that he was there until he had
put fingers into his wounds, thereby establishing himself as the
prototype and patron saint of all the "discoverers" who, as the
Irish say, "would guess eggs if they saw the shells." Darwin's was
an exceptionally exasperating case, because he not only got the
credit of having discovered Evolution, which had been promulgated
and thoroughly established in the period of Goethe and Darwin's
grandfather (1790–1830), but had actually substituted for this
great general conception an elaborate study of that pseudo-evolution
which is produced by external accident (as if a tree could be
properly said to have been "evolved" into firewood by the storm
which blew it down). This was not Darwin's fault: he did not call
the process he demonstrated Evolution, but Natural Selection; still,
Darwinism was none the less irritating and disastrous because Darwin was not a Darwinist. The intelligent people jumped wildly at
Natural Selection because it knocked Paley and the Book of Genesis
clean out. The stupid people took it up because, like St Thomas,

they could understand a soulless mechanical process, but could not conceive a vital process like Evolution. The result was half a century of bedevilment, folly, pessimism, despair, and cowardice, of which we are now reaping the fruits in Flanders; and against this Butler stood for years alone; for one cannot count the belated pietists who wanted to go back to the Garden of Eden. In a word, Butler stood alone for science against the purblind naturalists and biologists, with their following of miracle mongers, experiment jobbers, and witch doctors, all absurdly claiming to be *the* men of science. And I contend that Mr Cannan, belonging as he does to Butler's camp, should stand to his guns and defend the apprehensive mind and the intuitive imagination against the peering eyes and the groping fingers. Besides, Butler has won. Why does Mr Cannan, like Frederick at Molwitz, throw up the sponge for him?

Reviews of *Samuel Butler, Author of Erewhon (1835–1902): A Memoir*, by Henry Festing Jones, in *Manchester Guardian*, November 1, 1919, and of *Samuel Butler: A Critical Study*, by Gilbert Cannan, in *New Statesman*, May 8, 1915.

Mr. Arnold Bennett Thinks
Play-Writing Easier than Novel Writing

A Shavian satire, based upon a belated review of Arnold Bennett's
The Author's Craft *(1914), on the comparative artistic challenges
of writing novels and writing plays.*

I did not at first understand why the Editor of The Nation sent
me Mr Bennett's book as one which I might like to review. Mr
•Bennett talks shop and debits harmless tosh about technique for the
entertainment of literary amateurs in a very agreeable and suggestive manner, as he has every right to do, being so distinguished a
master of the craft. But why on earth should I join in the conversation and snatch a professional job from some young reviewer whose
week's board and lodging it would provide?

I found the solution of the enigma on page 76, which begins with
the words, "One reason why a play is easier to write than a novel."
That fetched me. I did not want to know "one reason" for so outrageous a stroke of novelist's bluff. But the impetus of my reading
carried me on, in spite of the shock; and so I learnt that this one
reason is "that a play is shorter than a novel." It is; and so is the
Bible shorter than the London Directory. "Excuse the length of my
letter," said Pascal: "I had no time to write a short one."

Now, I am not going to argue. I never do. I will simply take one
of the shortest, most intense, and most famous scenes in English
dramatic literature, and rewrite it as a chapter in a novel in the
style of my friends Bennett and Galsworthy when they are too lazy
to write plays:

Macbeth
A Play. By William Shakespear. Act V. Scene 8
The precinct of Macbeth's Castle on Dunsinane Hill

Enter Macbeth

MACBETH: Why should I play the Roman fool, and die
On mine own sword? Whiles I see lives, the gashes
Do better upon *them.*

Enter Macduff

MACDUFF: Turn, hell-hound, turn.

MACBETH: Of all men else I have avoided thee;
But get thee back: my soul is too much charg'd
With blood of thine already.

MACDUFF: I have no words,
My voice is in my sword, thou bloodier villain
Than terms can give thee out! *(They fight.)*

MACBETH: Thou losest labor.
As easy may'st thou the intrenchment air
With thy keen sword impress, as make me bleed.
Let fall thy blade on vulnerable crests:
I bear a charmed life, which must not yield
To one of woman born.

MACDUFF: Despair thy charm;
And let the angel whom thou still hast serv'd
Tell thee, Macduff was from his mother's womb
Untimely ripp'd.

MACBETH: Accursèd be that tongue that tells me so;
For it hath cow'd my better part of man.
And be these juggling fiends no more believ'd
That palter with us in a double sense;
That keep the word of promise to our ear,
And break it to our hope. I'll not fight with thee.

MACDUFF: Then yield thee, coward;
And live to be the show and gaze o' the time.
We'll have thee, as our rarer monsters are,
Painted upon a pole; and, underwrit,
"Here may you see the tyrant."

MACBETH: I'll not yield,
To kiss the ground before young Malcolm's feet,
And to be baited with the rabble's curse.
Though Birnam wood *be* come to Dunsinane,
And thou oppos'd, being of no woman born,
Yet I will try to last: before my body
I throw my warlike shield. Lay on, Macduff;
And damn'd be him that first cries, "Hold! Enough!"
                                     (Exeunt fighting.)

Macbeth

A Novel. By Arnold Bennett, John Galsworthy, or
Anybody. The Last Chapter

He was to fail, after all, then. The day was going against him.
His men were not really fighting. They had conveyed to Old Siward
that they were open to an offer of quarter; and the hint had not
been lost on that ancient campaigner, whose son he had just slain.

What was the use of killing? Duncan, Banquo, the Macduff
people: he had waded through their blood; and how much better
would it not be if it were all a dream and they were alive and kind
to him?

How the martins were singing! Banquo, always a bit of a fool,
had been sentimental about the martins. Gruach, the dear dead wife
whom the southrons persisted in calling Lady Macbeth, had argued
with Banquo about them, telling him that their habits were insani-
tary, and that they were infested with small bugs which got into the
castle, already too rich in insect life. But Duncan had agreed with
Banquo; and when Gruach became queen she would not let the
martins' nests be broken down, being anxious to copy Duncan's
tastes in every way, lest anyone should say that the Macbeths did
not know how kings lived. And so the martins were singing, singing,
always singing when they were not fly-catching.

It came to him, with a twist at the heart, that he had never told
Gruach the truth about Banquo. He had left her to believe that he
had killed him because the witches had foretold that his posterity
should be kings. But the real reason was that Banquo had given

himself moral airs. That is hard to bear at any time; but when you
are within ten minutes of committing a murder, it is insufferable.
Morality is easy for a man who does not intend to do anything; but
a man of action cannot stand on scruples. These idle thanes who
sat down on their little patrimonies and had no ambition: they had
invented this moral twaddle to excuse their laziness.

What an exquisite morning it was! Was there anything so blue as
a blue sky, anything so white as a white cloud, any gold so golden
as the gold of the gorse? From the summit of Dunsinane he could
see almost to the Roman wall on the south and to the Forth Bridge
on the north. The wind had backed a little to the north: perhaps
it would rain later. But no such foreboding troubled the wood
pigeon that now called to him, "Tak two coos, Taffy: tak two coos,
Taffy." He smiled grimly. He had taken from first to last not less
than a thousand coos; and this funny bird kept on exhorting him
to take two. And yet he did not throw a stone at it as he once would
have done. It seemed all so useless. You strove and strove, and killed
and killed, and made journeys to consult witches; and at the end
of it all the wood pigeon had no more to say to you than before;
and the sky was no bluer, the cloud no whiter, the whins no yellower.
Curse the sky! Curse the whins! Doubly damn the wood pigeon!
Why not make an end of it, like the Roman fool at Philippi? He
stood his claymore on its hilt on the flags and bent over the point.
Just to lean on it, and let it go through him: then the wood pigeon
might coo itself black in the face: Macbeth would be at rest with
Duncan. Where had he heard about Philippi? It seemed unlikely
that he could have learned Roman history; and yet he found that
he did know. Do men know everything before death? He shuddered.
Strange, that he, who rather enjoyed killing other people, should
feel an intense repugnance to kill himself! Yet there was one canny
thing about killing yourself: it relieved you of all concern for the
future. You could kill as many other people as you liked first without
considering the consequences. He would, please God, spit a few
more of his enemies on that sword before his own turn came. He
tossed it into the air by the point, and caught the hilt as it came
down. He no longer heard the wood pigeon.

And yet, what was that? Had the wood pigeon called him a hell-hound? He turned, and saw Macduff there, between him and the sun, glaring at him. If the sun had been in his eyes, he could not have glared. It was clever of him to come that way and get the advantage of the sun.

Macduff! Yes, Macduff: the man of whom the spirit called up by the witches had bade him beware. The man whose wife and child he had slaughtered. Could he blame him for glaring? Would not any man glare after such an experience? Banquo had glared even after his death, but with no speculation in his eyes. There was speculation enough in Macduff's: he was speculating on the sun being in the eyes of his adversary.

How the martins were singing! How fresh the air tasted! How good life was! How many pleasant paths there were on those hillsides, paths that had led his feet and Macduff's to this one spot of all spots in the world! Well, if Macduff had not come by one path he would have come by another. That was life, always inscrutable, sometimes a little ironical. The wind dropped: the banner had ceased to flap, and hung inert. A number of birds and crickets, no longer scared into silence by its flapping, joined the concert of the martins. Again came the wood pigeon's incitement, "Tak two coos, Taffy: tak——" What was that? A sharp, rasping sound called Macbeth from the landscape. He looked again at the man against whom he had been warned.

Macduff had stooped to sharpen his claymore on the flags. He was squatting down in an attitude which brought his boney knees into prominence just below his kilt, and drawing his blade to and fro with a harsh, rhythmical grating on the granite. By the mere instinct of imitation, Macbeth did the same. His knees were fleshier; and it was harder for him to stoop; but he did it. It is never easy for a king to stoop; but Fate will have it so sometimes. Now there were two blades scraping. The birds stopped singing, and listened in astonished suspicious silence. Only a jay laughed.

Macbeth heard it. Something stirred in him, and distorted his lips into a grin. It seemed to him that he suddenly opened a book that had always been sealed to him. When Gruach was dying he had asked the doctor for some physic for the mind; and the doctor had failed him. Then he had asked the porter, because he had noticed that the porter, alone among all the men of his acquaintance, was light-hearted, and would laugh, even when nobody was being hurt or ridiculed, and seemed to despise ambition. And the porter had told him that life is not so bad if you can see the fun of it. Old Siward had nailed the porter to the door that morning because he refused to open it to the enemy. Did he see the fun of that, Macbeth wondered? Yet here, as he squatted before Macduff, and they both sharpened their blades on the flags, a dim sense of something laughable in the situation touched him, though, God knows, there was nothing to laugh at if the warning of the witches were trustworthy. The spirits had said that no man born of woman should harm Macbeth. That seemed pretty conclusive. But they had also said that he would not be vanquished until Birnam Wood came to Dunsinane. That also seemed conclusive; yet the thing had happened: he had seen the wood walking.

He decided to give Macduff a chance. He was tired of killing people named Macduff. He said so. He advised Macduff to go away.

Macduff tried to speak; gulped; and came on. His voice was in his sword.

Macbeth was not afraid, though he knew he was not the man he had been. He had drunk heavily since he seized the throne: the Scots expected that from a king. But he could fight as well as ever for forty-five seconds; and then he could clinch, and try to get in his dirk somewhere. After all, Macduff was no teetotaller, if one might judge by his nose, which was red and swollen. Only, the doubt came: was the redness and the swelling from drink, or from weeping over his slaughtered family? With that thought came Macduff's first blow: a feint, followed by a vicious thrust at the groin.

Macbeth was quick enough to drop his targe and stop the thrust, even while he guarded the blow that did not come. That reassured him, and took some of the bounce out of Macduff. He was equally successful the next time, and the next. He became elated. At last his pride in his charmed life got the better of his prudence. He told Macduff that he was losing his labor, and told him why.

The effect was exactly the contrary of what he had anticipated. A gleam of savage delight came into Macduff's eyes.

What did it mean?

Macbeth was not left long in doubt. He stood petrified, whilst a tale poured from Macduff's lips such as had never before blasted the ears of mortal man. It cannot be repeated here: there is such a thing as the library censorship. Let it suffice that it was a tale of the rude but efficient obstetric surgery of those ancient times, and that it established beyond all question the fact that Macduff had never been born.

After that, Macbeth felt that he simply could not fight with him. It was not that he was afraid, even now. Nor was it that he was utterly disgusted at the way the witches had let him down again. He just could not bring himself to hack at a man who was not natural. It was like trying to eat a cat. He flatly refused further combat.

Of course, Macduff called him Coward. He did not mind that so much; for he had given his proofs, and nobody would believe Macduff; nor, indeed, would any reasonable Scot expect him to fight an unborn adversary. But Macduff hinted at unbearable things: at defeat, disgrace, the pillory even.

There was a lark singing now. Far down the hillside, where the rugged road wound up to the barbican, the last of Birnam Wood was still on the march. A hawk hovered motionless over a walking oak: he could see the glint of the sun on its brown back. The oak's legs must be those of an old soldier, he thought, who had cunningly taken the heaviest tree so that he might be late for the fighting. But, old or young, the soldier was now anxious lest he should be late for the plunder and the other sequels to the sack of a castle; for the oak was coming up at a rattling pace. There were nests in it, too. Curious, to wonder how those nesting pairs took their moving!

A surge of wrath went through Macbeth. He was, above all things, a country gentleman; and that another country gentleman should move his timber without acquiring any rights infuriated him. He became reckless. Birnam Wood—*his* wood—had been taken to Dunsinane: was that a thing he could be expected to stand? What though Macduff had not been properly born: was it not all the more likely that he had a weak constitution and could not stick it out if he were pressed hard in the fight? Anyhow, Macbeth would try. He braced himself; grasped his claymore powerfully; thrust his shield under the chin of his adversary; and cried, "Lay on, Macduff."

He could not have chosen a more unfortunate form of defiance. When the news had come to Macduff of the slaughter of his wife and boy, he had astonished the messenger by exclaiming, "What! All my pretty chickens and their dam at one fell swoop!" Accustomed from his earliest youth to deal with horses, he knew hardly anything of poultry, which was a woman's business. When he applied the word dam, properly applicable only to a mare, to a hen, Malcolm, though deeply moved by his distress, had a narrow escape of a fit of hysterics; for the innocent blunder gave him an impulse of untimely laughter. The story had been repeated; and something of it had come to Macduff's ears. He was a highly-strung man, exquisitely sensitive to ridicule. Since that time the slightest allusion to chickens had driven him to transports of fury. At the words "Lay on," he saw red. Macbeth, from the instant those fatal words passed his lips, had not a dog's chance.

In any case, he would not have been ready to meet a sudden attack. All his life he had been subject to a strange discursiveness which sent his mind wandering to the landscape, and to the fauna and flora of the district, at the most exciting crises of his fate. When he meant to tell Gruach that he had arranged to have Banquo killed, he had said to her instead, "Light thickens; and the crow makes wing to the rooky wood." His attention had already strayed to the wood pigeon when Macduff's yell of fury split his ears; and at the same moment he felt his foe's teeth snap through his nose and his foe's dirk drive through his ribs.

When Malcolm arrived, there was little left of Macbeth but a pile of mince. Macduff was panting. "That will teach him," he said, and stopped, exsufflicate.

They laid Macbeth beside Gruach in God's quiet acre in the little churchyard of Dunsinane. Malcolm erected a stately tomb there, for the credit of the institution of kingship; and the epitaph, all things considered, was not unhandsome. There was no reproach in it, no vain bitterness. It said that Macbeth had "succeeded Duncan."

The birds are still singing on Dunsinane. The wood pigeon still coos about the coos; and Malcolm takes them frankly and generously. It is not for us to judge him, or to judge Macbeth. Macbeth was born before his time. Men call him a villain; but had the press existed in his day, a very trifling pecuniary sacrifice on his part would have made a hero of him. And, to do him justice, he was never stingy.

Well! Well!

(The end)

There! that is what is called novel writing. I raise no idle question as to whether it is easy or not. Fine art of any sort is either easy or impossible. But that sort of thing I can write by the hundred thousand words on my head. I believe that if I turned my attention to mechanics for a month or two, I could make a typewriter attachment that would do it, like the calculating attachment that has lately come into use. The odd thing is that people seem to like it. They swallow it in doses of three hundred pages at a time; and they are not at all keen on Shakespear. Decidedly, when my faculties decay a little further, I shall go back to novel writing. And Arnold Bennett can fall back on writing plays.

Nation, March 11, 1916.

First Public Conference
on Mr. H. G. Wells' "Samurai"

*A newspaper report of a panel discussion about a controversial
and polemical novel by H. G. Wells, in which both Wells and Shaw
participated and were quoted at great length.*

On Thursday evening, April 11, in the New Reform Club, under
the auspices of the Fabian Arts Group, Mr H. G. Wells conducted
the first public discussion on the subject of the Samurai of his
Modern Utopia. In opening the discussion, Mr Wells said:—

> The conversation to-night is to be about the idea of the
> Samurai, an idea which I broached in a book of mine, A Mod-
> ern Utopia.[1] Some years ago I made a series of formal and
> inadequate studies of social development. In them I tried to
> view the whole social process as a vast conflict of personalities;
> and so soon as I came to look at social development I perceived
> that the social process has an air of being aimless, wasteful, and
> in many aspects cruel, and that there was a crying need to have
> some sort of plan to which individual aims could be subordi-
> nated, which would make the whole process less aimless and
> less confused. That ordering of the social process seemed to me
> to be Socialism. However, the more I thought of the disorder
> of human affairs the more skeptical I became as to the practica-
> bility of the remedy, and this scepticism which I found creeping
> into my mind was as to whether man's impulse could be so

1. *A Modern Utopia* had been published two years before, in 1905, to
great controversy. Wells at the time had been the darling of the Fabians;
but by 1908, the year after the conference on the "Samurai," he was convinced that the Fabian Society would not follow his revolutionary lead,
and resigned.

enlarged as to make the whole of Society able to sustain a new ordering of life in which the disintegrating forces making for renewed confusion would be subordinated and controlled. Is it possible to educate the community so that Socialism becomes the form of the thought of that community? I am not at all sure that we are going to get Socialism. I am not cock-sure that it is an inevitable consequence of the present condition of affairs. Still, that it is possible to get human beings to work together to an extent they do not now—to work together for the realisation of Socialism—is something concerning which I entertain no doubt whatever. Therefore, at the outset, I was confronted with the problem of the provision of a personal culture which would make this thing which was a dream and an ideal at last a possibility and a reality.

Now that opened up two questions. First, what should be the culture of the citizen which would enable a community to realise Socialism? Second, how to get that culture? It became clear that it was necessary to get people with a fine enthusiasm for social reconstruction, who would have faith in the ideas which that enthusiasm inspired. They would need to produce a new model of citizenship suited to the reconstructed state. They must work out by experience those attributes of good citizenship which would best contribute to the advancement of a better and more sane ordering of life, and having worked out their conception of the Socialist citizen who will fit the Socialist State, that new culture must be propagated; they must try and infect people with it. The question first is to work out the Socialist State and then to make a propaganda of that ideal citizen, so that the number of these self-trained and self-disciplined Socialist citizens may increase and at last become the administrative forces of the reconstructed State. Therefore the literature of the propagandist, as it becomes enlarged, must become the literature of the future; must become the leading thought of the emancipated mind. If we cannot elaborate this system of personal discipline, it seems to me Socialism must remain a dream. Any other system would be a superficial caricature.

In this book, A Modern Utopia, my Samurai represented the class who were running that Socialist State, my first crude sketch of the citizen of the ideal State to come. It was an unsatisfactory sketch, but it appealed to a large number of readers; and their response has been some justification of the attempt. Then, if we are really going to try to work out such a system as I have suggested, we have got first to form out a number of precedents, and in all human experience it seemed that some sort of discipline was necessary. One has to invent a rule for our Samurai, and in that first projection I made the rules fall under three classifications.

First. Rules to secure personal efficiency, such as to maintain perfect health, habits of industry, and rules aiming at the physical development of the Samurai, at keeping the Samurai in a condition of courage and nervous fitness. Second. System of rules for the sake of discipline that would serve as reminders of the purpose for which the order of Samurai existed. I made some grotesque little suggestions which I think may still have some considerable value—petty abstinences and things to remind the Samurai of some distinction in their order, of having vowed themselves in the direction of social service. I also suggested that these Samurai should wear a uniform which should be distinctive and confined to their order. Under this head the rules would aim at administrative efficiency, at discipline and co-ordinate action. The third set of rules would be more difficult. There would be rules that aim at the moral and intellectual training of the members of the Samurai. The whole aim in attempting the culture of the Socialist citizen is to take the spirit of service which is latent in every human being and to develop that, and, on the other hand, to discourage and check the spirit of personal gain which is the most stimulated side of the human being to-day, and to irradiate that spirit of service with which the Samurai would be inspired with a distinctive religious quality. Well, how is this to be achieved?

The most important thing of all is the creation of an atmosphere round about this idea of service which will prevent the new order of citizen from breaking away and check the mass of self-seeking to which at present the human race is devoted, and to do this thing is extraordinarily difficult. Something is needed then which will restore the individual and keep him in touch with the very impulse of the movement. I suggest that a system of private devotions may be necessary, and at any rate if we are going to have a religious Socialist movement, a movement which is powerful enough to stir men's hearts and nerve their wills, some sort of simple ritual will be needed to be the common inspiration of that movement.

Another rule, another duty, in addition to insistence on the moral and religious side of the Socialist movement, is the intellectual obligation. For the Socialist it is not sufficient to mean well. Something more than that is required of him. Clear and definite study, understanding, reading and constant discussion become a duty for the Socialist, for the really earnest and organised propagandist of Socialism. We have to create, for ourselves first of all and then for the movement, a circle of ideas. That is an imperative necessity. There would therefore be rules as between the members of the Samurai for the purpose of keeping all in touch with every side of contemporary effort and thought. Then I would lay stress on the importance of having some code of behaviour. There must be a fine attitude of mind between the Samurai.

Now these three groups—rules to secure personal efficiency, rules to secure discipline and co-ordinate action, and rules for intellectual training—the complete order of Samurai would have to possess. Possibly the whole scheme will be no more than discussed by the present generation. Premature attempts to found an order of Samurai will only end in arrogance and stupidity. At present we have not enough ideas. It would be a stupid and presumptuous thing to attempt to realise the idea. The danger of priggishness, for example, is enormous, and though it is better to be a prig than a pig, it is better to be neither. Essentially a prig is a person who substitutes the letter for the spirit, and the only correction is to remember constantly the object of the rule. In any case, some such organised and conscious force will be necessary as an alternative to the go-as-you-please procedure of to-day. Individual and uncoordinated efforts may afford opportunities for bright and brilliant personal displays; but something more will be needed to take us outside into the collective area. If we are to develop this idea of the Samurai into something which will be workable and possible, we have to bear in our mind some sort of corrective to our conscious endeavours to be good and do right. We shall never achieve any collective result unless we have some organised effort.

After a lengthy discussion, in which Mrs Sidney Webb, Dr Lake of Leyden, Dr Guest, Mr Aylmer Maude, Mrs Montefiore and others took part, Mr Bernard Shaw said:

I have listened to this discussion with a certain personal restiveness. The discipline described by Mr Wells falls ridiculously short of the discipline I have put upon myself. Multiply any one of his disciplines by ten, and I'll undertake to do it on my head. The error is the outcome of the curious habit of supposing that character and morals are simple things; but they are outrageously difficult things. And our absurd method of juvenile education doesn't help matters a bit; it makes them worse. For instance, in the matter of truth-telling, if a child steals a lump of sugar and is asked about it and says "Yes," it is punished for stealing; if the child says "No," then the parents punish it for lying. So long as that kind of thing goes on, truth will be a very rare and difficult quality. Pontius Pilate had the good sense to ask the question—What is Truth? Well, that was a good question, and a very knotty question to answer. It is perfectly true that education ruins two-thirds of our children. In the name of education we do not hesitate to impose on the very weakest members of the community a burden of work that Lord Kelvin would kick against.

I put it to Mr Wells that the present state of our civilisation has been brought about precisely as the result of a sort of Samurai idea. Why, every Tory would cordially agree with

Mr Wells; only he would say that in the English gentleman we have already got our Samurai. He is sent to Oxford where he undergoes most of Mr Wells's discipline, including the cold bath and daily shave. He is duly turned out with a degree certifying his proficiency as a gentleman; and then, in the Church, he is provided with an elaborate system of reminders that he must always be a gentleman and nothing else.

But this is just the very thing that every superior mind does his very best to avoid. I claim to be an undeniably superior person; and my superiority has been shown and won by flying in the face of every single one of these disciplines. As for that system of reminders, there is only one effectual method of reminding people of anything, and that is to tell them in a startling way every five years or so. Tell anybody the same thing three times a day for a year and you kill the very thing you wish to develop. The Church has been taken as an example. But the Church doesn't remind anybody of anything. I am told that in India, where some of the Anglo-Indians can only get to church once in six months, the people positively complain that they don't get enough church. I've suggested to my clergy-men friends that the best thing they could do for their religion would be to tell the people that they weren't fit to come to church and then to lock up the building and hold no services for six months. I am sorry Mr Wells abandoned his technical training for his Samurai. I think he should put it in again. It is vitally important that people who are to become rulers should know from experience how to earn their own living. It is no use having good intentions. Everybody is positively bursting with good intentions, but very few know how to carry them out. Then, in regard to the question of God. We want a reconstruction of our theories. We've got to conceive of God as a powerless power unless it operates through man. Just as steam is no good without the steam engine, the world-will is useless without man. Man is the only possible executant; he is God in operation. This belief screws up the sense of responsi-bility and self-respect. We want to organise Being. If we are told that God is all-pow___ ' ' ll-good, and that man is nothing, a sensible man sits down and does nothing; but if he believes that God is no more powerful than himself he buckles to and does some work.

As for rules. You know perfectly well that if the Samurai were instituted to-morrow the first rule that they would make would be to compel members to wear a starch collar and change it daily. The fact is we are suffering from a universal aspiration to be ladies and gentlemen, and while we are doing that we can't expect to be any better.

Mr Edward Carpenter said that the heart of Mr Wells's proposal was this: How are we to get the Socialist idea into the people at large. Mr Wells suggested an order of Samurai. But the great danger was prigs and priests. The main way of inculcating the spirit of the common life was by education. The children were to be got hold of. He had observed the pride children took in making themselves useful. It wasn't necessary to discuss theology; the fact of solidarity was enough. In a thousand ways our essential unity was demonstrated. But this fact and sentiment of common life had been veiled by excessive individualism; and it needed to be nourished and reproduced in modern life. A voluntary Socialism was the heart of the matter. Once get that and forms would not matter. The more they varied the better.

Mrs Sidney Webb said that all the good in the world had been done by either priests or prigs. Most of the great reformers had been consummate prigs. A prig was a person selected by himself to guide the world. The French encyclopaedists were prigs. The Benthamites were a set of prigs who gathered round the two consummately priggish Mills. The Fabians were prigs. Mr Shaw was a prig. Mr Wells was a prig. Her husband was, perhaps, the best prig of the lot. But it was only when discipline was lost that priests became false priests, and prigs became a nuisance. Socialists would not succeed till they had become practical mystics. There was one maxim which summed up for her the whole rules of physiology and economy:—no one should ever consume anything that did not add to efficiency.

New Age, May 2, 1907.

Charles Lever: Real Life
and the Romantic Imagination

Charles Lever's novel A Day's Ride: A Life's Romance *(1863) is Shaw's springboard for a discussion of the romantic imagination in life (including his own) and in literary art.*

About half a century ago, an Irish novelist, Charles Lever, wrote a story entitled A Day's Ride: A Life's Romance. It was published by Charles Dickens in Household Words, and proved so strange to the public taste that Dickens pressed Lever to make short work of it. I read scraps of this novel when I was a child; and it made an enduring impression on me. The hero was a very romantic hero, trying to live bravely, chivalrously, and powerfully by dint of mere romance-fed imagination, without courage, without means, without knowledge, without skill, without anything real except his bodily appetites. Even in my childhood I found in this poor devil's unsuccessful encounters with the facts of life, a poignant quality that romantic fiction lacked. The book, in spite of its first failure, is not dead: I saw its title the other day in the catalogue of Tauchnitz.

Now why is it that when I also deal in the tragi-comic irony of the conflict between real life and the romantic imagination, critics never affiliate me to my countryman and immediate forerunner, Charles Lever, whilst they confidently derive me from a Norwegian author of whose language I do not know three words, and of whom I knew nothing until years after the Shavian *Anschauung* was already unequivocally declared in books full of what came, ten years later, to be perfunctorily labelled Ibsenism? I was not Ibsenist even at second hand; for Lever, though he may have read Henri Beyle, *alias* Stendhal, certainly never read Ibsen. Of the books that made Lever popular, such as Charles O'Malley and Harry Lorrequer, I know nothing but the names and some of the illustrations. But the story of the day's ride and life's romance of Potts (claiming alliance with Pozzo di Borgo) caught me and fascinated me as something

strange and significant, though I already knew all about Alnaschar
and Don Quixote and Simon Tappertit and many another romantic
hero mocked by reality. From the plays of Aristophanes to the tales
of Stevenson that mockery has been made familiar to all who are
properly saturated with letters.

Where, then, was the novelty in Lever's tale? Partly, I think, in a
new seriousness in dealing with Potts's disease. Formerly, the contrast between madness and sanity was deemed comic: Hogarth
shews us how fashionable people went in parties to Bedlam to laugh
at the lunatics. I myself have had a village idiot exhibited to me as
something irresistibly funny. On the stage the madman was once
a regular comic figure: that was how Hamlet got his opportunity
before Shakespear touched him. The originality of Shakespear's
version lay in his taking the lunatic sympathetically and seriously,
and thereby making an advance towards the eastern consciousness
of the fact that lunacy may be inspiration in disguise, since a man
who has more brains than his fellows necessarily appears as mad to
them as one who has less. But Shakespear did not do for Pistol and
Parolles what he did for Hamlet. The particular sort of madman
they represented, the romantic make-believer, lay outside the pale
of sympathy in literature: he was pitilessly despised and ridiculed
here as he was in the east under the name of Alnaschar, and was
doomed to be, centuries later, under the name of Simon Tappertit.
When Cervantes relented over Don Quixote, and Dickens relented
over Pickwick, they did not become impartial: they simply changed
sides, and became friends and apologists where they had formerly
been mockers.

In Lever's story there is a real change of attitude. There is no
relenting towards Potts: he never gains our affections like Don
Quixote and Pickwick: he has not even the infatuate courage of
Tappertit. But we dare not laugh at him, because, somehow, we
recognize ourselves in Potts. We may, some of us, have enough
nerve, enough muscle, enough luck, enough tact or skill or address
or knowledge to carry things off better than he did; to impose on
the people who saw through him; to fascinate Katinka (who cut
Potts so ruthlessly at the end of the story); but for all that, we

know that Potts plays an enormous part in ourselves and in the world, and that the social problem is not a problem of story-book heroes of the older pattern, but a problem of Potts's, and of how to make men of them. To fall back on my old phrase, we have the feeling—one that Alnaschar, Pistol, Parolles, and Tappertit never gave us—that Potts is a piece of really scientific natural history as distinguished from funny story-telling. His author is not throwing a stone at a creature of another and inferior order, but making a confession, with the effect that the stone hits each of us full in the conscience and causes our self-esteem to smart very sorely. Hence the failure of Lever's book to please the readers of Household Words. That pain in the self-esteem nowadays causes critics to raise a cry of Ibsenism. I therefore assure them that the sensation first came to me from Lever and may have come to him from Beyle, or at least out of the Stendhalian atmosphere. I exclude the hypothesis of complete originality on Lever's part, because a man can no more be completely original in that sense than a tree can grow out of air.

It is reserved for some great critic to give us a study of the psychology of the XIX century. Those of us who as adults saw it face to face in that last moiety of its days when one fierce hand after another—Marx's, Zola's, Ibsen's, Strindberg's, Turgenieff's, Tolstoy's—stripped its masks off and revealed it as, on the whole, perhaps the most villainous page of recorded human history, can also recall the strange confidence with which it regarded itself as the very summit of civilization, and talked of the past as a cruel gloom that had been dispelled for ever by the railway and the electric telegraph. But centuries, like men, begin to find themselves out in middle age. The youthful conceit of the nineteenth had a splendid exponent in Macaulay, and, for a time, a gloriously jolly one during the nonage of Dickens. There was certainly nothing morbid in the air then: Dickens and Macaulay are as free from morbidity as Dumas *père* and Guizot. Even Stendhal and Prosper Mérimée, though by no means burgess optimists, are quite sane. When you come to Zola and Maupassant, Flaubert and the Goncourts, to Ibsen and Strindberg, to Aubrey Beardsley and George Moore, to D'Annunzio and Echegaray, you are in a new and morbid atmosphere. French litera-

ture up to the middle of the XIX century was still all of one piece
with Rabelais, Montaigne, and Molière. Zola breaks that tradition
completely: he is as different as Karl Marx from Turgot or Darwin from Cuvier.

In this new phase we see the bourgeoisie, after a century and a
half of complacent vaunting of its own probity and modest happiness (begun by Daniel Defoe in Robinson Crusoe's praises of "the
middle station of life"), suddenly turning bitterly on itself with
accusations of hideous sexual and commercial corruption. Thackeray's campaign against snobbery and Dickens's against hypocrisy
were directed against the vices of respectable men; but now even
the respectability was passionately denied: the bourgeois was depicted as a thief, a tyrant, a sweater, a selfish voluptuary whose marriages were simple legalizations of unbridled licentiousness. Sexual
irregularities began to be attributed to the sympathetic characters
in fiction not as the blackest spots in their portraits, but positively
as redeeming humanities in them.

I am by no means going here either to revive the old outcry
against this school of iconoclasts and disillusioners, or to join the
new reaction against it. It told the world many truths: it brought
romance back to its senses. Its very repudiation of the graces and
enchantments of fine art was necessary; for the artistic morbidezza
of Byron and Victor Hugo was too imaginative to allow the Victorian bourgeoisie to accept them as chroniclers of real facts and
real people. The justification of Zola's comparative coarseness is
that his work could not have been done in any other way. If Zola
had had a sense of humor, or a great artist's delight in playing
with his ideas, his materials, and his readers, he would have become
either as unreadable to the very people he came to wake up as
Anatole France is, or as incredible as Victor Hugo was. He would
also have incurred the mistrust and hatred of the majority of
Frenchmen, who, like the majority of men of all nations, are not
merely incapable of fine art, but resent it furiously. A wit is to them
a man who is laughing at them: an artist is a man of loose character who lives by telling lying stories and pandering to the voluptuous passions. What they like to read is the police intelligence,

especially the murder cases and divorce cases. The invented murders and divorces of the novelists and playwrights do not satisfy them, because they cannot believe in them; and belief that the horror or scandal actually occurred, that real people are shedding real blood and real tears, is indispensable to their enjoyment. To produce this belief by works of fiction, the writer must disguise and even discard the arts of the man of letters and assume the style of the descriptive reporter of the criminal courts. As an example of how to cater for such readers, we may take Zola's Bête Humaine. It is in all its essentials a simple and touching story, like Prévost's Manon Lescaut. But into it Zola has violently thrust the greatest police sensation of the XIX century: the episode of Jack the Ripper. Jack's hideous neurosis is no more a part of human nature than Caesar's epilepsy or Gladstone's missing finger. One is tempted to accuse Zola of having borrowed it from the newspapers to please his customers just as Shakespear used to borrow stories of murder and jealousy from the tales and chronicles of his time, and heap them on the head of convivial humorists like Iago and Richard III, or gentle poets like Macbeth and Hamlet. Without such allurements, Shakespear could not have lived by his plays. And if he had been rich enough to disregard this consideration, he would still have had to provide sensation enough to induce people to listen to what he was inspired to say. It is only the man who has no message who is too fastidious to beat the drum at the door of his booth.

Still, the Shakespearian murders were romantic murders: the Zolaesque ones were police reports. The old mad heroines, the Ophelias and Lucies of Lammermoor, were rhapsodists with flowers in their hands: the new ones were clinical studies of mental disease. The new note was as conspicuous in the sensational chapters as in the dull chapters, of which there were many. This was the punishment of the middle class for hypocrisy. It had carried the conspiracy of silence which we call decorum to such lengths that when young men discovered the suppressed truths, they felt bound to shout them in the streets. I well remember how when I was a youth in my teens I happened to obtain access to the papers of an Irish crown solicitor through a colleague who had some clerical work to do upon them.

The county concerned was not one of the crimeless counties: there was a large camp in it; and the soldier of that day was not the respectable, rather pious, and very low-spirited youth who now makes the King's uniform what the curate's black coat was then. There were not only cases which were tried and not reported: there were cases which could not even be tried, the offenders having secured impunity by pushing their follies to lengths too grotesque to be bearable even in a criminal court—also because of the silly ferocity of the law, which punished the negligible indecencies of drunken young soldiers as atrocious crimes. The effect produced by these revelations on my raw youth was a sense of heavy responsibility for conniving at their concealment. I felt that if camp and barrack life involved these things, they ought to be known. I had been caught by the great wave of scientific enthusiasm which was then passing over Europe as a result of the discovery of Natural Selection by Darwin, and of the blow it dealt to the vulgar Bible worship and redemption mongering which had hitherto passed among us for religion. I wanted to get at the facts. I was prepared for the facts being unflattering: had I not already faced the fact that instead of being a fallen angel I was first cousin to a monkey? Long afterwards, when I was a well-known writer, I said that what we wanted as the basis of our plays and novels was not romance, but a really scientific natural history. Scientific natural history is not compatible with taboo; and as everything connected with sex was tabooed, I felt the need for mentioning the forbidden subjects, not only because of their own importance, but for the sake of destroying taboo by giving it the most violent possible shocks. The same impulse is unmistakeably active in Zola and his contemporaries. He also wanted, not works of literary art, but stories he could believe in as records of things that really happen. He imposed Jack the Ripper on his idyll of the railwayman's wife to make it scientific. To all artists and Platonists he made it thereby very unreal; for to the Platonists all accidents are unreal and negligible; but to the people he wanted to get at—the anti-artistic people—he made it readable.

The scientific spirit was unintelligible to the Philistines and repulsive to the dilettanti, who said to Zola: "If you must tell us stories about agricultural laborers; why tell us dirty ones?" But Zola did not want, like the old romancers, to tell a story. He wanted to tell the world the scientific truth about itself. His view was that if you were going to legislate for agricultural laborers, or deal with them or their business in any way, you had better know what they are really like; and in supplying you with the necessary information he did not tell you what you already knew, which included pretty nearly all that could be decorously mentioned, but what you did not know, which was that part of the truth that was tabooed. For the same reason, when he found a generation whose literary notions of Parisian cocotterie were founded on Marguerite Gauthier,[1] he felt it to be a duty to shew them Nana. And it was a very necessary thing to do. If some Irish writer of the seventies had got himself banished from all decent society, and perhaps convicted of obscene libel, by writing a novel shewing the side of camp life that was never mentioned except in the papers of the Crown Solicitor, we should be nearer to a rational military system than we are today.

It is, unfortunately, much easier to throw the forces of art into a reaction than to recall them when the reaction has gone far enough. A case which came under my own notice years ago illustrates the difficulty. The wife of an eminent surgeon had some talent for drawing. Her husband wrote a treatise on cancer; and she drew the illustrations. It was the first time she had used her gift for a serious purpose; and she worked hard enough at it to acquire considerable skill in depicting cancerous proliferation. The book being finished and published, she resumed her ordinary practice of sketching for pleasure. But all her work now had an uncanny look. When she drew a landscape, it was like a cancer that accidentally looked like a landscape. She had acquired a cancerous technique; and she could not get rid of it.

This happens as easily in literature as in the other arts. The men

1. Marguerite Gauthier ("Camille") was the prostitute-heroine of Alexandre Dumas's *Dame Aux Camelias*, first published as a novel in 1848 and dramatized in 1852. Verdi turned the sentimental tragedy into his opera *La Traviata*.

who trained themselves as writers by dragging the unmentionable
to light, presently found that they could do that so much better
than anything else that they gave up dealing with the other subjects.
Even their quite mentionable episodes had an unmentionable air.
Their imitators assumed that unmentionability was an end in itself
—that to be decent was to be out of the movement. Zola and Ibsen
could not, of course, be confined to mere reaction against taboo.
Ibsen was to the last fascinating and full of a strange moving
beauty; and Zola often broke into sentimental romance. But neither
Ibsen nor Zola, after they once took in hand the work of unmasking
the idols of the bourgeoisie, ever again wrote a happy or pleasant
play or novel. Ibsen's suicides and catastrophes at last produced the
cry of "People dont do such things," which he ridiculed through
Judge Brack in Hedda Gabler. This was easy enough: Brack was
so far wrong that people do do such things occasionally. But on
the whole Brack was right. The tragedy of Hedda in real life is not
that she commits suicide but that she continues to live. If such acts
of violent rebellion as those of Hedda and Nora and Rebecca and
the rest were the inevitable or even the probable consequences of
their unfitness to be wives and mothers, or of their contracting
repugnant marriages to avoid being left on the shelf, social reform
would be very rapid; and we should hear less nonsense as to women
like Nora and Hedda being mere figments of Ibsen's imagination.
Our real difficulty is the almost boundless docility and submission to
social convention which is characteristic of the human race. What
balks the social reformer everywhere is that the victims of social
evils do not complain, and even strongly resent being treated as
victims. The more a dog suffers from being chained the more dangerous it is to release him: he bites savagely at the hand that dares
touch his collar. Our Rougon-Macquart families are usually enormously proud of themselves; and though they have to put up with
their share of drunkards and madmen, they do not proliferate into
Jack-the-Rippers. Nothing that is admittedly and unmistakably horrible matters very much, because it frightens people into seeking a
remedy: the serious horrors are those which seem entirely respectable and normal to respectable and normal men. Now the formula

of tragedy had come down to the nineteenth century from days
in which this was not recognized, and when life was so thoroughly
accepted as a divine institution that in order to make it seem tragic,
something dreadful had to happen and somebody had to die. But the
tragedy of modern life is that nothing happens, and that the resul-
tant dulness does not kill. Maupassant's Une Vie is infinitely more
tragic than the death of Juliet.

Preface to *Major Barbara* (London, 1906).

Realism, Real and Unreal

Observations on realism and naturalism in fiction, based upon a review of William Edward Norris's Major and Minor *(1887). Norris (1847–1925) was a prolific author of commercial and forgettable fiction from 1877 until after World War I.*

Were Mr Norris, without further explanation, set down here as a realistic novelist, misunderstanding would inevitably ensue. Mr George Moore might amazedly demand why Mr Norris was classed with him; and it is not impossible that Mr Norris might second him very strongly in the inquiry. The Real has always been a hard bird to catch. Plato did not succeed in getting it under his hat until he had divested it of everything that is real to the realists of noveldom to-day: these gentlemen are not Platonic realists. They do not seem to have got much further than an opinion that the romance of the drawing-room is less real than the romance of the kitchen, the romance of the kitchen than that of the slum, that of the slum than that of the sewer, and, generally, that reality is always in inverse proportion to self-control, education, health, and decency. For this discouraging view M Zola and his "tail"—which seems to grow, by-the-by, faster than he can bite it off—are less to blame than society, in which, quite unquestionably, conditions discreditable to civilization make up the greater part of our national life. Nor is there any form of toleration of evil more contemptible than the "good taste" which pretends not to know this, and strives to boycott those who refuse to join the conspiracy of silence. Whilst the slums exist and the sewers are out of order, it is better to force them on the attention even of the polite classes than to engage in the manufacture of eau-de-cologne for sprinkling purposes, and sedulously ignore, like Mrs General, everything that is not perfectly proper, placid, and pleasant. But it must not, in the heat of reaction against Mrs General, be forgotten that the proper, the placid, and the pleasant, even when quantitatively less than the improper, the hysterical, and the noisome, are quite as real. And when the separate question as to which is fitter for the three-volume treatment arises, it is to be considered that no born romancer can help imparting a certain attraction, morbid or healthy, to his subject matter; and that when he treats of the improper, the hysterical, and the noisome, he must, whether he will or no, clothe them with the fascinations of his art. If, for example, he takes a culpable prostitute for his heroine, he makes a heroine of a culpable prostitute; and no mechanical heaping of infamy and disease upon her in the third volume will quite despoil her of that glamour. And as to the prostitute whom it is inhuman to call culpable—the woman who can only save herself and her family from starvation by eking out her miserable wage by prostitution—it is not clear that she can be helped by serving her up as a new sensation for the novel-reading classes. The corruption of society to-day is caused by evils which can be remedied only by the aspiration of the masses towards better things, and not by the shrinking of the classes from horror known to them only by clever descriptions. Besides, one cannot help suspecting that those who shrink do not read, and that the rest dreadfully enjoy, the paper sensation. When, on any definite issue, the apathy or selfishness of the classes stands in the way of needed reform, then have at their consciences by all means, without the very slightest regard for their "delicacy." But to persist in showing the classes repulsive pictures of evils which they are powerless to abolish, without ever striving to show the masses the better conditions which they have the power to make real as soon as they have the will, is shallow policy put forward as an excuse for coarse art.

So much for the present concerning the realistic school to which Mr Norris does not belong. There is a naturalist school to which he does belong; and its founder was Anthony Trollope. Society has not yet forgiven that excellent novelist for having worked so many hours a day, like a carpenter or tailor, instead of periodically going mad with inspiration and hewing Barchester Towers at one frenzied stroke out of chaos, that being notoriously the only genuine artistic method. Yet, if we except the giants of the craft, he is entitled to rank among English writers as the first sincerely naturalistic novelist of our day. He delivered us from the marvels, senseless accidents, and cat's-cradle plots of old romance, and gave us, to the best of his ability, a faithful picture of the daily life of the upper and middle classes. If any contemptuously exclaim here, "Aha! The upper and middle classes! Why did not the snob give us the daily life of the slum and the gutter, on which all society rests to-day?" the answer is simple and convincing. He, as an honest realist, only told what he knew; and, being a middle-class man, he did not and could not know the daily life of the slum and gutter. And it must be added, at the risk of giving a violent shock to literary slummers, that every middle-class novelist who professes to arrive at his descriptions of that daily life by the inductive or Zolaistic method, is to that extent a flagrant humbug, although he may, through the ignorance of his readers, be as safe from exposure as an East-end dog-stealer would be if he undertook the fashionable intelligence for a paper circulating exclusively in Bethnal-green.

Mr Norris is by no means Anthony Trollope over again, though he exploits the same region, and produces good work rapidly enough to suggest that he, too, must turn out so much manuscript per hour, rain or shine. But, standing on Trollope's shoulders and belonging to a later generation, he is droller and brighter than Trollope; he knows the time of day in the political and social movement better; and he can, on emergency, go deeper into human motive, though it is hardly fair to say that his average profundity is greater. In Major and Minor he has taken the world easily. Major and Minor are brothers, who, since one is virtuous and the other rascally, would in an ordinary novel run a heavy risk of being very much underdone and overdone respectively. Mr Norris has done both to a turn, never overstepping the modesty of nature in his treatment of them except for a moment in the third volume, where he has indulged himself with a superfluous blackening of the villain's eye, very much as Dickens, in one of the most ridiculous moments of his immaturity, set the elder Chuzzlewit belabouring Mr Pecksniff with a nobby stick. In the first volume, too, there is a chapter or so of unpleasant suspense for the reader. When the father of the brothers disinherits

the elder; settles the estate on the younger; and then relents, it becomes evident to experienced readers that he must die before he
carries out his intention of revoking the will. A horrible curiosity
as to how Mr Norris is going to polish off this hale old man takes
possession of the imagination, and is so demoralizing that one is fain
to say, as Macbeth did in a similar mental attitude, that " 'twere
well it were done quickly." Mr Norris finally does the deed with a
chunk of old red sandstone, but contrives to avoid suspicion of
plagiarism from a well-known passage in Bret Harte. On the whole,
the worst that can be said of Major and Minor is that it might have
been better in two volumes only, like My Friend Jim. But it is an
amusing and sensible novel; and its realism is perfectly sincere and
in no way offensive.

Pall Mall Gazette, September 29, 1887.

III. POETS

Shaming the Devil about Shelley

Observations on Shelley as radical and heretic based upon a local celebration of the centenary of his birth.

When I first saw the proposal that Shelley's native county should celebrate the centenary of his birth by founding a Shelley Library and Museum at Horsham, I laughed: not publicly, because that would have been the act of a spoil-sport, but in my sleeve. The native county in question was Sussex, which had just distinguished itself at the General Election by a gloriously solid Conservative vote which had sent to Parliament a lord (son of a duke), an admiral, two baronets (one of them ex-Groom-in-Waiting to the Queen, and the other an ex-Dragoon officer), and two distinguished commoners (one of them son to a lord and the other to a Canon, once Her Majesty's chaplain): all of them high Tories. Now the difficulty of inducing so true-blue a corner of England to express any feeling towards Shelley but one of indignant abhorrence, can only be appreciated by those who are in possession of a complete and unexpurgated statement of what Shelley taught. Let me, therefore, draw up such a statement, as compendiously as may be.

In politics Shelley was a Republican, a Leveller, a Radical of the most extreme type. He was even an Anarchist of the old-fashioned Godwinian school, up to the point at which he perceived Anarchism to be impracticable. He publicly ranged himself with demagogues and gaol-birds like Cobbett and Henry Hunt (the original "Man in the White Hat"), and not only advocated the Plan of Radical Reform which was afterwards embodied in the proposals of the Chartists, but denounced the rent-roll of the landed aristocracy as the true pension list, thereby classing himself as what we now call a Land Nationalizer. He echoed Cobbett's attacks on the National Debt and the Funding System in such a manner as to leave no reasonable doubt that if he had been born half a century later he would have been advocating Social-Democracy with a view to its development into the most democratic form of Communism practically attainable and maintainable. At the late election he would certainly have vehemently urged the agricultural laborers of Sussex to procure a candidate of the type of John Burns and to vote for him against the admiral, the lord, the two baronets, and against Messrs Gathorne Hardy and Brookfield.

In religion, Shelley was an Atheist. There is nothing uncommon in that; but he actually called himself one, and urged others to follow his example. He never trifled with the word God: he knew that it meant a personal First Cause, Almighty Creator, and Supreme Judge and Ruler of the Universe, and that it did not mean anything else, never had meant anything else, and never whilst the English language lasted would mean anything else. Knowing perfectly well that there was no such person, he did not pretend that the question was an open one, or imply, by calling himself an Agnostic, that there might be such a person for all he knew to the contrary. He did know to the contrary; and he said so. Further, though there never was a man with so abiding and full a consciousness of the omnipresence of a living force, manifesting itself here in the germination and growth of a tree, there in the organization of a poet's brain, and elsewhere in the putrefaction of a dead dog, he never condescended to beg off being an Atheist by calling this omnipresent energy God, or even Pan. He lived and died professedly, almost boastfully, godless. In his time, however, as at present, God was little more than a word to the English people. What they really worshipped was the Bible; and our modern Church movement to get away from Bible fetishism and back to some presentable sort of Christianity (*vide* Mr Horton's speech at Grindelwald the other day, for example) had not then come to the surface. The preliminary pickaxing work of Bible smashing had yet to be done; and Shelley, who found the moral atmosphere of the Old Testament murderous and abominable, and the asceticism of the New suicidal and pessimistic, smashed away at the Bible with all his might and main.

But all this, horrifying as it is from the Sussex point of view, was mere eccentricity compared to Shelley's teaching on the subject of the family. He would not draw any distinction between the privilege of the king or priest and that of the father. He pushed to its extremest consequences his denial that blood relationship altered by one jot or tittle the relations which should exist between human beings. One of his most popular performances at Eton and Oxford was an elaborate curse on his own father, who had thwarted and oppressed him: and the entirely serious intention of Shelley's curses may be seen in his solemn imprecation against Lord Eldon, ending with the words:

"I curse thee, though I hate thee not."

His determination to impress on us that our fathers should be no more and no less to us than other men, is evident in every allusion of his to the subject, from the school curse to The Cenci, which to this day is refused a license for performance on the stage.

But Shelley was not the man to claim freedom of enmity, and say nothing about freedom of love. If father and son are to be as free in their relation to one another as hundredth cousins are, so must sister and brother. The freedom to curse a tyrannical father is not more sacred than the freedom to love an amiable sister. In a word, if filial duty is no duty, then incest is no crime. This sounds startling even now, disillusioned as we are by Herbert Spencer, Elie Reclus, and other writers as to there being anything "natural" in our code of prohibited degrees; but in Shelley's time it seemed the summit of impious vice, just as it would to the Sussexers to-day, if they only knew. Nevertheless, he did not shrink from it in the least: the hero and heroine of Laon and Cythna are brother and sister; and the notion that the bowdlerization of this great poem as The Revolt of Islam represents any repentance or withdrawal on Shelley's part, cannot be sustained for a moment in the face of the facts. No person who is well acquainted with Shelley's work can suppose that he would have thought any the worse of Byron if he had known and believed everything that Mrs Beecher Stowe alleged concerning him. And no one who has ever reasoned out the consequences of such views can doubt for a moment that Shelley regarded the family, in its legal aspects, as a doomed institution.

So much for the opinions which Shelley held and sedulously propagated. Could Sussex be reconciled to them on the ground that they were mere "views" which did not affect his conduct? Not a bit of it. Although Shelley was the son of a prosperous country gentleman, his life was consistently disreputable except at one fatal moment of his boyhood, when he chivalrously married a girl who had run away from school and thrown herself on his protection. At this time he had been expelled from Oxford for writing and circulating a tract called The Necessity of Atheism. His marriage, as might have been expected, was a hopeless failure; and when this fact was fully established the two parted; and Shelley was fallen in love with by the daughter of Mary Wollstonecraft and Godwin. Shelley took young Mary Godwin abroad, and started housekeeping with her without the least scruple; and he suggested that his wife should come and make one of the household, a notion which did not recommend itself to either of the ladies. The courts then deprived him of the custody of his children, on the ground that he was unfit to have charge of them; and his wife eventually committed suicide. Shelley then married Mary Godwin, solely, as he explained, because the law forced him to do so in the interest of his son. The rest of his life was quite consistent with the beginning of it; and it is not improbable that he would have separated from his second wife as from his first, if he had not been drowned when he was twenty-nine.

It only remains to point out that Shelley was not a hot-headed nor an unpractical person. All his writings, whether in prose or verse, have a peculiarly deliberate quality. His political pamphlets are unique in their freedom from all appeal to the destructive passions; there is neither anger, sarcasm, nor frivolity in them; and in this respect his poems exactly resemble his political pamphlets. Other poets, from Shakespear to Tennyson, have let the tiger in them loose under pretext of patriotism, righteous indignation, or what not: he never did. His horror of violence, cruelty, injustice, and bravery was proof against their infection. Hence it cannot for a moment be argued that his opinions and his conduct were merely his wild oats. His seriousness, his anxious carefulness, are just as obvious in the writings which still expose their publishers to the possibility of a prosecution for sedition or blasphemy as in his writings on Catholic Emancipation, the propriety and practical sagacity of which are not now disputed. And he did not go back upon his opinions in the least as he grew older. By the time he had begun The Triumph of Life, he had naturally come to think Queen Mab a boyish piece of work, not that what it affirmed seemed false to him or what it denied true, but because it did not affirm and deny enough. Thus there is no excuse for Shelley on the ground of his youth or rashness. If he was a sinner, he was a hardened sinner and a deliberate one.

The delicate position of the gentlemen who invited Sussex to honor Shelley on the 4th of last month will now be apparent, especially when it is added that the facts are undeniable, accessible to all inquirers, and familiar to most fanciers of fine literature. The success of the celebration evidently depended wholly on the chances of inducing the aforesaid fanciers to wink and say nothing in as many words as possible. A conspiracy to keep an open secret of so scandalous a character seems extravagant; and yet it almost succeeded. The practical question was not whether Shelley could be shewn to be infamous, but whether anyone wished to undertake that demonstration. In Shelley's case it appeared that everybody— that is, everybody whose desire weighed two straws with the public —was anxious to make Shelley a saint. Mr Cordy Jeaffreson's attempt to prove him the meanest of sinners had been taken in such uncommonly bad part that no literary man with any regard for his own popularity cared to follow up Mr Jeaffreson's line. The feeblest excuses for Shelley had been allowed to pass. Matthew Arnold had explained how poor Percy had the misfortune to live in a low set, as if he had not been more free to choose his own set than most other men in England. Others had pleaded that he was young; that he was a poet; that you would find his works full of true piety if you only read them in a proper spirit; and—most exquisite of all— that the people who persisted in raking up the story of Harriet must be low-minded gossips, to allude to so improper a story. On all sides there went up the cry, "We want our great Shelley, our darling Shelley, our best, noblest, highest of poets. We will not have it said

that he was a Leveller, an Atheist, a foe to marriage, an advocate
of incest. He was a little unfortunate in his first marriage; and we
pity him for it. He was a little eccentric in his vegetarianism; but
we are not ashamed of that; we glory in the humanity of it [with
morsels of beefsteak, fresh from the slaughter house, sticking between our teeth]. We ask the public to be generous—to read his
really great works, such as the Ode to a Skylark, and not to gloat
over those boyish indiscretions known as Laon and Cythna, Prome-
theus, Rosalind and Helen, The Cenci, The Masque of Anarchy,
etc., etc. Take no notice of the Church papers; for our Shelley was
a true Christian at heart. Away with Jeaffreson; for our Shelley was
a gentleman if ever there was one. If you doubt it, ask—"

That was just the difficulty: who were we to ask when the Centenary came round? On reflection, the Horsham Committee decided
that we had better ask Mr Gosse. It was a wise choice. The job was
one which required a certain gift of what is popularly called cheek;
and Mr Gosse's cheek is beyond that of any man of my acquaintance. I went down to Horsham expressly to hear him; and I can
certify that he surpassed himself. I confess I thought he was going
to overdo it, when, extolling the poet's patriotism in selecting England for his birth-place, he applied to Shelley a brilliant paraphrase
of Mr Gilbert's

"For he might have been a Rooshan," etc.,

but no: it came off perfectly. A subsequent fearless assertion that
there was surprisingly little slime—he said slime—on Shelley's reputation, and that the "sordid" details of his career were really not so
very numerous after all, hit off to a nicety the requirements of the
occasion; and when he handsomely remarked that for his part he
thought that far too much talk had already been made about Harriet, we all felt that a gentleman could say no less. It was a happy
thought also to chaff Shelley as an eater of buns and raisins, the
satirist being no doubt stoked up for the occasion with gobbets of
cow or sheep, and perhaps a slice or two of pig. But what fairly
banged everything in his address was his demonstration that Shelley
was so fragile, so irresponsible, so ethereally tender, so passionate a

creature that the wonder was that he was not a much greater rascal. The dodge of making allowances for a great man's differences with small men on the plea of his being a privileged weakling is one which I have of course often seen worked; but I never saw it brought to such perfection as by Mr Gosse at Horsham. It was a triumph not only of audacity but of platform manner. At the stiffest parts of the game Mr Gosse contrived to get on a sort of infatuated pomposity which is quite indescribable. Whilst it completely imposed on the innocents, there was yet lurking behind it a sly relish for the fun of the situation which disarmed those out-and-out Shelleyans who half expected to see Mr Gosse struck by lightning for his presumption. For my own part, I have seldom been worse misunderstood than by the gentleman who wrote to a daily paper alleging, in proof of my sympathy with his own outraged feelings, that I walked out of the room in disgust. I protest I only went to catch the 5:17 train to London, where I had to act as the best available substitute for Mr Gosse at the proletarian celebration of Shelley in the easterly parish of St Luke's.

In a rougher, homelier, style, the chairman, Mr Hurst, Justice of the Peace and Deputy Lieutenant for the county, gave Mr Gosse an admirable lead. The judicious way in which he dwelt on the central fact that Shelley had been born in the neighbourhood; his remarks on the intellectual value of a free public library to the working classes, and his declaration that if Shelley were alive he would be the first to support a free library; his happy comparison of Horsham to Stratford-on-Avon (which brought the house down at once); his deprecation of the harshness of Oxford University in expelling Shelley for a "mere dialectical view" (meaning The Necessity of Atheism); and his genial peroration on the theme of "boys will be boys," pitched so as to half confess that he himself had held quite desperate views when he was young and foolish; all this was so ingenious that when I described it in the evening at the Hall of Science it established my reputation in St Luke's as a platform humorist of the first order. But his point about the free library was really the essential one. It was for the sake of the library that I refused to blow the gaff by speaking at Horsham when Mr Stanley

Little, with characteristic intrepidity, invited me to do so. It was presumably for the sake of the library that Mr Hurst, Mr Gosse, and Mr Frederic Harrison deliberately talked bogus Shelleyism to the reporters. Miss Alma Murray and Mr Herbert Sims Reeves may have recited and sung for the sake of the real Shelley; and Professor Nicholl, as I gather, shewed an alarming disposition to let the cat out of the bag in moving a vote of thanks to the chair; but the rest were solid for the library, even if the front were to be decorated with a relief representing Shelley in a tall hat, Bible in hand, leading his children on Sunday morning to the church of his native parish.

Of the meeting in the evening at the Hall of Science I need say but little. It consisted for the most part of working men who took Shelley quite seriously, and were much more conscious of his opinions and of his spirit than of his dexterity as a versifier. It was summoned without the intervention of any committee by Mr G. W. Foote, the President of the National Secular Society, who, by his own personal announcement and a few handbills, got a meeting which beat Horsham hollow. The task of the speakers was so easy that Mr Gosse and Mr Frederic Harrison might well have envied us. Mr Foote, a militant Atheist like Shelley himself, and one who has suffered imprisonment under the outrageous Blasphemy Laws which some people suppose to be obsolete, was able to speak with all the freedom and force of a man who not only talks Shelley but lives him. Dr Furnivall, incorrigible in the matter of speaking his mind, frankly stated how far he went with Shelley, which was far enough to explain why he was not one of the Horsham orators. As for me, my quotations from the Horsham proceedings came off so immensely that I could not but feel jealous of Mr Hurst. For the rest, I had nothing to do but give a faithful account of Shelley's real opinions, with every one of which I unreservedly agree. Finally Mr Foote recited Men of England, which brought the meeting to an end amid thunders of applause. What would have happened had anyone recited it at Horsham is more than I can guess. Possibly the police would have been sent for.

Mr Foote's meeting, which was as spontaneous as the absence of committee and advertisement could make it, was composed for the most part of people whose lives had been considerably influenced by Shelley. Some time ago Mr H. S. Salt, in the course of a lecture on Shelley, mentioned on the authority of Mrs Marx Aveling, who had it from her father, Karl Marx, that Shelley had inspired a good deal of that huge but badly managed popular effort called the Chartist movement. An old Chartist who was present, and who seemed at first much surprised by this statement, rose to confess that, "now he came to think of it" (apparently for the first time), it was through reading Shelley that he got the ideas that led him to join the Chartists. A little further inquiry elicited that Queen Mab was known as The Chartists' Bible; and Mr Buxton Forman's collection of small, cheap copies, blackened with the finger-marks of many heavy-handed trades, are the proofs that Shelley became a power —a power that is still growing. He made and is still making men and women join political societies, Secular societies, Vegetarian societies, societies for the loosening of the marriage contract, and Humanitarian societies of all sorts. There is at every election a Shelleyan vote, though there is no means of counting it. The discussion of his life, which makes our literary *dilettanti* so horribly uneasy, cannot be checked, no matter how exquisitely they protest. He is still forcing us to make up our minds whether the conventional judgment of his life as that of a scoundrel is the truth or only a *reductio ad absurdum* of the conventional morality. That is a vital question; and it is pitifully useless for the exponents of the fashionable culture to deprecate it as "chatter about Harriet," when no sensible man can hear any chattering except that of their own teeth at the prospect of having to face Shelley's ideas seriously.

Without any ill-conditioned desire to rub the situation into those who have offered Shelley a carnival of humbug as a centenary offering, I think no reasonable man can deny the right of those who appreciate the scope and importance of Shelley's views to refuse to allow the present occasion to be monopolized by triflers to whom he was nothing more than a word-jeweller. Besides, the Horsham affair has been a failure: nobody has been taken in by it. Mr Foote scores heavily; and Mr Gosse and Mr Frederic Harrison are left sitting down, rather pensively, even though no newspaper except the Pall Mall Gazette and the Daily Chronicle dared to prick the bubble. I now venture to suggest that in future the bogus Shelley be buried and done with. I make all allowances for the fact that we are passing through an epidemic of cowardice on the part of literary men and politicians which will certainly make us appear to the historians of 1992 the most dastardly crew that has ever disgraced the platform and the press. It seems that as the march of liberty removes concrete terrors from our path, we become the prey of abstract fear, and are more and more persuaded that society is only held together by the closest trade unionism in senseless lying and make-believe. But it is vain to lie about Shelley: it is clear as day that if he were nothing more than what we try to make him out, his Centenary would be as little remembered as that of Southey. Why not be content to say, "I abhor Shelley's opinions; but my abhorrence is overwhelmed by my admiration of the exquisite artistic quality of his work," or "I am neither an Atheist nor a believer in Equality nor a Free Lover; and yet I am willing to celebrate Shelley because I feel that he was somehow a good sort," or even "I think Shelley's poetry slovenly and unsubstantial, and his ideas simply rot; but I will celebrate him because he said what he thought, and not what he was expected to say he thought." Instead of this, each of us gets up and says, "I am forced for the sake of my wife and family and social position to be a piffler and a trimmer; and as all you fellows are in the same predicament, I ask you to back me up in trying to make out that Shelley was a piffler and a trimmer too." As one of the literary brotherhood myself, I hope I am clubbable enough to stand in with any reasonable movement in my trade; but this is altogether too hollow. It will not do: the meanest Shelley reader knows better. If it were only to keep ourselves from premature putrefaction, we must tell the truth about somebody; and I submit that Shelley has pre-eminent claims to be that somebody. Hence this article.

Albemarle Review, September, 1892.

The *English Poems* of Richard Le Gallienne

When Richard Le Gallienne's English Poems *was published in September, 1892, it was offered to Shaw for review, rather than to an outside literary critic, apparently because he once reviewed the poet's* The Book-Bills of Narcissus, *and had been kind. Shaw—less generous this time—reviewed the book under his music-critic byline of* Corno di Bassetto.[1]

I wonder why I, of all *Star* reviewers, should have been asked to deal with this book, I, di Bassetto, most prosaic of critics. For I do not enthuse readily over the smaller fancy wares of art: the builder, not the jeweller, is the man for my money; and your miniatures and fan paintings, your ballads and *morceaux de salon,* make but a finicking appeal to the Bassettian spirit, nursed upon cathedrals, frescoes, and giant Wagnerian music-epics. Besides, it is against my vow to let any man off cheaply in the arts. I am no smirking verger to let all comers who look good for a tip into the choir and among the tombs of the mighty dead, there to pose and scratch their names until Time, Death and Judgment come down out of Mr Watts's picture, and

1. A name sufficiently well known in London to enable Le Gallienne to react to what he first called "Bernard Shaw's bludgeoning of my little song bird" with a good-humored poem:

To C. di B.

Poor little book that only yesterday
Fluttered new-born in delicate array,
How bruised and broken in the mud you lie—
Surely some elephant was passing by!
Or those mad herds of Galilean swine
Have hoofed across that pretty page of thine;
A nightingale within Minotaur's paw—
So seemed my little book within the grasp of Shaw.

inexorably eject them. Rather let me stand at the gate I guard, fell, grim, and venomous, not to say downright unpopular, holding it against all who are not strong enough to make a doormat of me. And yet Mr Le Gallienne is such an uncommonly likely young man, and so easily able to do me a good turn some day—for is he not a professed logroller?[2]—that I am half tempted to do what so many of the other vergers do, and make a pretty exhibition of tact and good nature by passing him quietly in after a little coquetry with his claims. But in England this cannot safely be done without a careful investigation of the applicant's moral character; and I regret to say that the most cursory examination of Mr Le Gallienne's hymn-book is enough to convince any verger that a more abandoned youth has seldom presented himself at the choir gates of an English cathedral. Just listen to this, for instance—page 91, the first and third verse (the second is too awful for quotation)

> Let me take thy hair down, sweetheart,
>   loosed little pin by pin,
> Let me feel it tumbling o'er me,
>   drinking all its fragrance in.
> Let me wrap thee all within it,
>   kiss thee through its golden thread—
> O I shall go mad with kissing,
>   kissing, kissing thy dear head.
>
> O thy body, sweet, sweet body,
>   let me drink and drink and drink!
> Canst thou let me, like the minstrel,
>   die upon the fountain's brink?
> Love, O Love, what *art* Thou? Tell me:
>   is this heaven, hell or where?
> All I know is that I kiss thee,
>   lying in thy yellow hair.

Now I ask, is this proper? Is it moral? The answer depends, obviously, on whether Mr Le Gallienne is legally married to the lady.

2. Le Gallienne wrote book reviews in the *Star* under the pen name of "Logroller."

On this subject I proceed to collect the evidence. Let me admit at once that I found none to justify me in doubting that the above was addressed to the same lady as "Hesperides," which I pass unquoted with a blush, merely observing for the reader's convenience that it is to be found on page 72. But what about the following lines from the poem beginning, "Dear desk, farewell!" on pp. 115–116?

> How many queens have ruled and passed
> Since first we met; how thick and fast
> The letters used to come at first, how thin at last;
> Then ceased, and winter for a space!
> Until another hand
> Brought spring into the land, &c., &c.

Can any man of experience believe that the author of this passage is a strict monogamist? Further evidence is to be found in the series of poems called "Love Platonic" (Platonic indeed!) in which Mr Le Gallienne, after betraying the fact that the heroines are several and not one by little discrepancies which cannot be detailed here for lack of space, gets so confused by their multiplicity that he forgets which is which, and exclaims—

> Who is the lady I sing?
> Ah, how can I tell thee her praise?
> For whom all my life's but the string
> Of a rosary painful of days.

But the worst is to come. One of the ladies is unquestionably a married woman. The poem entitled 'Why Did She Marry Him?' will set a good many of Mr Le Gallienne's domesticated friends speculating rather dubiously as to which of them is the subject of it. At any rate, since she did marry him, Mr Le Gallienne's duty was plain. Instead of doing it he persevered in his address in the following fashion:—

> Yea, let me be "thy bachelere,"
> Tis sweeter than thy lord.
>   *(note this preference)*

> How should I envy him, my dear,
>   The lamp upon his board.
> Still make his little circle bright,
> With boon of dear domestic light,
>   While I afar,
> Watching his windows in the night,
>   Worship a star
> For which he hath no bolt or bar
>   Yea, dear,
>   Thy "bachelere."

I wonder what people would say of me if I wrote such things! It is all very well for Mr Le Gallienne to call his poems "Platonic," and to pitch into the "Decadent poets" in his virtuous intervals; but if he came round watching my windows in that fashion, I should have a serious talk with Madame di Bassetto on the head of it. Apart from these considerations of personal morality, which must ever come first with me, my chief quarrel with Mr. Le Gallienne arises out of a certain commonplaceness and banality of material, which is not altogether compensated by his dainty workmanship. . . . If Mr Le Gallienne thinks his verse fresh enough for me, he greatly under-rates my literary experience. . . . The commonplaceness is due to the usual cause—unconscious insincerity; leading to a preference for secondhand ideas. Mr. Le Gallienne ought to know that a writer should never read anything but the book of life. Yet he is not ashamed to call himself a "passionate reader." . . . Mr. Le Gallienne's estimate of himself I rather like. He boldly says in an apostrophe to Song that his verses are

> Stars that may linger yet
> When I, their master, shall have come to die.

My own opinion is that immortality is not so cheap. It really does take a most tremendous equipment to survive oneself as a poet. In fact, the demand is so unreasonable that I do not myself consider immortality worth having at the price. For you must not only make good verses, but you must write poetry which the very cleverest poets of succeeding generations shall not be able to renew and replace. Looking at Mr Le Gallienne's valentines and rhymed love letters and dedications, his prayers and pleas and songs, I can appreciate his delicate ear and fine literary taste, and feel in his works a charm of character that even his cleverness and wit have not been able to spoil; but I think, nevertheless, that there will always be three or four men in England able to do as well as he in poesy, especially when they fall in love; and these three or four, by renewing and replacing his poems (so far), will rob them of immortality. But then, what a ridiculous criticism that is, after all! It is as if I had been asked my opinion of a diamond bracelet, and had replied that its weight fell far short of a ton. However, I declared honestly at the outset that I was not the man for the job. If Mr Le Gallienne will send me along something in five acts and in blank verse, or in thirty cantos or so, then I shall be in my element. In the meantime my overtrial of him may amuse him; whilst my quotations, though they are by no means the plums of the book, may help the reader to form his own more sympathetic judgment.   c. di b.

London Star, October 27, 1892.

Keats

Observations on Keats elicited from Shaw by a committee seeking material for a volume commemorating the centenary of the poet's death.

It is very difficult to say anything about Keats except that he was a poet. His merits are a matter of taste. Anyone who can read his best lines without being enchanted by them is verse-deaf. But whether the enchantment works or fails there is nothing more to be said. Other poets have other strings to their bows. Macaulay could have written a very interesting essay on Shelley without liking or even mentioning a line of his verse. He did write a very interesting essay on Byron, which would have been equally readable had Byron been an amateur like Count D'Orsay. Societies have been established to discuss Browning; and they would not have held a meeting the less if Browning had been a revivalist preacher who had never penned a rhyme in his life. But out of Keats Macaulay could not have made two pages; and a Keats Society would be gravelled for lack of matter half-way through its first sitting unless it resolved itself into a Fanny Brawne Society, when it might conceivably make good for a few evenings of gossip. Being at this moment asked to write about Keats, a thing I should never have dreamt of doing on my own initiative, I find myself with nothing to say except that you cannot write about Keats.

Another way of putting this is to say that he was the most literary of all the major poets: literary to the verge of being but the greatest of the minor poets; only, if you go over that verge you achieve a *reductio ad absurdum;* for the strength of a poet is the strength of his strongest lines; and Keats's strongest lines are so lovely, and there are so many of them, that to think of him as a minor poet is impossible. Even his worst lines: for example,

> A bunch of blooming plums
> Ready to melt between an infant's gums,

have nothing minor about them; they are not poor would-be lines: they are brazenly infamous, like Shakespear's

> In a most hideous and dreadful manner,

which I once accused Ellen Terry of having improvised to cover a lapse of memory, so incredible it seemed that Shakespear should have perpetrated it.

What I mean by a literary poet is one who writes poetry for the sake of writing poetry; who lisps in numbers because he prefers that method of utterance; who wants to be a poet as if that were an end in itself. Such a one will force the forms and graces of poetry on the most prosaic subject matter, and turn a page of prose into a thousand lines of epic. Poe, a master of both prose and verse, complained that epics are not really homogeneous poems, but patches of poetry embroidered on long stretches of prosaic fabric disguised as poetry by the arts of versification. Even Milton did this, though no man knew better than he that prose has a music of its own, and that many pensters write verses because their ears are not good enough to enable them to write readable prose, and because, though nobody will give them any credit for calling a window a window, lots of people will take them for poets if they call it a casement.

Now Keats was the sort of youth who calls a window a casement. That was why the reviewers told him to go back to his gallipots. Critics who are only waiting for a chance to make themselves disagreeable trip themselves by jumping at the chance, when it comes, without looking before they leap. If an apothecary's apprentice happens to be born a poet, one of the first symptoms of his destiny will be a tendency to call windows casements (on paper). The fact that if he is born a poetaster the symptoms will be just the same, may mislead a bad critic, but not a good one, unless the good one (as often happens) is such a snob that when he has to review the poems of a shopman the critic in him is killed by the snob. If Keats had ever described a process so remote from Parnassus as the taking down and putting up of the shop shutters, he would have described them in terms of a radiant sunrise and a voluptuous sunset, with the red and green bottles as heavenly bodies and the medicines as Arabian Balsams. What a good critic would have said to him was not "Go back to your gallipots," but "If you can call a window a casement with such magical effect, for heaven's sake leave your gallipots and do nothing but write poetry all your life."

The other sort of poet is the one for whom poetry is only a means to an end, the end being to deliver a message which clamors to be revealed through him. So he secures a hearing for it by clothing it with word-garments of such beauty, authority, and eternal memorableness, that the world must needs listen to it. These are prophets rather than poets; and for the sake of being poets alone would not take the trouble to rhyme love and dove or bliss and kiss.

It often happens that a prophet-poet begins as a literary poet, the prophet instinctively training himself by literary exercises for his future work. Thus you have Morris exercising himself in his youth by re-writing all the old stories in very lovely verses, but conscientiously stating at the beginning that he is only "the idle singer of an empty day." Later on he finds his destiny as propagandist and prophet, the busy singer of a bursting day. Now if Morris had lived no longer than Keats, he would have been an even more exclusively literary poet, because Keats achieved the very curious feat of writing one poem of which it may be said that if Karl Marx can be imagined as writing a poem instead of a treatise on Capital, he would have written Isabella. The immense indictment of the profiteers and exploiters with which Marx has shaken capitalistic civilization to its foundations, even to its overthrow in Russia, is epitomized in

> With her two brothers this fair lady dwelt
> Enrichéd from ancestral merchandise;
> And for them many a weary hand did swelt
> In torchéd mines and noisy factories;
>
> And many once proud-quivered loins did melt
> In blood from stinging whip: with hollow eyes
> Many all day in dashing river stood
> To take the rich-ored driftings of the flood.

For them the Ceylon diver held his breath,
    And went all naked to the hungry shark:
For them his ears gushed blood: for them in death
    The seal on the cold ice with piteous bark
Lay full of darts: for them alone did seethe
    A thousand men in troubles wide and dark.
Half ignorant, they turned an easy wheel
That set sharp racks at work to pinch and peel.

Why were they proud? Because their marble founts
    Gush'd with more pride than do a wretch's tears?
Why were they proud? Because fair orange-mounts
    Were of more soft ascent than lazar stairs?
Why were they proud? Because red-lin'd accounts
    Were richer than the songs of Grecian years?
Why were they proud? Again we ask aloud,
Why in the name of Glory were they proud?

Everything that the Bolshevik stigmatizes when he uses the epithet
"bourgeois" is expressed forcibly, completely, and beautifully in
those three stanzas, written half a century before the huge tide of
middle-class commercial optimism and complacency began to ebb
in the wake of the planet Marx. Nothing could well be more literary than the wording: it is positively euphuistic. But it contains all
the Factory Commission Reports that Marx read, and that Keats
did not read because they were not yet written in his time. And so
Keats is among the prophets with Shelley, and, had he lived, would
no doubt have come down from Hyperions and Endymions to tin
tacks as a very full-blooded modern revolutionist. Karl Marx is
more euphuistic in calling the profiteers *bourgeoisie* than Keats with
his "these same ledger-men." Ledger-men is at least better English
than bourgeois: there would be some hope for it yet if it had not
been supplanted by profiteer.

Keats also anticipated Erewhon Butler's gospel of Laodicea in
the lines beginning (Shakespeareanly) with

How fever'd is the man who cannot look
Upon his mortal days with temperate blood!

triumphantly driving home the nail at the end with (Wordsworthily)

> Why then should Man, teasing the world for grace,
> Spoil his salvation for a fierce miscreed?

On the whole, in spite of the two idle epics, voluptuously literary, and the holiday globe-trotting "from silken Samarcand to cedar'd Lebanon," Keats manages to affirm himself as a man as well as a poet, and to win a place among the great poets in virtue of a future he never lived to see, and of poems he never lived to write. And he contributed a needed element to that august Communion of Saints: the element of geniality, rarely associated with lyrical genius of the first order. Dante is not notably genial. Milton can do a stunt of geniality, as in L'Allegro; but one does not see him exuberantly fighting the butcher, as Keats is said to have done. Wordsworth, cheerful at times as a pious duty, is not genial. Cowper's John Gilpin is a turnpike tragedy. Even the thought of Shelley kills geniality. Chesterton's resolute conviviality is about as genial as an *auto da fé* of teetotallers. Byron's joy is derision. When Moore is merry he ceases to be a poet so utterly that we are tempted to ask when did he begin. Landor and Browning are capable of Olympian joviality: their notion of geniality is shying thunderbolts. Mr Pecksniff, saying "Let us be merry" and taking a captain's biscuit, is as successful as most of them. If Swinburne had attempted to be genial he would have become a mere blackguard; and Tennyson would have been like a jeweler trying to make golliwogs. Keats alone remains for us not only a poet, but a merry soul, a jolly fellow, who could not only carry his splendid burthen of genius, but swing it round, toss it up and catch it again, and whistle a tune as he strode along.

But there is no end to talking about poets; and it often prevents people reading them; so enough.

The John Keats Memorial Volume (London: Keats House Committee, Hampstead, 1921).

Edgar Allan Poe

A rare extended Shavian comment upon an American writer, written to mark the centenary of Poe's birth.

There was a time when America, the Land of the Free, and the birthplace of Washington, seemed a natural fatherland for Edgar Allan Poe. Nowadays the thing has become inconceivable: no young man can read Poe's works without asking incredulously what the devil he is doing in *that* galley. America has been found out; and Poe has not; that is the situation. How did he live there, this finest of fine artists, this born aristocrat of letters? Alas! he did not live there: he died there, and was duly explained away as a drunkard and a failure, though it remains an open question whether he really drank as much in his whole lifetime as a modern succcessful American drinks, without comment, in six months.

If the Judgment Day were fixed for the centenary of Poe's birth, there are among the dead only two men born since the Declaration of Independence whose plea for mercy could avert a prompt sentence of damnation on the entire nation; and it is extremely doubtful whether those two could be persuaded to pervert eternal justice by uttering it. The two are, of course, Poe and Whitman; and there is between them the remarkable difference that Whitman is still credibly an American, whereas even the Americans themselves, though rather short of men of genius, omit Poe's name from their Pantheon, either from a sense that it is hopeless for them to claim so foreign a figure, or from simple Monroeism. One asks, has the America of Poe's day passed away, or did it ever exist?

Probably it never existed. It was an illusion, like the respectable Whig Victorian England of Macaulay. Karl Marx stripped the whitewash from that sepulchre; and we have ever since been struggling with a conviction of social sin which makes every country in which industrial capitalism is rampant a hell to us. For let no

American fear that America, on that hypothetic Judgment Day, would perish alone. America would be damned in very good European company, and would feel proud and happy, and contemptuous of the saved. She would not even plead the influence of the mother from whom she has inherited all her worst vices. If the American stands today in scandalous pre-eminence as an anarchist and a ruffian, a liar and a braggart, an idolater and a sensualist, that is only because he has thrown off the disguises of Catholicism and feudalism which still give Europe an air of decency, and sins openly, impudently, and consciously, instead of furtively, hypocritically, and muddleheadedly, as we do. Not until he acquires European manners does the American anarchist become the gentleman who assures you that people cannot be made moral by Act of Parliament (the truth being that it is only by Acts of Parliament that men in large communities can be made moral, even when they want to); or the American ruffian hand over his revolver and bowie knife to be used for him by a policeman or soldier; or the American liar and braggart adopt the tone of the newspaper, the pulpit, and the platform; or the American idolater write authorized biographies of millionaires; or the American sensualist secure the patronage of all the Muses for his pornography.

Howbeit, Poe remains homeless. There is nothing at all like him in America; nothing, at all events, visible across the Atlantic. At that distance we can see Whistler plainly enough, and Mark Twain. But Whistler was very American in some ways: so American that nobody but another American could possibly have written his adventures and gloried in them without reserve. Mark Twain, resembling Dickens in his combination of public spirit and irresistible literary power with a congenital incapacity for lying and bragging, and a congenital hatred of waste and cruelty, remains American by the local color of his stories. There is a futher difference. Both Mark Twain and Whistler are as Philistine as Dickens and Thackeray. The appalling thing about Dickens, the greatest of the Victorians, is that in his novels there is nothing personal to live for except eating, drinking, and pretending to be happily married. For him the great synthetic ideals do not exist, any more than the great preludes

and toccatas of Bach, the symphonies of Beethoven, the paintings of
Giotto and Mantegna, Velasquez and Rembrandt. Instead of being
heir to all the ages, he came into a comparatively small and smutty
literary property bequeathed by Smollet and Fielding. His criticism
of Fechter's Hamlet, and his use of a speech of Macbeth's to illus-
trate the character of Mrs Macstinger, shew how little Shakespear
meant to him. Thackeray is even worse: the notions of painting he
picked up at Heatherley's school were further from the mark than
Dickens's ignorance; he is equally in the dark as to music; and
though he did not, when he wished to be enormously pleasant and
jolly, begin, like Dickens, to describe the gorgings and guzzlings
which make Christmas our annual national disgrace, that is rather
because he never does want to be enormously pleasant and jolly than
because he has any higher notions of personal enjoyment. The truth
is that neither Dickens nor Thackeray would be tolerable were it not
that life is an end in itself and a means to nothing but its own perfection; consequently any man who describes life vividly will entertain us, however uncultivated the life he describes may be. Mark
Twain has lived long enough to become a much better philosopher
than either Dickens or Thackeray: for instance, when he immortalized General Funston by scalping him, he did it scientifically, knowing exactly what he meant right down to the foundation in the
natural history of human character. Also, he got from the Mississippi
something that Dickens could not get from Chatham and Pentonville.
But he wrote A Yankee at the Court of King Arthur just as Dickens
wrote A Child's History of England. For the ideal of Catholic chivalry he had nothing but derision; and he exhibited it, not in conflict
with reality, as Cervantes did, but in conflict with the prejudices of a
Philistine compared to whom Sancho Panza is an Admirable Crich-
ton, an Abelard, even a Plato. Also, he described Lohengrin as "a
shivaree," though he liked the wedding chorus; and this shews that
Mark, like Dickens, was not properly educated; for Wagner would
have been just the man for him if he had been trained to understand
and use music as Mr Rockefeller was trained to understand and use
money. America did not teach him the language of the great ideals,
just as England did not teach it to Dickens and Thackeray. Conse-

quently, though nobody can suspect Dickens or Mark Twain of lacking the qualities and impulses that are the soul of such grotesque makeshift bodies as Church and State, Chivalry, Classicism, Art, Gentility, and the Holy Roman Empire; and nobody blames them for seeing that these bodies were mostly so decomposed as to have become intolerable nuisances, you have only to compare them with Carlyle and Ruskin, or with Euripides and Aristophanes, to see how, for want of a language of art and a body of philosophy, they were so much more interested in the fun and pathos of personal adventure than in the comedy and tragedy of human destiny.

Whistler was a Philistine, too. Outside the corner of art in which he was a virtuoso and a propagandist, he was a Man of Derision. Important as his propaganda was, and admired as his work was, no society could assimilate him. He could not even induce a British jury to award him substantial damages against a rich critic who had "done him out of his job"; and this is certainly the climax of social failure in England.

Edgar Allan Poe was not in the least a Philistine. He wrote always as if his native Boston was Athens, his Charlottesville University[1] Plato's Academy, and his cottage the crown of the heights of Fiesole. He was the greatest journalistic critic of his time, placing good European work at sight when the European critics were waiting for somebody to tell them what to say. His poetry is so exquisitely refined that posterity will refuse to believe that it belongs to the same civilization as the glory of Mrs Julia Ward Howe's lilies or the honest doggerel of Whittier. Tennyson, who was nothing if not a virtuoso, never produced a success that will bear reading after Poe's failures. Poe constantly and inevitably produced magic where his greatest contemporaries produced only beauty. Tennyson's popular pieces, The May Queen and The Charge of the Six Hundred, cannot stand hackneying: they become positively nauseous after a time. The Raven, The Bells, and Annabel Lee are as fascinating at the thousandth repetition as at the first.

Poe's supremacy in this respect has cost him his reputation. This is a phenomenon which occurs when an artist achieves such perfec-

1. The University of Virginia, in Charlottesville.

tion as to place himself *hors concours*. The greatest painter England ever produced is Hogarth, a miraculous draughtsman and an exquisite and poetic colorist. But he is never mentioned by critics. They talk copiously about Romney, the Gibson of his day; freely about Reynolds; nervously about the great Gainsborough; and not at all about Rowlandson and Hogarth, missing the inextinguishable grace of Rowlandson because they assume that all caricatures of his period are ugly, and avoiding Hogarth instinctively as critically unmanageable. In the same way, we have given up mentioning Poe: that is why the Americans forgot him when they posted up the names of their great in their Pantheon. Yet his is the first—almost the only name that the real connoisseur looks for.

But Poe, for all his virtuosity, is always a poet, and never a mere virtuoso. Poe put forward his Eureka, the formulation of his philosophy, as the most important thing he had done. His poems always have the universe as their background. So have the figures in his stories. Even in his tales of humor, which we shake our heads at as mistakes, they have this elemental quality. Toby Dammit himself, though his very name turns up the nose of the cultured critic, is more impressive and his end more tragic than the serious inventions of most story-tellers. The shortsighted gentleman who married his grandmother is no common butt of a common purveyor of the facetious: the grandmother has the elegance and free mind of Ninon de l'Enclos, the grandson the *tenue* of a marquis. This story was sent by Poe to Horne, whose Orion he had reviewed as poetry ought to be reviewed, with a request that it might be sold to an English magazine. The English magazine regretted that the deplorable immorality of the story made it for ever impossible in England!

In his stories of mystery and imagination Poe created a world-record for the English language: perhaps for all the languages. The story of the Lady Ligeia is not merely one of the wonders of literature: it is unparalleled and unapproached. There is really nothing to be said about it: we others simply take off our hats and let Mr Poe go first. It is interesting to compare Poe's stories with William Morris's. Both are not merely stories: they are complete works of art, like prayer carpets; and they are, in Poe's phrase, stories of imagination. They are masterpieces of style: what people call Macaulay's style is by comparison a mere method. But they are more different than it seems possible for two art works in the same kind to be. Morris will have nothing to do with mystery. "Ghost stories," he used to say, "have all the same explanation: the people are telling lies." His Sigurd has the beauty of mystery as it has every other sort of beauty, being, as it is, incomparably the greatest English epic; but his stories are in the open from end to end, whilst in Poe's stories the sun never shines.

Poe's limitation was his aloofness from the common people. Grotesques, negroes, madmen with delirium tremens, even gorillas, take the place of ordinary peasants and courtiers, citizens and soldiers, in his theatre. His houses are haunted houses, his woods enchanted woods; and he makes them so real that reality itself cannot sustain the comparison. His kingdom is not of this world.

Above all, Poe is great because he is independent of cheap attractions, independent of sex, of patriotism, of fighting, of sentimentality, snobbery, gluttony, and all the rest of the vulgar stock-in-trade of his profession. This is what gives him his superb distinction. One vulgarized thing, the pathos of dying children, he touched in Annabel Lee, and devulgarized it at once. He could not even amuse himself with detective stories without purifying the atmosphere of them until they became more edifying than most of Hymns, Ancient and Modern. His verse sometimes alarms and puzzles the reader by fainting with its own beauty; but the beauty is never the beauty of the flesh. You never say to him as you have to say uneasily to so many modern artists: "Yes, my friend, but these are things that men and women should *live* and not write about. Literature is not a keyhole for people with starved affections to peep through at the banquets of the body." It never became one in Poe's hands. Life cannot give you what he gives you except through fine art; and it was his instinctive observance of this distinction, and the fact that it did not beggar him, as it would beggar most writers, that makes him the most legitimate, the most classical, of modern writers.

It also explains why America does not care much for him, and why he has hardly been mentioned in England these many years.

EDGAR ALLAN POE   143

America and England are wallowing in the sensuality which their
immense increase of riches has placed within their reach. I do not
blame them: sensuality is a very necessary and healthy and educa-
tive element in life. Unfortunately, it is ill distributed; and our
reading masses are looking on at it and thinking about it and longing
for it, and having precarious little holiday treats of it, instead of
sharing it temperately and continuously, and ceasing to be preoccupied with it. When the distribution is better adjusted and the pre-
occupation ceases, there will be a noble reaction in favor of the
great writers like Poe, who begin just where the world, the flesh,
and the devil leave off.

Nation (London), January 16, 1909.

In Five Acts and in Blank Verse

Shavian observations on blank-verse playwriting, based upon a review of three mediocre contemporary examples.

This is the sort of thing we have all done. We hardly know what blank verse is; and of the nature of an "act" we are utterly ignorant; yet we do it to give expression to the Shakspere in us. Nobody reads it when it is done—not even the reviewer who makes merry over it: there is always enough in the first page he chances on to inspire as many gibes as we are worth. No matter: gibe as he may, he has done it himself. In his bureau, pushed to the back of the drawer, over-littered and dusty, is his Cromwell, or Raleigh, or Caractacus, or Timour, "an historical tragedy, in five acts and in blank verse." If it was not published, that proves only that the author was poor. Had he possessed the needful spare cash, some bookseller of the High-street, Oxford, would have been the richer and the British Museum catalogue the longer for him. The present writer was poor, and gave in before the third act was finished. What is he that he should sit in judgment on others? Yet there were some fine lines in it—finer than any he has since reviewed.

What is blank verse?

ESTHER: Place a light in my uncle's study.

Is that blank verse? The author of Wiclif says it is. But, "be it not said, thought, understood"; for no actor that ever mouthed could make blank verse of it. It should run—

ESTHER: A light place in mine uncle's study.

Or, better still, to save the ambiguity and lack of distinction—
Yare, yare, good Esther;

144

Pour thou the petrol oil: snip thou the wick:
Light up the study.

This at least cannot be mistaken for sane prose. Mr David Graham, the author of King James the First, an Historical, &c, understands the matter better than the author of Wiclif. He featly turns the phrase "Italian minuet" into blank verse, thus—

                    A minuet
Straight from the sunny land of Italy.

This is the true blank manner. Mr Graham's characters even laugh in blank verse:—

QUEEN: And the tenth General Council would break up
    With—No decision come to. Ha! ha!
ABBOTT: Ha! ha! ha!

Here the measured cachinnation preserves the stately march of tragedy. There is one dangerous line in King James the First; and that, significantly enough, adorns a scene in which the author soars into prose. The King, early in the third act, says:—

This is of interest: go on.

In actual performance that line might bring down the house, very much as it was brought down by Kemble's delivery of—

And when this solemn mockery is o'er—

in Ireland's Vortigern, which, by-the-by, was really not a bad historical tragedy as such works go. Vortigern was a well-intended blend of what most people like in Macbeth and Cibber's Richard III. Should any of our popular plagiarists need a benefit Mr Irving might find a worse play to revive for the occasion.

The Elizabethan lymph does not seem to have taken satisfactorily

with the author of Wiclif. The late R. H. Horne would have thought
him a poor creature. His metaphors lack immensity; and his language is too little magniloquent. A successor of Chapman and Marlowe cannot afford to play the gentle student, avoid hyperbole, and
treat history in the modern sociological spirit. Nor must he so delude
himself as to hope that moderate prose, cut into lengths, will pass
as even Byronic blank verse. The following is a sample of Wiclif:—

> Yet had I wished a little more of life,
> A little longer still to ply the oar,
> To carry still yet further [*still yet further is really too bad*] on
>   her way
> The ship we sail by. We shall sleep at last
> Beneath the bunkers when our work is done,
> And go unconsciously to our longed haven.

Now, in cold blood, was this worth doing? Is the thought beyond
the capacity of a well-educated poodle? Is the expression specially
apt, harmonious, forcible, suggestive, or in any way interesting? Is
the metaphor not fitted to Tom Tug rather than to Wiclif? Were
bunkers known years before steam navigation? and are dead shipmen
buried in them? Is the power to write such lines any excuse for the
error of thinking them worth writing? Above all, does the consciousness of having written an historical tragedy compensate one
for the publisher's bill, and the unpleasantness of being publicly
asked such questions as the foregoing?

Mr W. W. Aldred, in his "drama of an Ancient Democracy," has
lain low for his reviewers in a singular fashion. We have all heard
of the gentlemen who send rolls of blank paper to theatrical managers, and receive them again with neat notes to the effect that
"their play" has been read attentively, but is not suitable for presentation on the boards. Mr Aldred, having so poor an opinion of
human nature as to suspect that reviewers, lost to all professional
honour, criticise dramas in blank verse without having anxiously
scrutinized every line, has laid a trap. On page 176, in the middle
of the fifth act, the scene being ancient Rome, the time 82 B.C., and

the personages Sulla, Pompey, Caesar, Cato, &c., he has interpolated, without connection, warning, or explanation, a ballad, as follows:—

POMPEIUS: Ah, do not jest, Tullius. I am too anxious in mind
    to laugh with you.

Ballad.
The last shots are growing more distant,
   Hushed is the cannon's roar,
And he lies with his soldiers around him,
   All silent for evermore. &c., &c., &c.

In the flush of triumph at having escaped this ambush, one may magnanimously admit that there are gleams of nature, of wit, of observation, and even of verse, in The Love Affair. The style is free from mere verbiage and line padding; and it changes with freedom from the old and stately to the modern and familiar. For example—

Oh, now methinks the Fates look at the clock
And wait the hour which is to change the world—

is Marlovian. But the following smacks of our own time:—

CENTURION (to soldiers): Halt! Shoulder arms! Fall out!
SPY: You understand?
CENTURION: No; I'm damned if I do. But I will carry out the
orders. Fall in! Dress your ranks! Left wheel! Quick march!

Review of *King James the First: An Historical Tragedy*, by David Graham; *Wiclif: An Historical Drama* (Anon.); and *The Love Affair*, by W. W. Aldred, in *Pall Mall Gazette*, July 14, 1887.

Blank Versifiers

Observations on poetry and playwriting extracted from a Shavian play preface.

It may be asked why I wrote The Admirable Bashville in blank verse. My answer is that the operation of the copyright law of that time (now happily superseded) left me only a week to write it in. Blank verse is so childishly easy and expeditious (hence, by the way, Shakespear's copious output), that by adopting it I was enabled to do within the week what would have cost me a month in prose.[1]

Besides, I am fond of blank verse. Not nineteenth century blank verse, of course, nor indeed, with a very few exceptions, any post-Shakespearean blank verse. Nay, not Shakespearean blank verse itself later than the histories. I am quite sure that anyone who is to recover the charm of blank verse must go back frankly to its beginnings, and start a literary pre-Raphaelite Brotherhood. I like the melodious sing-song, the clear simple one-line and two-line sayings, and the occasional rhymed tags, like the half closes in an eighteenth century symphony, in Peele, Kyd, Greene, and the histories of Shakespear. Accordingly, I poetasted The Admirable Bashville in the primitive Elizabethan style. And lest the literary connoisseurs should declare tht there was not a single correct line in all my three acts, I stole or paraphrased a few from Marlowe and Shakespear (not to mention Henry Carey); so that if any man dared quote me derisively, he should do so in peril of inadvertently lighting on a purple patch from Hamlet or Faustus.

I also endeavored in this little play to prove that I was not the

1. What Shaw set out to do was race unauthorized stage adaptors of his 1882 novel *Cashel Byron's Profession* to a copyright performance which theoretically protected his English interests. In the United States, where his prize-fighting novel had already been pirated, the hero was played by such ring heroes as James J. Corbett.

heartless creature some of my critics took me for. I observed the established laws of stage popularity and probability. I simplified the character of the heroine, and summed up her sweetness in the one sacred word: Love. I gave consistency to the heroism of Cashel. I paid to Morality, in the final scene, the tribute of poetic justice. I restored to Patriotism its usual place on the stage, and gracefully acknowledged The Throne as the fountain of social honor. I paid particular attention to the construction of the play, which will be found equal in this respect to the best contemporary models.

And the result was that the British playgoer, to whom Elizabethan English is a dead language, only half understood nine-tenths of the play, and applauded the other tenth (the big speeches) with a seriousness that was far funnier than any burlesque.

The play, by the way, should be performed on an Elizabethan stage, with traverses for the indoor scenes, and with only one interval after the second act.

On reading over the above after a lapse of thirty years I am not quite so sure as I was that Elizabethan English may not again become a living language to the ordinary playgoer. To people who never read anything but newspapers and popular magazines, a good deal of Shakespear's more euphuistic blank verse is hardly more intelligible than classical Greek. Even actors may be heard repeating it by rote with an air that persuades the public that they understand what they are saying; but it cannot impose any such illusion on a professionally skilled listener.

Then there are the people who do not go to Protestant churches nor read anything at all, and consequently understand no English except modern vernacular English. This class is by no means a negligible one even in the theatre; for it includes a large body of intelligent manual and open air workers and sportsmen who, though after their day's exertions they fall asleep in less than a minute if they sit down with an open book in their hands, can be kept awake and alert very effectually in the theatre by a play. Only, it must be a play in the vernacular. Otherwise it does not exist for them except as an incomprehensible bore.

There was a time when not only the theatres but the newspapers

addressed themselves to the literate alone. Hunt up an old melodrama (say Sweeney Todd the Demon Barber of Fleet Street) or
an old newspaper file; and you will at once see that the writers of
the play and of the contemporary leading articles, though they may
have been the seediest of Bohemians, had learnt Latin grammar and
read books written by persons similarly schooled. They had literally
the benefit of clergy, and wrote accordingly. With the advent of
compulsory education sixty years ago, and the creation thereby of a
class which could read and write, but had no Latin and less Greek,
newspapers and plays alike soon came to be written by illiterate
masters of the vernacular; and I myself welcomed the change and
discarded my early very classical style for a vernacular one. Nowadays, when I read typewritten plays by young authors, as I sometimes have occasion to do, I find in them such illiteracies as He
exits, She exits, They exit etc. etc. Chapman, who wrote all his stage
directions in Latin, or Ben Jonson, who deplored the slenderness
of Shakespear's classical education, would have risen up and roared
for a birchrod to castigate such execrable solecisms. By the end of
the nineteenth century the press and the theatre had lost all their
Latinity; and this was why, whenever The Admirable Bashville was
performed, men of letters like Maurice Hewlett would chuckle de-
lightedly over it almost line by line, whilst the ordinary playgoers
would listen with a puzzled and troubled stare, wondering what on
earth it was all about and how they ought to take it, and the unfortunate persons who had been forced to "get up Shakespear" as part
of an academic course on English literature, sat with a scowl of
malignant hatred that poisoned the atmosphere. When Bashville
was followed by a piece in the vernacular the relief of the audience
was so great that there was always a burst of applause at the very
first sentence.

And yet, whenever the meaning of the words was clear, the lis-
teners shewed unmistakably that they liked hyperbolical rhetoric and
deliberately artificial language. My parodies of the Elizabethan man-
nerism, and funny echoes of pet lines from the Elizabethan playwrights were, as such, quite lost on them; but Ben Webster brought
down the house with Cashel Byron's declamatory repudiation of the

name of gentleman, and James Hearn's lamentation over the tragedy of Cetewayo[2] came off, not as a mockery, but as genuine tragedy, which indeed it also is. It was the literary fun that proved a mere puzzle, in spite of the acting of casts which included such accomplished comedians as Charles Quatermaine, William Wyes, Lennox Pawle, Henrietta Watson, Marie Lohr, and Fanny Brough.

Another significant fact pointed in the same direction. In no country is the worship of the old authorized version of the Bible carried to greater lengths than in the United States of America. To alter a single word of it was, it was believed, to incur the curse in the last chapter of Revelations. Even in England the very timid official revision of 1885 shocked our native Fundamentalists (a ridiculous but convenient name not then invented). Yet it was in the United States that the ministers of religion first found themselves compelled to produce versions in modern vernacular and journalese under stress of the flat fact that their flocks often could not understand the old authorized version, and always found the style so artificial that though it could produce an unintelligent reverence it brought no intimate conviction to the reader.

Sometimes, however, the simple and direct passages were not sentimental enough to satisfy people whose minds were steeped in modern literary sob stuff. For instance, such bald statements about Barabbas as that he was a robber, or that he had killed a certain man in a sedition, quite failed to interest anyone in him; but when Marie Corelli expanded this concise information into a novel in her own passionate and richly colored style it sold like hot cakes.

I must make a personal confession in this matter. Though I was saturated with the Bible and with Shakespear before I was ten years old, and the only grammar I ever learned was Latin grammar, so that Elizabethan English became a mother tongue to me, yet when I first read such vivid and unaffected modern versions as Dr James Moffatt's New Translation of the New Testament I at once got from them so many lights on the Bible narratives which I had missed

2. The Zulu king in the novel, who is brought to England after his capture. Shaw gives him his real name in the play, as he was taken from real life; but in the novel he is unnamed.

in the authorized version that I said to myself "Some day I will translate Hamlet into modern vernacular English." But indeed if the alienation of our young from Elizabethan English continues it will be necessary to produce revised versions not only of Shakespear but of Sir Walter Scott and even of my own early novels.

Still, a revival of Elizabethan literature may be possible. If I, as an Irish child in the eighteen-sixties, could without enforced study become so familiar with it that I had some difficulty as a journalist later on in getting rid of it, it must be possible for the same thing to occur to an English child in the nineteen-sixties. The Elizabethan style has many charms for imaginative children. It is bloody, bombastic, violent, senselessly pretentious, barbarous and childish in its humor, and full of music. In short, the taste for it, as anyone can observe at the Old Vic or the Stratford Festivals, is essentially half childish, half musical. To acquire it, all that is necessary is access to it. Now the opportunities for such access are enormously wider than they used to be. Of course as long as we persist in stuffing Shakespear and the Bible down our children's throats with threats of condign punishment if they fail to answer silly questions about them, they will continue to be loathed as they very largely are at present. But if our children, when they have been simply taught to read, have plenty of dramatically illustrated Bibles and Shakespears left in their way, with the illustrated passages printed under the pictures, it will soon be possible to find a general audience which can laugh at The Admirable Bashville as heartily as Maurice Hewlett did, and for repertory theatres to amuse themselves and their congregations with occasional performances of Carey's Chrononhotonthologos, Fielding's Tom Thumb, and even Bombastes Furioso.

I shall not here raise the question of whether such a revival is desirable. It would carry me too far and plunge me too deep for a volume of trifles and tomfooleries. But as the Elizabethan style is unquestionably both musical and powerful, I may at least say that it is better to have a sense of it and a fancy for it than to have no sense of style or literary fancy at all.

Preface to *The Admirable Bashville* (London, 1909); afterwards revised.

IV.   MEMOIRISTS

Super-Tramp

Shaw was not the discoverer of the offbeat Edwardian poet W. H. Davies, but his appreciative prefatory critique to Davies's autobiography was instrumental in enlarging the poet's reputation.

I hasten to protest at the outset that I have no personal knowledge of the incorrigible Super-tramp who wrote this amazing book.[1] If he is to be encouraged and approved, then British morality is a mockery, British respectability an imposture, and British industry a vice. Perhaps they are: I have always kept an open mind on the subject; but still one may ask some better ground for pitching them out of window than the caprice of a tramp.

I hope these expressions will not excite unreasonable expectations of a thrilling realistic romance, or a scandalous chronicle, to follow. Mr Davies' autobiography is not a bit sensational: it might be the Post Office Directory for the matter of that. A less simple minded super-tramp would not have thought it worth writing at all; for it mentions nothing that might not have happened to any of us. As to scandal, I, though a most respectable author, have never written half so proper a book. These prudent pages are unstained with the

1. Davies wrote in his own preface:

> This Autobiography was written on the advice of a number of friends who claimed that my life of adventure would have an interest for the public, distinct from any merit I might have as a poet. Taking their advice, I began the book at once, and, as the incidents were fresh in my memory, the work was ready for a publisher in a couple of months.
>
> When the book was done it was suggested that a Preface by a well-known man would bring it into notice. A couple of friends, Edward Thomas and Edward Garnett, who had a good opinion of my poetry up till then, suggested the name of G. Bernard Shaw. Mr. Shaw, in spite of his busy life, came forward with fine sympathy and kindness, and with his Preface the immediate popularity of the book was assured.

frightful language, the debased dialect, of the fictitious proletarians of Mr Rudyard Kipling and other genteel writers. In them the patrons of the casual ward and the doss-house argue with the decorum of Socrates, and narrate in the style of Tacitus. They have that pleasant combination of childish freshness with scrupulous literary conscientiousness only possible to people for whom speech, spoken or written, but especially written, is still a feat to be admired and shewn off for its own sake. Not for the life of me could I capture that boyish charm and combine it with the *savoir vivre* of an experienced man of the world, much less of an experienced tramp. The innocence of the author's manner and the perfection of his delicacy is such, that you might read his book aloud in an almshouse without shocking the squeamishness of old age. As for the young, nothing shocks the young. The immorality of the matter is stupendous; but it is purely an industrial immorality. As to the sort of immorality that is most dreaded by school-mistresses and duennas, there is not a word in the book to suggest that tramps know even what it means. On the contrary, I can quite believe that the author would die of shame if he were asked to write such books as Adam Bede or David Copperfield.

The manuscript came into my hands under the following circumstances. In the year 1905 I received by post a volume of poems by one William H. Davies, whose address was The Farm House, Kennington, S.E. I was surprised to learn that there was still a farmhouse left in Kennington; for I did not then suspect that the Farmhouse, like the Shepherdess Walks and Nightingale Lanes and Whetstone Parks of Bethnal Green and Holborn, is so called nowadays in irony, and is, in fact, a doss-house, or hostelry where single men can have a night's lodging for, at most, sixpence.

I was not surprised at getting the poems. I get a gift of minor poetry once a week or so; and yet, hardened as I am to it, I still, knowing how much these little books mean to their authors, can seldom throw them aside without a twinge of compunction which I allay by a glance at one of the pages in the faint but inextinguishable hope of finding something valuable there. Sometimes a letter accompanies the book; and then I get a rapid impression, from the

handwriting and notepaper as well as from the finding and type in
the book, or even from the reputation of the publisher, of the class
and type of the author. Thus I guess Cambridge or Oxford or Maida
Vale or West Kensington or Exeter or the lakes or the east coast;
or a Newdigate prizeman, a romantic Jew, a maiden lady, a shy
country parson or whom not, what not, where not. When Mr Davies'
book came to hand my imagination failed me. I could not place him.
There were no author's compliments, no publisher's compliments,
indeed no publisher in the ordinary channel of the trade in minor
poetry. The author, as far as I could guess, had walked into a
printer's or stationer's shop; handed in his manuscript; and ordered
his book as he might have ordered a pair of boots. It was marked
"price half a crown." An accompanying letter asked me very civilly if
I required a half crown book of verses; and if so, would I please send
the author the half-crown: if not, would I return the book. This was
attractively simple and sensible. Further, the handwriting was remarkably delicate and individual: the sort of handwriting one might
expect from Shelley or George Meredith. I opened the book, and
was more puzzled than ever; for before I had read three lines I perceived that the author was a real poet. His work was not in the
least strenuous or modern: there was in it no sign that he had ever
read anything later than Cowper or Crabbe, not even Byron, Shelley
or Keats, much less Morris, Swinburne, Tennyson, or Henley and
Kipling. There was indeed no sign of his ever having read anything
otherwise than as a child reads. The result was a freedom from
literary vulgarity which was like a draught of clear water in a
desert. Here, I saw, was a genuine innocent, writing odds and ends
of verse about odds and ends of things, living quite out of the world
in which such things are usually done, and knowing no better (or
rather no worse) than to get his book made by the appropriate
craftsman and hawk it round like any other ware.

Evidently, then, a poor man. It horrified me to think of a poor
man spending his savings in printing something that nobody buys:
poetry, to wit. I thought of Browning threatening to leave the country when the Surveyor of Taxes fantastically assessed him for an
imaginary income derived from his poems. I thought of Morris, who,

even after The Earthly Paradise, estimated his income as a poet at a hundred a year. I saw that this man might well be simple enough to suppose that he could go into the verse business and make a living at it as one who makes a living by auctioneering or shopkeeping. So instead of throwing the book away as I have thrown so many, I wrote him a letter telling him that he could not live by poetry. Also, I bought some spare copies, and told him to send them to such critics and verse fanciers as he knew of, wondering whether they would recognise a poet when they met one.

And they actually did. I presently saw in a London newspaper an enthusiastic notice of the poems, and an account of an interview with the author, from which I learnt that he was a tramp; that "the farm house" was a doss-house; and that he was cut off from ordinary industrial pursuits by two circumstances: first, that he had mislaid one of his feet somewhere on his trampings, and now had to make shift as best he could with the other; second, that he was a man of independent means—a *rentier*—in short, a gentleman.

The exact amount of his independent income was ten shillings a week. Finding this too much for his needs, he devoted twenty percent of it to pensioning necessitous friends in his native place; saved a further percentage to print verses with; and lived modestly on the remainder. My purchase of eight copies of the book enabled him, I gathered, to discard all economy for about three months. It also moved him to offer me the privilege (for such I quite sincerely deem it) of reading his autobiography in manuscript. The following pages will enable the world at large to read it in print.

All I have to say by way of recommendation of the book is that I have read it through from beginning to end, and would have read more of it had there been any more to read. It is a placid narrative, unexciting in matter and unvarnished in manner, of the commonplaces of a tramp's life. It is of a very curious quality. Were not the author an approved poet of remarkable sensibility and delicacy I should put down the extraordinary quietness of his narrative to a monstrous callousness. Even as it is, I ask myself with some indignation whether a man should lose a limb with no more to-do than a lobster loses a claw or a lizard his tail, as if he could grow a new one at his next halting place! If such a thing happened to me, I should begin the chapter describing it with "I now come to the event which altered the whole course of my life, and blighted etc. etc." In Mr Davies' pages the thing happens as unexpectedly as it did in real life, and with an effect on the reader as appalling as if he were an actual spectator. Fortunately it only happened once: half a dozen such shocks would make any book unbearable by a sensitive soul.

I do not know whether I should describe our super-tramp as a lucky man or an unlucky one. In making him a poet, Fortune gave him her supremest gift; but such high gifts are hardly personal assets: they are often terrible destinies and crushing burdens. Also, he chanced upon an independent income: enough to give him reasonable courage, and not enough to bring him under the hoof of suburban convention, lure him into a premature marriage, or deliver him into the hands of the doctors. Still, not quite enough to keep his teeth in proper repair and his feet dry in all weathers.

Some flat bad luck he has had. I suppose every imaginative boy is a criminal, stealing and destroying for the sake of being great in the sense in which greatness is presented to him in the romance of history. But very few get caught. Mr Davies unfortunately was seized by the police; haled before the magistrate; and made to expiate by stripes the bygone crimes of myself and some millions of other respectable citizens. That was hard luck, certainly. It gives me a feeling of moral superiority to him; for I never fell into the hands of the police—at least they did not go on with the case (one of incendiarism), because the gentleman whose property I burnt had a strong sense of humour and a kindly nature, and let me off when I made him a precocious speech—the first I ever delivered— on the thoughtlessness of youth. It is remarkable what a difference it makes, this matter of the police; though it is obviously quite beside the ethical question. Mr Davies tells us, with his inimitable quiet modesty, that he begged, stole, and drank. Now I have begged and stolen; and if I never drank, that was only an application of the principle of division of labour to the Shaw clan; for several members of it drank enough for ten. But I have always managed to keep out of the casual ward and the police courts; and this gives me an inef-

fable sense of superior respectability when I read the deplorable
confessions of Mr Davies, who is a true poet in his disregard for
appearances, and is quite at home in tramp wards.

Another effect of this book on me is to make me realise what a
slave of convention I have been all my life. When I think of the
way I worked tamely for my living during all those years when Mr
Davies, a free knight of the highway, lived like a pet bird on titbits,
I feel that I have been duped out of my natural liberty. Why had I
not the luck, at the outset of my career, to meet that tramp who
came to Mr Davies, like Evangelist to Christian, on the first day of
his American pilgrim's progress, and saved him on the very brink
of looking for a job, by bidding him to take no thought for the
morrow; to ask and it should be given to him; to knock and it should
be opened to him; and to free himself from the middle-class assumption that only through taking a ticket can one take a train. Let every
youth into whose hands this book falls ponder its lesson well, and,
when next his parents and guardians attempt to drive him into
some inhuman imprisonment and drudgery under the pretext that
he should earn his own living, think of the hospitable countrysides
of America, with their farm-houses overflowing with milk and honey
for the tramp, and their offers of adoption for every day labourer
with a dash of poetry in him.

And then, how much did I know about hotels until I read this
book! I have often wondered how the poor travel; for it is plain
that the Ritzes and Metropoles, and even the hotels noted by
Baedeker as "unpretending," are not for them. Where does the man
with sixpence in his pocket stay? Mr Davies knows. Read and learn.

It is to be noted that Mr Davies is no propagandist of the illusions

---

2. *Lavengro* (1851) was a romantic, mannered, picaresque yet scholarly
fictional autobiography by George Borrow (1803–1881) about his travels
among gypsies, tinkers, and other itinerants of the English roads. *Lavengro*
is the Gypsy for philologist. Theodore Watts-Dunton (1832–1914), a solicitor
turned literary critic, and a friend of George Borrow, wrote often about
gypsies, who figure prominently in his best-known novel, *Aylwin* (1898).

of the middle-class tramp fancier. You never suspect him of having read Lavengro, or got his notions of nomads from Mr Theodore Watts Dunton.[2] He does not tell you that there is honour among tramps: on the contrary, he makes it clear that only by being too destitute to be worth robbing and murdering can a tramp insure himself against being robbed and murdered by his comrade of the road. The tramp is fastidious and accomplished, audacious and self-possessed; but he is free from divine exploitation: he has no orbit: he has the endless trouble of doing what he likes with himself, and the endless discountenance of being passed by as useless by the Life Force that finds superselfish work for other men. That, I suppose, is why Mr Davies tramps no more, but writes verses and saves money to print them out of eight shillings a week. And this, too, at a moment when the loss of a limb has placed within his reach such success in begging as he had never before dared to dream of!

Mr Davies is now a poet of established reputation. He no longer prints his verses and hawks them: he is regularly published and reviewed. Whether he finds the change a lucrative one I venture to doubt. That the verses in The Soul's Destroyer and in his New Poems will live is beyond question; but whether Mr Davies can live if anything happens to his eight shillings a week (unless he takes to the road again) is another matter. That is perhaps why he has advised himself to write and print his autobiography, and try his luck with it as Man of Letters in a more general sense. Though it is only in verse that he writes exquisitely, yet this book, which is printed as it was written, without any academic corrections from the point of view of the Perfect Commercial Letter Writer, is worth reading by literary experts for its style alone. And since his manner is so quiet, it has been thought well by his friends and his publishers to send a trumpeter before him the more effectually to call attention to him before he begins. I have volunteered for that job for the sake of his poems. Having now done it after my well-known manner, I retire and leave the stage to him.

Preface to *Autobiography of a Super-tramp*, by W. H. Davies (London, 1907).

The Latest from Colonel Lawrence

T. E. Lawrence's Seven Pillars of Wisdom *was edited and cut about 13 percent (with G.B.S.'s help) from a 330,000-word original for the sumptuous Subscription Edition of 1926. In order to help pay the costs of the private edition (about 127 copies), Lawrence (1888-1935) the next year published a trade edition pruned to 130,000 words. It was this version,* Revolt in the Desert, *which Shaw was reviewing.*

This abridgement of the famous Seven Pillars (itself an abridgement) contains as much of the immense original as anyone but an Imam has time to read. It is very handsomely and readably printed, and has not a dull or empty sentence from end to end. It contains sixteen reproductions of the illustrations to the Seven Pillars, including a portrait of Feisal, the superb drawing of Mr D. G. Hogarth, and a magical one of the author by Mr Augustus John; a remarkable Chino-Johnion group by Mr Cosmo Clark; three portraits by Mr W. Roberts, which are triumphs of the draughtsmanship that sprang from Cubism; and seven of the portraits of Arab chiefs which Mr Eric Kennington went into the desert to make so consummately and humorously skilful in their combination of the popular style of the pavement artist (to disarm the chiefs) with his own very original and independent modernity: the Perfect Futurist turned Perfect Screever. The book does not, like the original, leave you with a sense of having spent many toilsome and fateful years in the desert struggling with Nature in her most unearthly moods, tormented by insomnia of the conscience: indeed it is positively breezy; but that will not be a drawback to people who, having no turn for "salutary self-torture," prefer a book that can be read in a week to one that makes a considerable inroad on a lifetime.

Among the uncommon objects of the worldside, the most uncommon include persons who have reached the human limit of literary genius, and young men who have packed into the forepart of their lives an adventure of epic bulk and intensity. The odds against the occurrence of either must be much more than a million to one. But what figure can estimate the rarity of the person who combines the two? Yet the combination occurs in this amazing age of ours in which we sit holding our breaths as we await wholesale destruction at one another's hands. In Mr Apsley Cherry-Garrard's Worst Journey in the World we have a classic on Antarctic exploration written by a young man who endured it at its blackest. And within ten years of that we have "Colonel Lawrence" (the inverted commas are his own) appearing first in the war news from Arabia as a personage rather more incredible than Prester John, and presently emerging into clear definition as the author of one of the great histories of the world, recording his own conquests at an age at which young company officers are hardly allowed to speak at the mess table.

The fate of the man who has shot his bolt before he is thirty, and has no more worlds to conquer, may be compared curiously with that of the genius who dies unwept, unhonored, and unsung, and is dug up and immortalized a century later. Nobody will ever be able to decide which is the more enviable. But it is mitigated if the hero has literary faculty as a second string to his bow; and Colonel Lawrence has this with a vengeance. He can re-create any scene, any person, any action by simple description, with a vividness that leaves us in more complete possession of it than could "the sensible and true avouch of our own eyes." He packs his narrative with detail that would escape nine hundred and ninety-nine out of a thousand observers; so that when he has made you see the start of Feisal's motley legions as plainly as he saw it himself, he has also left you with an exact knowledge of how an Arab mounts a camel and arranges his outlandish clothes for riding, and how he manages to carry a slave with him (when he has one) as a westerner might carry a portmanteau. As to the landscape painting, no padding novelist gravelled for lack of matter ever approached Col. Lawrence's feats in this art. And the descriptions are not interpolated: they are so woven into the texture of the narrative, that the sense of the track underfoot, the mountains ahead and around, the vicissitudes of the weather, the night, the dawn, the sunset and the meridian, never leaves you for a moment.

You feel, too, the characters of the men about you: you hear the inflections of their voices, the changes in their expression, all without an instant of reader's drudgery. There is a magical brilliance about it; so that you see it at once with the conviction of reality and with the enchantment of an opera. Auda after his roaring camel charge, with his horse killed, his field glasses shattered, and six bullet holes through his clothes, unhurt and ascribing his escape (under Allah) to an eighteen-penny Glasgow Koran which he had bought as a talisman for a hundred and twenty pounds, is at once a squalidly realistic Arab chieftain and a splendid leading baritone. The description has the quality of orchestration. Lawrence's own famous camel charge, which was checked by his having the camel shot under him, and ended, after a whole Arab tribe had thundered over him, in the irresistible anti-climax of the discovery that he had shot the camel himself, makes a page that reduces Tennyson's Charge of the Light Brigade to minor poetry.

These blazing climaxes of adventure stand out from an inferno of tormented bodies and uneasy souls in which one is glad to meet a rascal for the sake of laughing at him. The subjective side which gives Miltonic gloom and grandeur to certain chapters of The Seven Pillars, and of the seventy and seven pillars out of which they were hewn, plays no great part in this abridgement: Lawrence's troublesome conscience and agonizing soul give place to his impish humor and his scandalous audacities; but it will interest the latest French school of drama to know that their effect remains, and imparts an otherwise unattainable quality to the work, even though they are not expressed.

The political side of the revolt, important and extraordinary as it is, need not be dwelt on here: it is now public property; and the value of the national service rendered by its author is patent to everybody, except, apparently, those whose function it is to give official recognition to such services. It is characteristic of the author and hero of this book that he has provided most effectively against the possibility of his ever making a farthing by it; and it is equally

characteristic of the powers that be, to assume that he is amply
provided for by it. He is left in his usual ultra-scrupulous attitude;
but the nation can hardly claim to have left itself in a generous one.[1]
For it is England's way to learn young men not to know better than
their elders. Nothing could have been more irregular than the
methods by which Lawrence disabled Turkey in the Great War by
hurling an Arab revolt on her rear; and to encourage and reward
irregularity would be to set a bad example to the young.

Review of *Revolt in the Desert*, by T. E. Lawrence, in *Spectator* (London),
March 12, 1927; and in *Evening Post Literary Review* (New York), April
16, 1927.

1. Lawrence's contract with his London publisher, Jonathan Cape, provided that sales of the abridgment, *Revolt in the Desert*, would be halted
once the author had earned sufficient royalties to pay off the indebtedness
incurred in the expensive private printing of *Seven Pillars*. (Overages which
were unavoidable would go to the R.A.F. Benevolent Fund.) Shaw's accusations of national ungenerosity referred to T. E.'s former situation as a private
in the Tank Corps. T. E., who wanted neither his old colonelcy nor any
government pension (the latter Shaw's own idea), wanted only to serve in
the ranks in the R.A.F., which the government at first resisted and which
T. E. achieved with Shaw's help by publication time.

Ace Morality: A Document

A review of a World War I flying memoir, Cecil Lewis's Sagittarius Rising *(1936).*

This is a book which everybody should read. It is the autobiography of an ace, and of no common ace, either. We are all much concerned just now with the danger of being bombed, gassed, and burnt alive, women, children and all, with our water and electricity cut off when we have become helplessly dependent on them. Well, the hand that can release these judgments on us is the hand of the ace. And the ace may be a lad of 17. Indeed, it is not clear that such an age limit is necessary. The late Sir Horace Plunkett learnt to fly when he was over 80, having been recommended to take mountain air for sleeplessness. I believe I could have taken a plane into the air and released a bomb when I was 15.

Under such circumstances the moral training of our lads might be expected to rouse some concern or at least some curiosity. Apparently it is not even thought worth mentioning. When Prime Ministers and Secretaries of State for War in their great rearmament speeches proposed the enlistment and training of several thousand youths to rain destruction on the capital cities of the world, it never occurred to them to give any particulars as to the course of Diabolonian education which is to fit them for a delight and pride in this new and very startling department of human activity. How are we to test and select for the requisite high spirits, sense of mischievous humour, and moral irresponsibility which must go to make a boy ready to convert a city of God (more or less) into a City of Destruction?

Mr Lewis solved that problem for himself without any misgivings. At the age of 16 he found himself so "air minded' that he transferred himself from his famous public school to the Flying Corps in the spring of 1915 without consulting anyone. Now, if the public

167

school had been Eton, Harrow, Winchester, Rugby or the like, Mr Lewis would have been a ready-made Diabolonian. But it was not: it was Oundle: Oundle under Sanderson the Great, who cordially agreed with me as he showed me round the scene of his triumphs that Eton and all the rest of them should be razed to the ground and their foundations sown with salt. Thus Mr Lewis had a quite special Sandersonian-Wellsian pacifist schooling. His father was and is a distinguished sky pilot, not a bomber, but one who has never left the ground, nor rained anything but sermons on his fellow-creatures. The boy was not the usual young public-school Caliban whom nothing can tame or humanise: he had all the noble tastes and qualities, love of nature, love of beauty, love of poetry, soaring imagination, and physical gifts that eventually carried him to a height of six feet four inches, with a brilliant endowment of good looks. In short, one of the best, perhaps the very best, of all the recruits of 1915. He could have won his Military Cross and his promotions on his appearance alone.

As a matter of fact, he won them by committing all the atrocities of air warfare with an enjoyment that lasted until his demobilisation with unbroken nerve and unscathed limbs at the end of the war. He had a charmed life in every sense of the word. And throughout it all he never disliked a German except for twenty minutes on a black night when the Gothas were bombarding London, and somebody he loved was on the ground beneath. That brought on a fit of Berserker fury in which he deserted his defensive post and plunged vengefully into the thick of our own anti-aircraft barrage in search of a Gotha to bring down. But the Gothas eluded him in the darkness; and the fit passed very quickly.

And now comes the test question. How did the exceptional humanity of this prince of pilots react to the demand for atrocities made upon him by his duties? As it happened he was never a bomber. He won his cross on observation patrol, which needs daring, intelligence, reckless exposure to Archies, but has not slaughter for its direct object. In the second phase of his service, which was offensive patrol, he was a duellist, guiltless of the blood of women, children, and civilians. It was, as he puts it, Hector and Achilles, a battle of champions, fought in flying chariots with machine guns instead of Homeric spears. So far, nothing unpardonably Diabolonian.

Unfortunately, there was one incident which spoils the chivalrous picture. It reminds me of something that happened to myself one evening many years before the war. One cheerless evening, walking through Battersea Park, I came upon a vast ruin that had old associations for me. It was one of those enormous glass structures that came into vogue in the middle of last century with Paxton's Crystal Palace, originally the Hyde Park Exhibition. These monsters were as movable as bird cages. One of them appeared during my boyhood in Dublin as an exhibition building on the site now occupied by the Catholic University. It was taken away to England, where it was re-named The Albert Palace; and, after what wanderings I know not, got finally stranded and abandoned in Battersea Park, where it confronted me in the dusk like a ghost from my nonage. There was something spectral and tragic about it; for all Battersea's boys had thrown all Battersea's stones (there were stones in the streets in those macadamised days) at its million panes, leaving nothing unshattered save its monstrous and miserable skeleton. You can imagine with what bitter reflections on the wanton destructiveness of my species I passed on.

Suddenly an unbroken pane of glass caught my eye. It was irresistible. I believe I should have been shying stones at that pane to this day if the appearance of a park-keeper and the dignity of my professional position had not forced me to pass along harmlessly with every fibre of my being crying out against leaving that pane unshattered.

To return to Mr Lewis. He was in the sky on a bloodless observation patrol contemplating a desolated terrain over which the tides of war had swept in and out. I had a glimpse of it myself in 1917, when, sightseeing round the Front, I found places where villages had been with nothing left of them but a prostrate signpost with a name on it, or a wheelwright's emplacement showing through the snow. Mr Lewis's reflections were no less sombre, his generalisations no less tragic than mine in Battersea Park. The pilot in him sublimated into the poet and philosopher, as so often happened to him in the empyrean.

Suddenly he noticed a solitary house that had not been demolished. His observer saw it, too. And the same strange call of nature gripped them both. They had no bombs: bombing was not their business, nor was their machine equipped for carrying or launching any such projectile. No matter: they returned to their station, wangled a bomb, shipped it at great risk of being blown to pieces by it, and returned to hover over the dwelling that war at its worst had spared. Lewis brought all his mental powers into play to ensure a direct hit. He calculated his height, his distance, his speed and that of the wind with a conscientiousness which made success mathematically certain; and at his word the observer managed to heave the bomb overboard, again at considerable risk of its resenting such improper manhandling by a premature explosion.

The story lacks its tragic consummation. The house stands to this day presumably; and the pit dug in the earth by the bomb a mile or two away has long since been filled up. But the page from the real psychology of war remains. Mr Lewis, like all sane men, loathes war. Nobody could sing more fervently than he: "How beautiful are the feet of them that bring the gospel of peace!" But he had a shot at that house all the same. Had the war lasted another month he would have bombed Berlin. So should I, I suppose, had I been in his place. Mr Lewis has a good deal to say about it, and says it very well; for he is a thinker, a master of words, and a bit of a poet. But there are the facts at first hand. The funniest passage in the book deals with the disappearance from the dinner table of two of his messmates who were smashed by one of our own shells. The passage is: "The battery rang up to apologise." Why must we laugh? Because, I suppose, if we took war seriously we should all go mad.

Some people like war. There is to all of us a side that likes it. We should provide for the gratification of that liking as a sport, even if we have to suppress its political exploitation. It could be done every year on Salisbury Plain. And as there is no fun in poison gas, and mechanised warfare has reduced courage to absurdity, we might reconsider Fielding's remark that battles might be fought just as well with fists as with musketry.

Mr Lewis was clearly not deficient in natural tenderness. He was apparently always in love with some lady; and it cannot be doubted that many ladies were always in love with him. Touching these matters with an admirable delicacy, he never tells us that it was not always the same lady; but as his heart was broken again and again by tragic partings seen dimly through his vein of poetry, one may suspect him of inconstancy, but not accuse him of indiscretion or insensibility.

New Statesman and Nation, August 1, 1936.

V. SOCIOLOGY AND SEX

Nineteenth-Century Writers

If you read Sociology, not for information but for entertainment (small blame to you!), you will find that the nineteenth-century poets and prophets who denounced the wickedness of our Capitalism exactly as the Hebrew prophets denounced the Capitalism of their time, are much more exciting to read than the economists and writers on political science who worked out the economic theory and political requirements of Socialism. Carlyle's Past and Present and Shooting Niagara, Ruskin's Ethics of the Dust and Fors Clavigera, William Morris's News from Nowhere (the best of all the Utopias), Dickens's Hard Times and Little Dorrit, are notable examples: Ruskin in particular leaving all the professed Socialists, even Karl Marx, miles behind in force of invective. Lenin's criticisms of modern society seem like the platitudes of a rural dean in comparison. Lenin wisely reserved his most blighting invectives for his own mistakes.

But I doubt whether nineteenth-century writers can be as entertaining to you as they are to me, who spent the first forty-four years of my life in that benighted period. If you would appreciate the enormous change from nineteenth-century self-satisfaction to twentieth-century self-criticism you can read The Pickwick Papers (jolly early Dickens) and then read Our Mutual Friend (disillusioned mature Dickens), after which you can try Dickens's successor H. G. Wells, who, never having had any illusions about the nineteenth century, is utterly impatient of its blunderings, and full of the possibilities of social reconstruction. When you have studied nineteenth-century country gentility in the novels of Anthony Trollope and Thackeray for the sake of understanding your more behindhand friends, you must study it up-to-date in the novels of John Galsworthy. To realise how ignorant even so great an observer as Dickens could be of English life outside London and the main coaching routes you can compare his attempt to describe the Potteries in Hard

Times with Arnold Bennett's native pictures of the Five Towns; but to appreciate his much more serious and complete ignorance of working-class history and organization in his own day you would have to turn from fiction to the Webbs' History of Trade Unionism.

The earlier nineteenth-century literature, for all its invective, satire, derision and caricature, made amiable by its generous indignation, was not a literature of revolt. It was pre-Marxian. Post-Marxian literature, even in its most goodhumored pages by men who never read Marx, is revolutionary: it does not contemplate the survival of the present order, which Thackeray, for instance, in his bitterest moods seems never to have doubted.

For women the division is made by Marx's Norwegian contemporary Ibsen rather than by Marx. Ibsen's women are all in revolt against Capitalist morality; and the clever ladies who have since filled our bookshelves with more or less autobiographical descriptions of female frustration and slavery are all post-Ibsen. The modern literature of male frustration, much less copious, is post-Strindberg. In neither branch are there any happy endings. They have the Capitalist horror without the Socialist hope.

The post-Marxian, post-Ibsen psychology gave way in 1914–18 to the postwar psychology. It is very curious; but it is too young, and I too old, for more than this bare mention of its existence and its literature.

Appendix to *The Intelligent Woman's Guide to Socialism and Capitalism* (London, 1928).

The Critics of The White Prophet

Hall Caine's novel The White Prophet *(1909) proved imme-diately controversial because of its apparent basis in contemporary events and people. Shaw's attitude of truculent support for the Caine point of view led him to write a preface to the second edi-tion of the novel.*

The fact that The White Prophet is a romance by an honest man is a guarantee of its political importance, because romances are the only documents that are now free to tell the truth and sure to be read.

In the Egyptian question, as in all questions of our Imperial foreign policy, nothing is genuine except the romance. The official reports are seldom sincere: they can be depended on only when the writers, infatuated by their class and color prejudices, their national conceit (which they call patriotism), their official self-importance, and their invincible ignorance of human nature, blurt out and even boast of deeds and views which men of normal outlook and un-blunted social conscience would be ashamed to commit or avow.

For example, the officials of the Occupation in Egypt, from Lord Cromer downwards, thought the Denshawai affair rather a fine thing.[1] Under this impression they themselves supplied the evidence that it was the most sensationally revolting villainy that has dis-graced English rule in our time. It was not founded on the popular theory that East and West are congenitally unlike, and that the

1. Evelyn Baring, first earl of Cromer (1841–1917), was British proconsul in Egypt. The affair of June, 1906, began when English officers, pigeon-shooting in the small village of Denshawai, were set upon by a mob outraged by their activities. Military punishment was unduly severe, and included hangings, floggings, and life imprisonment for selected villagers. Lord Cromer certified that the proceedings were "just and necessary," and Shaw never forgave him the brutality, protesting it in his preface to *John Bull's Other Island* and elsewhere.

177

methods that succeed with one will not succeed with the other. On the contrary, the argument was that as the Easterners are born murderers, torturers, perjurers, tyrants, and corrupters of justice, and understand nothing else, we must shew them that we are their masters in all these departments of despotic government, and can out-murder them, out-torture them, out-lie them, out-tyrannize them, out-corrupt them, and, generally, go one worse than they on all points of political conduct. When some of us pointed to the fact that the records of the Egyptian courts shewed a white-gloved absence of crime greatly to the credit of the Egyptians, and that this had been cited as a proof of our success in civilizing Egypt, we were told that the regular courts were a put-up bluff, and that the real work of "civilization" had been done by native lynching raids ("Brigandage Commissions"), in which the raiders tortured the Egyptians until they accused one another of whatever crimes were alleged to have been committed, then tortured the accused until they confessed, and finally dealt with the people thus convicted with such ferocity as the methods employed might have led the victims to expect. These facts were planked down by Lord Cromer the moment the alleged freedom of Egypt from crime was turned against him in argument instead of being held up as the glory of his administration.

But for the most part, the hard facts never reach us. What we get instead is the romance of the thing. The British boy reads with delight the stories of Kelly the Bushranger and Peace the Burglar. He thinks they were very fine fellows; and the more crimes they commit—especially fighting crimes—the more he admires them. The British adult reads stories of "prancing pro-Consuls," and the more hanging and flogging and bullying there is in the stories the prouder he feels of being an Englishman.

Then there is the romance of danger and terror. If an Egyptian were conceived as an agricultural laborer, a milkman, a shoemaker, a grocer, or anything ordinary or honest or real, England could no more be persuaded to care about him or read about him than if he were carrying on the same unexciting pursuits in New Cross as a native of Peckham. But conceive him as a human rattlesnake, a deadly and dangerous enemy of England, a fanatic eager to wade into paradise knee-deep in British blood, a member of a huge anti-Christian conspiracy known as Islam! Then the Briton who flogs and murders him, with or without a sham trial, is transfigured as a man of dauntless nerve and iron will, saving Western civilization from destruction, instead of the silly, mischievous, and panic-stricken grown-up schoolboy he actually is. What deluded us into the Denshawai abomination was puerile penny-number romance. Sir Edward Grey, who could have stopped it, is not at all a cruel or unamiable person—quite the contrary; but he belongs to a class in which the men and women never get out of leading-strings from their cradles to their graves; and he has a full share of the pleasant boyishness in fair weather and the petulant obstinacy in foul weather which such unremitted tutelage inevitably produces in the human subject. He was credulous enough to believe that there was a frightful conspiracy of Islam against Christendom just ready to explode in a universal St Bartholomew massacre, and—more jejune still—that the splendid and masterful counterstroke needed to decapitate the hydra at one blow was to seize on the inhabitants of a village in which some British officers had been mobbed for persisting in getting up shooting expeditions to kill the villagers' farm stock (on the ground that pigeons were made to be shot by British sportsmen), and, in the presence of their families and under the windows of their houses, hang them, flog them, and send the survivors to prison for life or for long-terms of penal servitude. Now if Sir Edward Grey were a Nero, if Lord Cromer were a fiend, this horrible business might at least have gratified them and the overfed people who have that specific lust for cruelty which pays an unacknowledged but influential part in modern science and politics. But that they should have been simply Tom Sawyer and Huckleberry Finn, wrecking an Empire to gratify their taste for the sort of romance that is sold in penny volumes by Limehouse stationers, is really enough to make one clamor for a statutory disqualification of the English country gentleman from any share whatever in affairs of State.

A Bedouin would not look at Denshawai in this way. He would see the finger of God in it. Oriental rulers, being subtler psychologists than English country gentlemen, have always known that the way to impress ignorant and thoughtless people with the greatness of a conqueror, a dynasty, or a religious movement, is to connect it with some horrifying sacrifice of human life. Thus a tribal king buries twenty people alive under the pillars of his hut-palace, and a conquering invader builds himself a monument of cut-off heads. Our pro-Consuls pick up the idea in the East rather too readily. Egyptian Nationalism needed just such a consecration of horror to drive it deep into the imaginations of the Egyptian people. Lord Cromer and Sir Edward Grey made Egypt a present of one which they intended for England's use. They forgot that when you get above the Hottentot or Kalmuck level the impression made is not on the side of the tyrants, but of the victims. The blood of the martyrs is the seed of the Church. The conscientious atrocities of "Bloody Mary" drove Protestantism into the very bones of the English people for three hundred years. The Crucifixion has been to Christianity what it was intended to be to Pharisaism and Roman Imperialism. Denshawai was the Crucifixion of Egyptian Nationalism. Henceforth, when an Egyptian wavers in his determination to recover Egypt for the Egyptians and drive out the Occupation bag and baggage, the word Denshawai will screw him up to the Nationalists mark like a magic spell.

The apology for Denshawai was as boyishly lighthearted as the crime itself. In the presence of their families we had hanged four men and given eight fifty lashes (the doctor forbidding one flogging of an epileptic). We sent two men to penal servitude for life because one of them struck a British officer who had just shot his wife (unintentionally, but the man did not know that). We sent one man to penal servitude for fifteen years, six men for seven years, and three to a year's hard labor in addition to their floggings. Until the blue books appeared, public opinion here was kept quiet by the usual expedient of inducing panic-stricken British gentlemen to preserve the Empire from destruction by lying like horse copers. But when the murder was out (literally), and Mr Wilfrid Scawen Blunt's protests were substantiated by the official reports, we all behaved charmingly, being good fellows at heart. "Dear me! Was it all a mistake?" we said. And with a delightful sense of behaving handsomely we released all the prisoners without a stain on their characters. And

no doubt if the hanged men could have been unhanged and the
flogged men unflogged, their cases would have received the kindest
consideration. As to Sir Edward Grey, his position was rather
improved than otherwise by an event which, in the opinion of the
Egyptians, should have made him for ever impossible as Foreign
Minister in any civilized country.

As to Lord Cromer, had he not restored the finances of Egypt?
We fell back on that whenever our consciences gave us a prick. It
is not clear how he could have helped himself. It is absolutely certain
that a wooden idol could have done the same. What was the history
of that part of the business? Whilst masses of English men, women
and children, were rotting in our slums and dying prematurely like
flies for want of English capital to be invested in the rebuilding and
sanitation of English cities, English capitalists were sending their
capital in millions out of the country to pay for the profligacies of
Ismail; and Ismail was extorting the interest from the starving
Egyptians by the kourbash. When he had ruined them so that he
could extort no more we took the land of Egypt in execution for the
debt, and sent Ismail about his business. As Egypt is a fertile land
with an industrious population, and as, after Ismail went and Baring
(now Lord Cromer) came, the sun shone and the Nile flowed and
the people worked without being robbed, matters righted themselves easily enough. But Lord Cromer's friends assured us that he
was the Sun, and the Nile, and the labor of the Egyptians; and we
patriotically and idiotically rejoiced in the superiority of the Englishman to Pharaoh. No doubt an intelligent biographer could shew
that Lord Cromer did not get his reputation for nothing, and that
there was some solid ability behind his unlucky panics and blunders;
but to say that he saved Egypt from ruin in any other sense than
that in which every policeman saves the lives of the people in
the street he patrols, is justifiable only at public dinners, where it is
polite to talk nonsense.

Sooner or later the grosser follies and falsehoods get exposed.
As we have seen, the fools and liars convict themselves boastfully out
of their own mouths because they conceive their folly as wisdom and
patriotism, believe their own lies, and know that their intentions are
good. But who is it that detects the exposure, and drives its lesson

home to the public? Usually the man of letters. Across the Channel, when the officers and gentlemen who represented the old nobility and the old religion of France had with the most patriotic and pious intentions perjured and forged their way through the Dreyfus affair, it was a novelist, Zola, who smashed their conspiracy up and brought the nation to its senses. In Egypt it was a poet, Mr Wilfrid Scawen Blunt, who released the survivors of Denshawai, and reduced the apologists who had certified it was "just and necessary" to giving equally credulous and well-meant, and equally mistaken certificates to the vivisectors of dogs and rabbits in England. And it is again a man of letters, Hall Caine,[2] who has gone deeper and put his finger on the real reason why our pro-Consuls get stuffed with these silly romances of a murderous conspiracy of Islam against Christendom.

That reason is that the situation of Pontius Pilate and Caiaphas is constantly and inevitably reproduced whenever we seize a foreign territory as Rome seized Judaea. Pontius Pilate becomes the catspaw of Caiaphas exactly as Dublin Castle is the catspaw of the Roman Catholic hierarchy in Ireland, or as, in Hall Caine's romance, the Consul-General becomes the catspaw of the Grand Cadi. When an original religious genius arises—Jesus, Mahomet, Savonarola, St Francis, or St Clare—his first attack is on the Temple, and whilst the people make him the leader of their eternal revolt against priestly tyranny and corruption, the priests accuse him of political conspiracy, and incite the military authorities to put him down with fire and sword. Thus they make Pontius Pilate crucify Jesus; Mahomet escapes them by the skin of his teeth, and seeing that he must smash or be smashed, comes back in arms and conquers both priest and soldier; Savonarola is burnt by the cardinals; St Francis dies young, before it becomes expedient to burn him; and St Clare, who survives him fights the Pope to the last because she wants her Clares to be Poor Clares, and he wants them to be women of property. This situation, with its explanation of the cry of Smash the Mahdi, and of the cock-and-bull story of the conspiracy of Islam which the Egyptian Caiaphases planted on Lord

2. Hall Caine (1853–1931) had written a number of popular novels before *The White Prophet*, notably *The Bondman* (1891), *The Manxman* (1894), *The Eternal City* (1901), and *The Prodigal Son* (1904).

Cromer and Sir Edward Grey, is the one which Hall Caine has presented in the form of a romance. In no other form would our credulous, pleasure-loving, intellectually lazy governing classes read it. Since romance is to carry the day, Hall Caine has used it on the right side, and beaten Caiaphas at his own game.

Hall Caine has also seen what none of our officials and Foreign Office Ministers have ever dreamt of—I mean the coming reconciliation between the best Christian and the best Mahometans. The greatest thing that the Empire has done is to knock out of us all the insular and insolent bigotry that used to assume that our share of inspiration and revelation was the whole, and that other people's prophets were impostors and other people's creeds damnable errors. Whilst Arab children were taught to respect Jesus in the name of Mahomet, English children were taught to despise and slander Mahomet in the name of Jesus. This is a heavy score to the credit of Mahomet. But the same fate finally overtook both prophets: the cults established on their teachings ended by claming their authority for most of the errors they strove against. Christianity has already undergone one Reformation, and is very badly in want of another. Mahometanism is in the same predicament. Now as the essential religious ideas by which both sects (they are only sects, big as they are) will be reformed are the same, the opportunity for a reconciliation is a golden one, and Hall Caine, in seeing and understanding it, has risen to the height of his profession. I myself tried for years to induce some publisher to reissue Rodwell's translation of the Koran, as I had found Sale's translation unreadable; and at last, thanks to Mr Ernest Rhys, the editor of Everyman's Library, we have a cheap and dainty edition of it which every traveller in the East ought to carry with him, if only to convince himself that the average Arab knows even less about it than the average Englishman knows about the Bible. True, he will find there the false doctrine of a material hell which Mahomet was driven to invent for the intimidation of those who could not be weaned from crude idolatry by his intellectual and spiritual appeal; but it does not lie with us to reproach him with that trick: we have used it too freely ourselves. For the rest, his doctrine rises far above the baser forms of Christianity; and it has, from the point of view of the sceptical educated Englishman of the Darwinian period (that is, of the governing class of to-day), the advantage that whereas many such Englishmen do not believe that Jesus ever existed, and, of those who do, many despise him because he was not "fit" to survive in the struggle for life, Mahomet's existence is as unquestionable as Henry the Eighth's, and his success was as solid as Mr Carnegie's. Also, when his followers persisted in trying to degrade him from the rank of prophet to that of a vulgar wizard (exactly as in the case of Jesus), he honestly and impatiently told them again and again that he was only a man, and could not perform miracles. Thus he appeals to men who are by temperament anti-Christian, just as he appealed to Napoleon, who said at St Helena that he thought Mahometanism was on the whole the most useful of the religions.

Now as to the definite charges made against Hall Caine for The White Prophet. I leave out of the question the hackneyed literary attack. Hall Caine sells a thousand copies where most other men of letters either sell a hundred or cannot escape from journalism into books at all. We console ourselves by taking advantage of the fact that his style is different from ours to declare publicly that he has no style at all. And when he does a stroke of important public work like The White Prophet, we disloyally join the official hue and cry against him, for which we ought to be shot as traitors to our profession. However, that matters to nobody but our petty selves. The public charges against Hall Caine are the important ones.

First, he is charged with using Lord Cromer as a model for one of his characters. Well, why should he not? He had to present a type of which Lord Cromer has been held up as the ideal representative. He has given his figure a private history that completely detaches it from Lord Cromer as a private man. And he has taken Lord Cromer's public traits at the highest valuation of Lord Cromer's most devoted flatterers. He has certainly not said an unfavorable word for which he has not Lord Cromer's own warrant in published official documents. It is true that the figure he draws is a character in a romance; but are the innumerable newspaper articles that told the tale of the conspiracy of Islam, and the strong, stern Englishmen who stamped it out by hanging and flogging helpless, unarmed, unorganized peasants, any the less romances, and very vile and silly romances too? If we refuse to read blue books, and insist on having romances, let us at least have them written by a master hand, with some knowledge and conscience behind it.

The next charge is that Hall Caine's picture of the British Occupation is not in accord with the facts. This is true. Hall Caine has neither the cynicism nor the specific talent for extravagant farce to paint the official Occupation as it really is. When I did it—when I told the story of how the officials demanded the suppression of the Egyptian newspapers and "a considerable increase in the army of occupation" because three thieves knocked a soldier off a donkey —everybody laughed, but nobody believed me. I quoted the official letters and gave the official references in vain: the facts were too absurd, too grotesquely comic, to be credible. There are truths too ridiculous to be thinkable except as jokes, just as there are truths too shameful to be mentioned by decent writers. Hall Caine has throughout represented Occupation officialism as public-spirited, high-minded, and earnestly patriotic even when misled and mistaken. There is no evidence that it deserves any such compliment. On its own shewing it is mostly snobbish, uppish, huffish, narrow, ignorant, conceited, and subject to paroxysms of panic in which it is capable of falsehood, cruelty, and injustice. But it is protected from exposure by the idolatry of officialism which has lately taken possession of England. Only the other day Mr Walkley, an upper division civil servant[3] and one of the most brilliant critical essayists in the country, told the Select Committee on stage plays, in effect, that he had no faith in the power of Decency, Honor, Virtue, the grace of God, or the common law to keep the English theatre from debauchery, but that all that these forces could not do could be done infallibly, omnisciently, and omnipotently—in short, divinely —by an official. And the Speaker of the House of Commons endorsed his opinion. Both gentlemen naïvely added that the theatre had become so corrupt under official despotism that they could not take their daughters to see officially licensed plays without careful inquiry beforehand as to their decency. What is to be done in

3. A. B. Walkley was not only dramatic critic of the *Times*, but held a senior position in the Post Office Department.

the face of such idolatrous infatuation? Had Hall Caine not generously attributed to the Occupation officials a large supply of his own conscience and public spirit, nobody would have believed him to be sane.

The next charge—a well-worn one—is that The White Prophet has inflamed sedition and provoked riot and insurrection. The curt reply that it hasnt is too trite to be interesting; besides, it is a mere fact, and facts are not popular in this country. Why does the official world always make this charge? For exactly the same reason that the lion-tamers at the music-halls always put up strong railings and carry terrible whips and iron bars when they enter the den and stand dauntlessly in the midst of twenty lions. If they revealed the fact that the lions have been carefully fed to such an extent that the offer of a nice, plump baby would simply nauseate them—if they reminded the audience that African travellers testify that it takes several days starvation to induce a lion to attack a man— people would not pay to see the performance. But it is more romantic to believe that the performer is facing a frightful danger with iron nerve. Even when the lady (it is more effective when a lady does it) has openly to slash a lion across the eyes with a whip before it can be persuaded even to growl at her, the audience still loves to think that she is taking her life in her hand. Now this is a very favorite official performance in Egypt, except that as our officials go through it with sheep instead of lions, more sensational steps have to be taken to persuade the public that the Egyptian sheep is the most savage of maneaters. It is lucky for the officials that the English are not logical; for the first half of the official story is that the Egyptians are such abject slaves and cowards that England had to rescue them from the most horrible oppression by Ismail, and could make soldiers of them only by giving them English officers; and the second half is that they are so desperately ferocious, bloody-minded and implacable, that at a word of encouragement from an English novelist they will rise and sweep the Occupation into the Nile after ravishing all the white women and massacring all the white men. But nobody sees the incoherence. As the first half shews the Englishman as magnificently superior, and the second as dauntlessly brave, he does not notice that they flatly contradict one another.

The truth is that if Hall Caine could really make tyranny dangerous he would be the greatest living benefactor of the human race. Men, whether white or red, yellow or black, are not too insurrectionary, but too docile, too sheepish, too cowardly, to keep the world decent. That is why their condition is so miserable and their history so dishonorable. If we could depend on a sanguinary revolution in England once a month until the crooked be made straight and the rough places plain, we should presently be a happy and prosperous nation. The real objection to The White Prophet is that it may make the Egyptians too patient and confiding, by persuading them that all Englishmen are as sympathetic and as high-minded as Hall Caine.

Finally, there is the objection that Hall Caine's hero, an Arab, has a "creeping" resemblance to Jesus, though why such a resemblance should give any Christian the creeps is not stated. Worse still, he has, in doing so, suggested that Jesus was a reality instead of a picture by Holman Hunt. Mr Gilbert Chesterton has just said very truly and forcibly that the one thing you must not assume in England is that God is something real, "like a tiger." If we have a god at all, we keep him as we keep a watchdog: he may bite everybody else—indeed that is what he is for—but he must not bite us. Hall Caine's prophet does not wag his tail at the door of the British Consulate and bark and bite at the door of the mosque. He is a humane and honorable preacher, who appears superhuman in England only because he is neither a snob or a sensualist. But suppose he *were* a reincarnation of Jesus! Does any Christian who has the faintest notion of what his religion means doubt that the spirit of Jesus is kept alive among us by continual reincarnation, and cannot be kept alive in any other way? What are we coming to when even professional writers are ignorant of this commonplace? The illiteracy which would forbid a man of letters to write an Imitation of Christ might be forgiven to the Irish peasant who is afraid to mention the fairies, and tremblingly alludes to them as "themselves" when the terrifying subject is forced on him; but that London journalists should have sunk to such an abyss of tribal ignorance is enough to make us ask, with a gasp, how long it will be before the civilized nations of Europe and Asia will come and conquer us for our own good as Caesar conquered us in the comparatively enlightened age of Boadicea.

Fortunately Hall Caine represents English feeling far more than the press or the governing class. He is comparatively a free man and can speak out. The press is not free. Its notion of foreign policy is to hold up as masterpieces of diplomacy such contemptible documents as the Anglo-Russian agreement, in which the speculators of England and Russia, conspiring to tempt capital out of their own countries into Persia, have made a "Keep off the Grass" compact for dividing the spoils, and have entrapped our Foreign Office into committing England to its enforcement. As far as I can ascertain, I am the only man in these Islands—not, I hope, excepting Sir Edward Grey himself—who has read this much puffed agreement, consequently I am the only man who blushes when it is mentioned. It is a characteristic product of the British foreign policy that made a deadly enemy of Russia by undertaking to make war on any Power that helped her against Japan, and then assured us that if we were not abjectly polite to the Tzar the tender friendship it had cemented between us and Russia would be shaken to the foundations. When our governing class loses the power of remembering yesterday and foreseeing to-morrow, and spends to-day in talking manifest folly, it is time for the man of letters to take the instruction of public opinion out of its hands. And it is extremely reassuring to find that there is at least one man of letters who is not shirking that duty. In bravely and disinterestedly shouldering it Hall Caine deserves well of his countrymen, and though it is perhaps too much to hope that they will have the political sagacity to appreciate his public spirit as a citizen, they may have imagination enough to come under his spell as a romancer, as they have done so often before when his books concerned them far less vitally than The White Prophet.

Preface to *The White Prophet*, by Hall Caine, 2d ed. (London, 1909).

Ruskin's Politics

Shaw's interest in Ruskin lay not in his style, but in his stance on economics and social welfare, on his attitudes toward the relationships of people to government. In emphasizing Ruskin as social critic he deliberately downplayed Ruskin as literary and art critic.

There have been very few men, I think, in whom our manifold nature has been more marked than in Ruskin. If you go round this exhibition, you will find several portraits exhibited as portraits of Ruskin, but it is surprising what a number of other people they are portraits of. Somewhere behind me on that wall there is a bronze dish, and on that bronze a portrait of Ruskin in profile. That is one of the most remarkable portraits in the exhibition, because whatever its merits may be as a portrait of Ruskin—and probably some of you will have said on seeing it, "That is not very like the Ruskin we are familiar with"—it is not at all a bad portrait of Mozart. Almost all the genuine portraits of Mozart are profiles. No doubt some of you have been taken in by the usual music-shop portrait of a handsome young nobleman who was a contemporary of Mozart. But in the genuine Mozart portraits there is a peculiar salience about the profile; you will see in them that Mozart's upper lip came out with a certain vivacity in it peculiar to the man, which spoils his beauty as compared with the portrait of the nobleman, but nevertheless gives you the great musician, who at the end of his life subordinated his music to his social enthusiasms and wrote his last opera nominally on the subject of freemasonry, but really on that social upheaval which was then preparing the French Revolution and has been developing ever since. Now look over there to my left, and you will see a portrait of Ruskin by Herkomer.[1] But it is more like John Stuart Mill. If you look at some

1. Sir Hubert von Herkomer (1849–1914) was a Royal Academician and after 1885 Slade Professor at Oxford.

of the photographs that were taken in the Lake country, when Ruskin was an elderly man, those of you who enjoyed the acquaintance of Grant Allen will be struck by the fact that they are very good portraits of Grant Allen: you feel that if Grant had lived a little longer, he would have been exactly like that.

Thus the portraits give you by their resemblances the evolution of the artist into the prophet. He begins as a painter, a lover of music, a poet and rhetorician, and presently becomes an economist and sociologist, finally developing sociology and economics into a religion, as all economics and sociology that are worth anything do finally develop. You follow him from Mozart to Mill, picking up on the way the man of science, Grant Allen, also a little in the sociological line, but very much interested in science and material things, and material forms and shapes, just as Ruskin is in Modern Painters. Finally, you have the portraits made by Mr Severn[2] of Ruskin in his latest time, when Ruskin was hardly a human being at all, when almost the nearest resemblance that occurs to you is his resemblance to God as depicted in Blake's Book of Job. You get, in short, to an almost divine condition.

I daresay you have already had lectures on all the phases of Ruskin represented in those portraits; and now it has come to my turn to deal with Ruskin as a politician. I think Ruskin was more misunderstood as a politician than in any other department of his activity. People complained that he was unintelligible. I do not think he was unintelligible. If you read his political utterances, the one thing that you cannot say of them is that they were unintelligible. You would imagine that no human being could ever have been under the slightest delusion as to what Ruskin meant and was driving at. But what really puzzled his readers—and incidentally saved his life, because he certainly would have been hanged if they had grasped what he was driving at, and believed that he believed it—was that he was incredible. You see, he appealed to the educated, cultivated, and discontented. It is true that he addressed himself to the working classes generally; and you can find among the work-

2. Arthur Severn, not the earlier Joseph Severn. Both were portrait painters.

ing classes, just as Mr Charles Rowley has found in the Ancoats quarter of Manchester, a certain proportion of workingmen who have intellectual tastes and artistic interests. But in all classes his disciples were the few who were at war with commercial civilization. I have met in my lifetime some extremely revolutionary characters; and quite a large number of them, when I have asked, "Who put you on to this revolutionary line? Was it Karl Marx?" have answered, "No, it was Ruskin." Generally the Ruskinite is the most thoroughgoing of the opponents of our existing state of society.

Now, the reason why the educated and cultured classes in this country found Ruskin incredible was that they could not bring themselves to believe that he meant what he was saying, and indeed shouting. He was even shouting in such terms that if I were to describe it merely as abusive I should underdo the description. Think of the way in which his readers were brought up! They were educated at our public schools and universities; they moved in a society which fitted in with those public schools and universities; they had been brought up from their earliest childhood as, above everything, respectable people; taught that what respectable people did was the right and proper thing to do, was good form and also high culture; that such people were the salt of the earth; that everything that existed in the way of artistic culture depended on their cultured and leisured existence. When you have people saturated from their childhood with views of that kind, and they are suddenly confronted with a violently contrary view, they are unable to take it in. For instance, to put it quite simply, they knew that there were the Ten Commandments, and that the Ten Commandments were all right; and they argued from this that as respectable people were all right in everything they did they must be living according to the Ten Commandments. Therefore, their consciences were entirely untroubled.

I have here a volume of Ruskin which I took up this morning, intending to read it, but had not time. I opened it at random, and happened on a page on which Ruskin gave the Ten Commandments according to which in his conception our polite and cultured society really lives. This is the only passage I shall read today, though I feel, of course, the temptation that every lecturer on Ruskin feels to get out of his job by reading, because anything he reads is likely to be better than anything he can say of his own. Ruskin says:

> Generally the ten commandments are now: Thou shalt have any other god but me. Thou shalt worship every bestial imagination on earth and under it. Thou shalt take the name of the Lord in vain to mock the poor; for the Lord will hold him guiltless who rebukes and gives not; thou shalt remember the sabbath day to keep it profane; thou shalt dishonor thy father and thy mother; thou shalt kill, and kill by the million, with all thy might and mind and wealth spent in machinery for multifold killing; thou shalt look on every woman to lust after her; thou shalt steal, and steal from morning till evening; the evil from the good, and the rich from the poor; thou shalt live by continual lying in millionfold sheets of lies; and covet thy neighbor's house, and country, and wealth and fame, and everything that is his. An finally, by word of the Devil, in short summary, through Adam Smith, a new commandment give I unto you: that ye hate oneanother.

If anybody is going to tell me, here or elsewhere, that this is unintelligible, I do not know what to think of that person's brains. Nothing could well be clearer. But, as I have said, and repeat, it was profoundly incredible to those to whom it was addressed.

Ruskin's political message to the cultured society of his day, the class to which he himself belonged, began and ended in this simple judgment: "Your are a parcel of thieves." That is what it came to. He never went away from that, and he enforced it with a very extraordinary power of invective. Ruskin was a master of invective. Compare him, for instance, with Cobbett. Cobbett had immense literary style, and when he hated a thing, he hated it very thoroughly indeed. Think of Cobbett's writing about the funding system—think of his writing about the spoliation of the Church by Henry VIII— think of his writing about the barrenness of Surrey, which cultured society likes so much and which Cobbett loathed as a barren place— think of what he said about "barbarous, bestial Malthus"—think of

Cobbett at the height of his vituperation. Then go on to Karl Marx. Karl Marx was a Jew who had, like Jeremiah, a great power of invective. Think of the suppression of the Paris Commune of 1871, and then of that terrific screed that Marx wrote, exposing the Empire, denouncing the Versaillese generals, execrating the whole order of things which destroyed the Commune so remorselessly. There you have a masterpiece of invective, a thing which, although it was not reproduced in any of the newspapers, or popular literary issues of the day, nevertheless did leave such an effect that when, thirty years after, a proposal was made in the French Chamber to put Galliffet[3] into a public position of some credit, the governing classes having forgotten that a word had ever been said against him, suddenly that terrible denunciation of Marx rose up against him and struck him absolutely out of public life. Yet when you read these invectives of Marx and Cobbett, and read Ruskin's invectives afterwards, somehow or other you feel that Ruskin beats them hollow. Perhaps the reason was that they hated their enemy so thoroughly. Ruskin does it without hatred, and therefore he does it with a magnificent thoroughness. You may say that his strength in invective is as the strength of ten because his heart is pure. And the only consequence of his denunciation of society was that people said, "Well, he cant possibly be talking about us, the respectable people"; and so they did not take any notice of it.

I must now go on to Ruskin's specific contribution to economics and sociology, because that, as you know, today means a contribution to politics. In Ruskin's own time this was not so clear. People did not understand then that your base in politics must be an economic base and a sociological base. We all know it today, and know it to our cost; and will know it to our still greater cost unless we find a way out, which, it seems, lies not very far from Ruskin's way. Ruskin took up the treatises of our classic political economy, the books by which our Manchester Capitalism sought to justify its existence. In this he did what Karl Marx had done before; and, like Marx, he did it in a way which I do not like exactly to describe as a corrupt way,

3. Gaston Alexandre Auguste Galliffet (1830–1909), once on the personal staff of Emperor Napoleon III, became a reformer and briefly was Republican war minister (1899–1900) in the cabinet of Waldeck-Rousseau.

because you cannot think of corruption in connection with Ruskin: nevertheless, he did not take it up as a man with a disinterested academic enthusiasm for abstract political economy. I think we must admit that, like Marx, he took it up because he was clever enough to see that it was a very good stick to beat the Capitalist dog with.

Marx took up the theory of value which had been begun by Adam Smith, and developed by Malthus, and, seeing that he could turn it against Capitalism, tried to re-establish it on a basis of his own. Thus we got his celebrated theory of value, which is now a celebrated blunder. What Ruskin did was this. He held up to us the definition of value given by the economists, and said: "These gentlemen define value as value in exchange. Therefore," he said,

> a thing that you cannot exchange has no value: a thing that you can exchange has value. Very well. When on my way to Venice I go through Paris, I can buy there for two francs fifty an obscene lithograph, produced by the French to sell to English tourists. When I reach Venice, I go to the Scuola di San Rocco and look at the ceiling painted there by Tintoretto, because it is one of the treasures of the world. But that ceiling cannot be sold in the market. It has no exchange value. Therefore, according to John Stuart Mill, the obscene lithograph has a higher value than the ceiling, which in fact has no value at all. After that, I have no further use for your political economy. If that is the way you begin, I hesitate to go on to the end; for I know where your journey must land you—in hell. You may be under the impression that after all hell is a thing you can think of later on; but you are mistaken: you are already at your destination; the condition in which you are living is virtually hell.

Then he gave his version of your Ten Commandments. If you had said to him, "We may be in hell; but we feel extremely comfortable," Ruskin, being a genuinely religious man, would have replied, "That simply shews that you are damned to the uttermost depths of damnation, because not only are you in hell, but you like being in hell."

Ruskin got no further than that in political economy. It was really a pregnant contribution, but he did not go on. Having knocked the spurious law of value into a cocked hat, he did not go on to discover a scientific law of value; and he took no interest in and never reached that other very revolutionary law, the law of economic rent. I see no sign in his writings that he ever discovered it.

When Karl Marx (let me make this contrast) demonstrated that, in his phrase, the workingman was being exploited by the Capitalist —and Karl Marx took a great deal of trouble to establish what he called the rate of surplus value: that is to say, the rate at which the Capitalist was robbing the workingman—he made a pretense of doing the thing mathematically. He was not a mathematician, but he had a weakness for posing as a mathematician and using algebraic symbols. He tried to determine the quantitative aspect of exploitation. That sort of thing did not interest Ruskin. Ruskin said to the Capitalist, "You are either a thief or an honest man. I have discovered that you are a thief. It does not matter to me whether you are a fifty percent thief or a seventy percent thief. That may be interesting to men of business who are interested in figures. I am not. Sufficient to me that you are a thief. Having found out that you are a thief, I can now tell you what your taste in art will be. And as I do not like a thievish taste in art I suggest you should become an honest man." And I daresay the Capitalists who read it said: "Aha! that serves Jones right!" I doubt if they ever applied it to themselves.

Though Ruskin was certainly not a completely equipped economist, I put him, nevertheless, with Jevons as one of the great economists, because he knocked the first great hole in classic economics by shewing that its value basis was an inhuman and unreal basis, and could not without ruin to civilization be accepted as a basis for society at all. Then Jevons came along and exploded the classic value theory from the abstract scientific side. Marx also never grasped the law of rent, never understood one bit of it any more than Ruskin did. Nevertheless, Marx did establish Marxism, a thing of which you hear a good deal, and which is therefore worth defining. Marxism does not mean this or that particular theory: it does mean that the economic question is fundamental in politics and sociology. No doubt some of Marx's disciples—after the way of disciples—have pushed that view a little hard.

You know that some of the curators of the Natural History Museum at South Kensington are eminent naturalists and paleontologists. In my youth—I do not know whether they do it still—their favorite swank was to say, "If you will bring us the smallest bone of any extinct monster, from that small bone we can reconstruct the whole monster." I remember in my youth being impressed by that—not so much by the wonderful thing they said they could do, as by their cleverness in discovering how safe it was to say they could do it: for when they had reconstructed the monster, who could come along and prove that it was not a bit like the original? Nobody could produce a live monster from his back garden and compare the two.

In the same way Marx said, in effect, "If you will bring me the tool or machine with which a man worked, I will deduce from it with infallible certainty his politics, his religion, his philosophy, and his view of history and morals." That, of course, like the South Kensington offer, was a great swank. Nevertheless, it epitomizes an important truth, and makes you feel the dramatic power with which Marx brought into economics and politics his view of the fundamental importance of economics. Our own historian, Buckle,[4] had taken very much the same line; but I think I can give you a simpler illustration of the importance of the economic basis, and why it was that Ruskin, beginning as an artist with an interest in art—exactly as I did myself, by the way—was inevitably driven back to economics, and to the conviction that your art would never come right whilst your economics were wrong.

The illustration I will give you is this. Here am I addressing you, a cultivated audience. I wish to keep before you the most elevated view of all the questions Ruskin dealt with. I am straining all my mental faculties and drawing on all my knowledge. Now suppose you were to chain me to this table and invite me to go on and on. What would happen? Well, after some hours a change would take place in the relative importance of the things presenting themselves to my mind. At first, I should be thinking of Ruskin, and attending

4. George Earle Buckle (1854–1935), historian and *Times* editor, edited Queen Victoria's *Letters* and completed W. F. Monypenny's massive biography of Disraeli.

to my business here as a lecturer on Ruskin. But at last my attention
would shift from the audience in front of me to that corner of the
room behind me, because that is where the refreshment room is.
I should, in fact, be thinking of nothing but my next meal. I should
finally reach a point at which, though I am a vegetarian, I should
be looking at the chubbiest person in the audience, and wishing I
could eat that chubby person.

That is the real soundness of Marxism and of Ruskin's change of
ground from art to economics. You may aim at making a man cultured and religious, but you must feed him first; and you must feed
him to the point at which he is reasonably happy, because if you
feed him only to the point at which you can make a bare drudge of
him and not make him happy, then in his need for a certain degree
of happiness he will go and buy artificial happiness at the public-
house and other places. Workingmen do that at the present day:
indeed we all do it to a certain extent, because all our lives are
made more or less unhappy by our economic slavery, whether we are
slaves or masters. Economics are fundamental in politics: you must
begin with the feeding of the individual. Unless you build on that,
all your superstructure will be rotten.

There you have the condition postulated by Marx and every
sensible man. That is why Ruskin, when he was twenty, gave you
Modern Painters, and at thirty, The Stones of Venice, also about
art, but very largely about the happiness of workingmen who made
the art; for the beauty of Venice is a reflection of the happiness of
the men who made Venice. When he was forty he wrote Unto this
Last, and there took you very far away from art and very close to
politics. At fifty he gave us the Inaugural Lectures, and, finally,
Fors Clavigera, in which you find his most tremendous invectives
against modern society.

Now, since Ruskin's contemporaries neglected him politically
because they found the plain meaning of his words incredible, I put
the question whether in the course of time there has developed any
living political activity on behalf of which you might enlist Ruskin
if he were living at the present time. It goes without saying, of course,
that he was a Communist.[5] He was quite clear as to that. But now

5. Shaw often used the term *Communist* as synonymous with *Socialist*,

comes the question, What was his attitude towards Democracy? Well, it was another example of the law that no really great man is ever a democrat in the vulgar sense, by which I mean that sense in which Democracy is identified with our modern electoral system and our system of voting. Ruskin never gave one moment's quarter to all that. He set no store by it whatever, any more than his famous contemporary, Charles Dickens—in his own particular department the most gifted English writer since Shakespear, and resembling Ruskin in being dominated by a social conscience. Dickens was supposed to be an extremely popular person, always on the side of the people against the ruling class, whereas Ruskin might, as a comparatively rich university man, have been expected to be on the other side. Yet Dickens gives no more quarter to Democracy than Ruskin. He begins by unmasking mere superficial abuses like the Court of Chancery and imprisonment for debt, imagining them to be fundamental abuses. Then, suddenly discovering that it is the whole framework of society that is wrong, he writes Hard Times, and after that becomes a prophet as well as a storyteller. You must not imagine that prophets are a dead race, who died with Habakkuk and Joel. The prophets are always with us. We have some of them in this room at the present time.[6] But Dickens the prophet is never Dickens the Democrat. Take any book of his in which he plays his peculiar trick of putting before you some shameful social abuse, and then asking what is to be done about it! Does he in any single instance say: "You workingmen who have the majority of votes: what are you going to do about it?" He never does. He always appeals to the aristocracy. He says: "Your Majesty, my lords and gentlemen, right honorables and wrong honorables of every degree: what have you to say to this?" When he introduces a workingman, he may make that workingman complain bitterly that society is all wrong; but when he plutocrats turn round on that man and say to him, "Oh, you think yourself very clever. What would you do? You complain

rarely using it to identify a member of the Communist party or a supporter of the Soviet Union. In this case it was deliberately and especially shocking because the Communist revolutionary government in Russia was new and had sent tremors of apprehension throughout Europe.

6. Shaw was noting the presence in the audience of his friend Dr. William Inge, the outspoken dean of St. Paul's.

about everything. What would you do to set things right?" he makes the workingman say, "It is not for the like of me to say. It is the business of people who have the power and the knowledge to understand these things, and take it on themselves to right them." That is the attitude of Dickens, and the attitude of Ruskin, and that really is my attitude as well. The people at large are occupied with their own special jobs, and the reconstruction of society is a very special job indeed. To tell the people to make their own laws is to mock them just as I should mock you if I said, "Gentlemen: you are the people: write your own plays." The people are the judges of the laws and of plays, but they can never be the makers of them.

Thus Ruskin, like Dickens, understood that the reconstruction of society must be the work of an energetic and conscientious minority. Both of them knew that the government of a country is always the work of a minority, energetic, possibly conscientious, possibly the reverse, too often a merely predatory minority which produces an illusion of conscientiousness by setting up a convention that what they want for their own advantage is for the good of society. They pay very clever people to prove it, and the clever people argue themselves into believing it. The Manchester or anti-Ruskin school had plenty of sincere and able apologists. If you read Austin's lectures on jurisprudence,[7] for instance, you will find a more complete acknowledgment of the horrors inevitable under Capitalism than in most Socialist writers, because Austin had convinced himself that they are the price of liberty and of progress. But then nobody in his day conceived Socialism as a practical alternative: indeed, it was not then practicable. Austin's argument, or rather his choice of evils, is no longer forced on us, so we need not concern ourselves about it except as a demonstration that Ruskin's skepticism as to government by the people as distinguished from government of the people for the people is shared by his most extreme and logical opponents as well as by his kindred spirits.

Is there, then, any existing political system in operation in Europe at this moment which combines Communism with a belief in government by an energetic and enlightened minority, and whose leaders

7. John Austin (1790–1859) published his *Province of Jurisprudence* in 1832.

openly say, "There is no use talking about Democracy. If reforms are to wait until a majority of the people are converted to an intelligent belief in them, no reforms will ever be made at all. If we, whose intentions are honest, wait for such an impossible conversion, the only result of our sitting down and doing nothing will be that another energetic majority, whose intentions are evil, will seize the lead and govern in our stead. Democracy in that sense would be merely an excuse to enable us to go on talking, without ever being called upon to take the responsibility of doing anything. Moreover, our opponents would kill us"?

Can you point to any political body in Europe which is now taking that line? Let me lead you to it gently.

In Germany, Socialism has been represented by the Social-Democrats, and they had a great apparent democratic success in the way of getting members into Parliament, and becoming the largest group there, besides founding many newspapers, and figuring as an established institution in the country. Their theoretic spokesman is Kautsky. Some years before the war there was a certain Internationalist Socialist Congress. As usual there was some controversy between the French and the Germans, the French being led by Jaurès, who was then happily still alive. The Germans claimed superior authority in the Socialist movement because they were so much more largely and systematically organized. They cited their numerous branches, their newspapers, their millions of votes, and their representation in Parliament, in which, by the way, they had a self-denying ordinance that none of them should take office until the Capitalist system was overthrown. This saved them much trouble. They had only to sit and criticize their opponents; and they criticized them very eloquently and very thoroughly. When the German leader, Bebel, had detailed all those advantages and thrown them at the head of the French, he said, "What have you French Socialists to shew in the way of Socialist organization comparable to that?" Jaurès simply said: "Ah, if we had all that in France, *something would happen*." Which shut up the German party.

You see, it had been driven in on Jaurès, himself a great talker, that mere talking is no use. It comes to no more than the talking about Christianity which has been going on for nineteen hundred

years, during which official Christianity has been incessantly trying
to find excuses for disregarding the teaching of Christ. I remember
when I was busy as an unpaid and quite sincere Socialist agitator
in this country—there were twelve years of my life during which I
delivered a long public address on Socialism certainly three times a
fortnight—one of the things that puzzled me at first was that I met
with so little opposition. I found that I was almost like a clergyman
talking pious platitudes. Nobody objected. Nothing happened. I apparently carried my audiences enthusiastically with me. Nevertheless,
Capitalism went on just the same. I began to understand that the
leaders of Socialism, the men with the requisite brains and political
comprehension, must not wait as Kautsky would have them wait on
the plea that you must do nothing until you have converted the
people, and can win a bloodless victory through the ballot-box.
The people seldom know what they want, and never know how
to get it.

As against Kautsky, Europe has in the field a very interesting
statesman named Nicholas Lenin. He says, "As long as you talk
like that, you will not do anything, and dont really mean to do anything. In this world things are done by men who have convictions,
who believe those convictions to be right, and who are prepared
with all the strength they have or can rally to them to impose
appropriate institutions on the vast majority who are themselves as
incapable of making the institutions as of inventing the telescope or
calculating the distance of the nearest fixed star."

Do not forget that this attitude of Lenin is the attitude not only
of all the prophets, but of, say, Mr Winston Churchill and Mr
Arthur Balfour. All our military and governing people who have
practical experience of State affairs know that the people, for good
or evil, must, whether they will or no, be finally governed by people
capable of governing, and that the people themselves know this
instinctively, and mistrust all democratic doctrinaires. If you like to
call Bolshevism a combination of the Tory oligarchism of Ruskin
and Mr Winston Churchill with the Tory Communism of Ruskin
alone, you may. So it comes to this, that when we look for a party
which could logically claim Ruskin today as one of its prophets,
we find it in the Bolshevist party. [*Laughter.*] You laugh at this.

You feel it to be absurd. But I have given you a demonstration, and I want you now to pick a hole in the demonstration if you can. You got out of the difficulty in Ruskin's own time by saying that he was a Tory. He said so himself. But then you did not quite grasp the fact that all Socialists are Tories in that sense. The Tory is a man who believes that those who are qualified by nature and training for public work, and who are naturally a minority, have to govern the mass of the people. That is Toryism. That is also Bolshevism. The Russian masses elected a National Assembly: Lenin and the Bolshevists ruthlessly shoved it out of the way, and indeed shot it out of the way as far as it refused to be shoved.

Some of you, in view of the shooting, repudiate Bolshevism as a bloodstained tyranny, and revolt against the connection of Ruskin's name with it. But if you are never going to follow any prophet in whose name governments have been guilty of killing those who resist them, you will have to repudiate your country, your religion, and your humanity. Let us be humble. There is no use in throwing these terms at oneanother. You cannot repudiate religion because it has been connected with the atrocities of the wars of religion. You cannot, for instance, ask any Roman Catholic to repudiate his Church because of the things that were done in the Inquisition, or any Protestant to admit that Luther must stand or fall by the acts of the soldiers of Gustavus Adolphus. All you can do is to deplore the atrocities. Lenin said the other day, "Yes: there have been atrocities; and they have not all been inevitable." I wish every other statesman in Europe had the same candor. Look at all that has been done, not only by Bolshevists, but by anti-Bolshevists, by ourselves, and by all the belligerents! There is only one thing that it becomes us to say, and that is, "God forgive us all."

Lecture delivered at the Ruskin Centenary Exhibition, held at the Royal Academy of Arts, London, November 21, 1919. Issued as a book by the Ruskin Centenary Council, London, 1921.

Literature and the Sex Instinct

Although Shaw opens with a theatrical reference, this extract from one of his prefaces is primarily concerned with the treatment of love in fiction.

* * * A heroine who atones in the last act by committing suicide may do all the things that Hedda [Gabler] only talked about, without a word of remonstrance from the press or the public. It is not murder, not adultery, not rapine that is objected to: quite the contrary. It is an unladylike attitude towards life: in other words, a disparagement of the social ideals of the poorer middle class and of the vast reinforcements it has had from the working class during the last twenty years. Let but the attitude of the author be gentlemanlike, and his heroines may do what they please. Mrs Tanqueray was received with delight by the public: Saint Teresa would have been hissed off the same stage for her contempt for the ideal represented by a carriage, a fashionable dressmaker, and a dozen servants.

Here, then, is a pretty problem for the manager. He is convinced that plays must depend for their dramatic force on appeals to the sex instinct; and yet he owes it to his own newly conquered social position that they shall be perfectly genteel plays, fit for churchgoers. The sex instinct must therefore proceed upon genteel assumptions. Impossible! you will exclaim. But you are wrong: nothing is more astonishing than the extent to which, in real life, the sex instinct does so proceed, even when the consequence is its lifelong starvation. Few of us have vitality enough to make any of our instincts imperious: we can be made to live on pretences, as the masterful minority well know. But the timid majority, if it rules nowhere else, at least rules in the theatre: fitly enough too, because on the stage pretence is all that can exist. Life has its realities behind its shows: the theatre has nothing but its shows. But can the theatre make a show of lovers' endearments? A thousand times no: perish the thought of such unladylike, ungentlemanlike exhibitions. You can have fights, rescues, conflagrations, trials-at-law, avalanches, murders and executions all directly simulated on the stage if you will. But any such realistic treatment of the incidents of sex is quite out of the question. The singer, the dramatic dancer, the exquisite declaimer of impassioned poesy, the rare artist who, bringing something of the art of all three to the ordinary work of the theatre, can enthral an audience by the expression of dramatic feeling alone, may take love for a theme on the stage; but the prosaic walking gentlemen of our fashionable theatres, realistically simulating the incidents of life, cannot touch it without indecorum.

Can any dilemma be more complete? Love is assumed to be the only theme that touches all your audience infallibly, young and old, rich and poor. And yet love is the one subject that the drawing room drama dare not present.

Out of this dilemma, which is a very old one, has come the romantic play: that is, the play in which love is carefully kept off the stage, whilst it is alleged as the motive of all the actions presented to the audience. The result is, to me at least, an intolerable perversion of human conduct. There are two classes of stories that seem to me to be not only fundamentally false but sordidly base. One is the pseudo-religious story, in which the hero or heroine does good on strictly commercial grounds, reluctantly exercising a little virtue on earth in consideration of receiving in return an exorbitant payment in heaven: much as if an odalisque were to allow a cadi to whip her for a couple of millions in gold. The other is the romance in which the hero, also rigidly commercial, will do nothing except for the sake of the heroine. Surely this is as depressing as it is unreal. Compare with it the treatment of love, frankly indecent according to our notions, in oriental fiction. In The Arabian Nights we have a series of stories, some of them very good ones, in which no sort of decorum is observed. The result is that they are infinitely more instructive and enjoyable than our romances, because love is treated in them as naturally as any other passion. There is no cast iron convention as to its effects; no false association of general depravity of character with its corporealities or of general elevation with its sentimentalities; no pretence that a man or woman cannot be courageous and kind and friendly unless infatuatedly in love with somebody (is no poet manly enough to sing The Old Maids of England?) : rather, indeed, an insistence on the blinding and narrowing power of lovesickness to make princely heroes unhappy and unfortunate. These tales expose, further, the delusion that the interest of this most capricious, most transient, most easily baffled of all instincts, is inexhaustible, and that the field of the English romancer has been cruelly narrowed by the restrictions under which he is permitted to deal with it. The Arabian storyteller, relieved of all such restrictions, heaps character on character, adventure on adventure, marvel on marvel; whilst the English novelist, like the starving tramp who can think of nothing but his hunger, seems to be unable to escape from the obsession of sex, and will rewrite the very gospels because the originals are not written in the sensuously ecstatic style. At the instance of Martin Luther we long ago gave up imposing celibacy on our priests; but we still impose it on our art, with the very undesirable and unexpected result that no editor, publisher, or manager, will now accept a story or produce a play without "love interest" in it. Take, for a recent example, Mr H. G. Wells's War of Two Worlds,[1] a tale of the invasion of the earth by the inhabitants of the planet Mars: a capital story, not to be laid down until finished. Love interest is impossible on its scientific plane : nothing could be more impertinent and irritating. Yet Mr Wells has had to pretend that the hero is in love with a young lady manufactured for the purpose, and to imply that it is on her account alone that he feels concerned about the apparently inevitable destruction of the human race by the Martians. Another example. An American novelist, recently deceased,[2] made a hit some years ago by compiling a Bostonian Utopia from the prospectuses of the little bands of devout Communists who have from time to time, since the days of Fourier and Owen, tried to establish millennial colonies outside our commercial civilization. Even in this economic Utopia we find the inevitable love affair. The hero, waking up in a distant

1. *The War of the Worlds* (1898).
2. Edward Bellamy (1850–1898), author of *Looking Backward* (1888).

future from a miraculous sleep, meets a Boston young lady, provided expressly for him to fall in love with. Women have by that time given up wearing skirts; but she, to spare his delicacy, gets one out of a museum of antiquities to wear in his presence until he is hardened to the customs of the new age. When I came to that touching incident, I became as Paolo and Francesca: "in that book I read no more." I will not multiply examples: if such unendurable follies occur in the sort of story made by working out a meteorological or economic hypothesis, the extent to which it is carried in sentimental romances needs no expatiation.

The worst of it is that since man's intellectual consciousness of himself is derived from the descriptions of him in books, a persistent misrepresentation of humanity in literature gets finally accepted and acted upon. If every mirror reflected our noses twice their natural size, we should live and die in the faith that we were all Punches; and we should scout a true mirror as the work of a fool, madman, or jester. Nay, I believe we should, by Lamarckian adaptation, enlarge our noses to the admired size; for I have noticed that when a certain type of feature appears in painting and is admired as beautiful, it presently becomes common in nature; so that the Beatrices and Francescas in the picture galleries of one generation, to whom minor poets address verses entitled To My Lady, come to life as the parlormaids and waitresses of the next. If the conventions of romance are only insisted on long enough and uniformly enough (a condition guaranteed by the uniformity of human folly and vanity), then, for the huge compulsorily schooled masses who read romance or nothing, these conventions will become the laws of personal honor. Jealousy, which is either an egotistical meanness or a specific mania, will become obligatory; and ruin, ostracism, breaking up of homes, duelling, murder, suicide and infanticide will be produced (often have been produced, in fact) by incidents which, if left to the operation of natural and right feeling, would produce nothing worse than an hour's soon-forgotten fuss. Men will be slain needlessly on the field of battle because officers conceive it to be their first duty to make romantic exhibitions of conspicuous gallantry. The squire who has never spared an hour from the

hunting field to do a little public work on a parish council will be
cheered as a patriot because he is willing to kill and get killed for
the sake of conferring himself as an institution on other countries.
In the courts cases will be argued, not on juridical but on romantic
principles; and vindictive damages and vindictive sentences, with
the acceptance of nonsensical, and the repudiation or suppression
of sensible testimony, will destroy the very sense of law. Kaisers,
generals, judges, and prime ministers will set the example of playing
to the gallery. Finally the people, now that their compulsory literacy
enables every penman to play on their romantic illusions, will be led
by the nose far more completely than they ever were by playing
on their former ignorance and superstition. Nay, why should I say
will be? they *are*. Ten years of cheap reading have changed the
English from the most stolid nation in Europe to the most theatrical
and hysterical.

Is it clear now, why the theatre was insufferable to me; why it
left its black mark on my bones as it has left its black mark on the
character of the nation; why I call the Puritans to rescue it again
as they rescued it before when its foolish pursuit of pleasure sunk
it in "profaneness and immorality"? I have, I think, always been
a Puritan in my attitude towards Art. I am as fond of fine music
and handsome building as Milton was, or Cromwell, or Bunyan;
but if I found that they were becoming the instruments of a systematic idolatry of sensuousness, I would hold it good statesmanship
to blow every cathedral in the world to pieces with dynamite, organ
and all, without the least heed to the screams of the art critics
and cultured voluptuaries. And when I see that the nineteenth
century has crowned the idolatry of Art with the deification of Love,
so that every poet is supposed to have pierced to the holy of holies
when he has announced that Love is the Supreme, or the Enough,
or the All, I feel that Art was safer in the hands of the most
fanatical of Cromwell's major generals than it will be if ever it gets
into mine. The pleasures of the senses I can sympathize with and
share; but the substitution of sensuous ecstasy for intellectual
activity and honesty is the very devil. It has already brought us to
Flogging Bills in Parliament, and, by reaction, to androgynous heroes

on the stage; and if the infection spreads until the democratic attitude becomes thoroughly Romanticist, the country will become unbearable for all realists, Philistine or Platonic. When it comes to that, the brute force of the strong-minded Bismarckian man of action, impatient of humbug, will combine with the subtlety and spiritual energy of the man of thought whom shams cannot illude or interest. That combination will be on one side; and Romanticism will be on the other. In which event, so much the worse for Romanticism, which will come down even if it has to drag Democracy down with it. For all institutions have in the long run to live by the nature of things, and not by childish pretendings.

From the Preface to *Three Plays for Puritans* (London, 1900).

Modern Novels and Sex

In the London Evening Standard on May 25, 1922, Dean Inge criticized the alleged vulgarity and indecency in much of contemporary English fiction, pointing in particular to "the corrupt taste of the moment" as he saw it in H. G. Wells's newest novel, The Secret Places of the Heart. *Wells wrote an instant rebuttal, and the* Evening Standard, *sensing a good thing, printed it the next day side-by-side with a defense of Wells which it had solicited from Shaw. "The homely reminders of the Anglican marriage service," Wells wrote, "should have taught him [Inge] better. Even among the higher clergy love is, I understand it, an affair between people of opposite sex, and it turns on that opposition. 'Lust' is a nasty word for the Dean to fling about, and I leave it to him, but it seems to me that people who profess to love and undertake to marry without strong sexual desires are the worst sort of unpleasant and intolerable people, and that love stories without a wholesome undertone of sensuousness are not so commendable as he would have us think." Shaw's statement is reprinted here in full.*

I agree with the Dean as to his first point, because, like him, I do not go to fiction to study pathological cases. The only fictitious characters which give me the satisfaction I look for in works of art are those with a full range of common human faculty.

I do not mind Don Quixote being a little crazy, and Sancho being totally illiterate; but the slightest touch of morbidity would spoil both. If people want to read about accidents and criminals and diseases they should read the daily papers: fiction should deal with healthy people in circumstances which are normal, or would be normal at the imagined period. To put it shortly, the Dean and I have the classic taste in literature.

But Victorian literature did not really comply with these conditions. Thackeray knew very well that his young men were incomplete, and therefore untrue to life as compared with Fielding's Tom

Jones. All the Victorians had to pretend that the marriage law was human nature, and that it was both unnatural and improper to lapse for an instant from perfect monogameity of sentiment.

The foulness of which the Dean complains is nothing but a violent reaction against this intolerable and dishonest affectation. The Victorian pretence that women had no legs or digestion is so exasperating that women are being provoked to strip off all their clothes in fiction to prove their right to adequate sanitary accommodation.

I doubt if there is a single excess in modern fiction that cannot be traced to a suppression in the reign of Queen Victoria. It is just because Mr James Joyce was brought up on the reticences of the heroes and heroines of Sir Walter Scott that he is so embarrassingly communicative as to the indiscretions of his own heroes and heroines.

I have just read Mr Wells's new book; and I swear it contains no "ugly story of seduction." Is Mr Wells to describe sexual human nature falsely, as the Victorians required it to be described, or is he to describe it as it actually is? In his book there are four men, including two who do not come upon the stage; 75 percent of them are as monogamic as the Master of Ravenswood or Rob Roy; 25 percent are polygamic.

Is this, taken as a picture of society, anything like so false in respect of sex as Victorian fiction was? It seems to me that when the Dean applies the word "seduction" to a perfectly natural attraction between two fully grown and highly capable adults, and qualifies it as ugly, he is for once in his life writing like a taboo-ridden Dean instead of like one of the mentally most gifted Englishmen now living.

Mr Wells does not shirk facts because they are considered scandalous, especially when the conventional foundation of that view of them is becoming more and more questionable; but I cannot find in his books a trace of that *morbidezza* which disgusts the Dean, and which is very largely produced by the fact that the writers have no real experience of what they are writing about, and are the victims of a baffled *libido* rather than of a Casanovesque excess of gallantry.

Evening Standard (London), May 26, 1922.

Romance and Real Sex

Collected in Table Talk of G.B.S. *(1925) were literary exchanges between Shaw and Archibald Henderson which had first appeared in the* Fortnightly Review. *Shaw had permitted his authorized biographer to piece together scraps of literary talk from letters, publications, and—in rare cases—conversation, into a mostly spurious dialogue on many subjects, to which G.B.S. provided additional material. The object was to furnish some needed income for Henderson, although Shaw shared the proceeds, in the process writing his own contract, in which he supplied an unusual clause which provided that if, within two years of publication, the book had not sold two thousand copies, the publishers should pay the authors the royalty on that number anyway. When Chapman and Hall protested, Shaw observed, "No book bearing my name has ever sold less than 2,000 copies. If you fail to sell that number, and thereby prove yourselves the world's worst publishers, you ought, upon every possible count, to pay the penalty of your incapacity." The clause remained, and remained unnecessary.*

Removed from the stuffy atmosphere of Table Talk, *some of the material retains its vitality as criticism. The best segments of the literary section are extracted below, minus Henderson's questions and pontifications.*

Very few books of any nationality are worth reading. People read to kill time; consequently it is no more objection to a book that it is not worth reading than it is to a pack of cards that it does not pile up treasures in heaven.

* * * What has happened is that there has been a great extension of the liberty of the press to deal with the sexual side of human life, followed by a rush to take advantage of it on the part of writers who, like a certain character in one of my plays, have only one subject. But their readers are finding out that crude sex, instead of being the most enthralling literary subject in the world, as they fancied when it was barred, is the dullest. The pleasures connected with it are pleasures to be enjoyed, not to be read about. What fun is there in staring at a young American film actor pretending to kiss Miss Mary Pickford at the happy ending of a movie play? It would no doubt be delightful to kiss Miss Pickford; and it is always pleasant to look at her when nobody is spoiling the view with his nose. But to watch another person kissing her is as indelicate as it is tantalizing. And how much stupider it is not even to see such things on the screen, but only to read about them in books and know the kisses only by description! The pornographic novel appeals to a want which literature cannot supply. It offers a hungry man a description of a dinner. Even if the descriptions were life-like, they could not satisfy his hunger. But almost all the descriptions seem written by people who are pitifully ignorant of what they are writing about, and they can appeal only to readers equally inexperienced. Compare these novels with Ivanhoe or Pickwick! It is like comparing cocktails with mountain torrents. In short, the pornographic novel is getting found out for the dull thing it is; and that is the long and short of it.

* * * We are only at the beginning of the subject. The old silence prevented us from realizing our own experiences; for it takes a tremendous lot of talking and writing to bring experience into clear intellectual consciousness. It also prevented us from discussing them: in fact we had no decent language to discuss them in. As the silence breaks, and we are forced to think and speak decently because we are thinking and speaking aloud, we are discerning a new world in sex.

There is never any real sex in romance. What is more, there is very little, and that of a very crude kind, in ninety-nine hundredths of our married life. The field of sexual selection is too narrowed by class and property divisions which forbid intermarriage to give anything like enough material for a genuine science of sex. I tell you you will never have a healthily sexed literature until you have a healthily sexed people; and that is impossible under Capitalism, which imposes commercial conditions on marriage as on everything else.

You cannot define the terms. One man's poetry is another man's pruriency. One woman's passion is another woman's impropriety. For goodness' sake let people have what they want. Read Sterne's Sentimental Journey. If that is not prurient, the word has no meaning. Well, are you going to warn people against A Sentimental Journey? When I read it—I was a boy at the time—I liked it. I conclude that I liked pruriency when it was well done. It has never occurred to me to try to prevent anyone else reading it. You must let people eat what agrees with them, even if it seems to you to be garbage.

I suppose you might call Manon Lescaut a sex novel just as you might call The Nigger of the *Narcissus* a sea novel. If you called Wagner's Tristan a sex opera or Romeo and Juliet a sex tragedy I should know what you meant, whereas if you called Dombey and Son or Macbeth sex stories I should conclude that you were mad. But the term taken by itself as a category conveys nothing.

A pornographic novelist is one who exploits the sexual instinct as a prostitute does. A legitimate sex novel elucidates it or brings out its poetry, tragedy, or comedy. But there is really no critical sense in such an expression as sex novel. The Victorian novel, which was sexless to the extent that Thackeray could not describe the sexual adventures of Pendennis as Fielding described those of Tom Jones, certainly did prove that the novel which says no more about sex than may be said in a lecture on the facts to a class of schoolgirls of fifteen can be enormously more entertaining than a novel wholly preoccupied with sexual symptoms. But readers of Don Quixote knew that already; and eight or more generations of readers had found Robinson Crusoe and The Pilgrim's Progress more readable than Moll Flanders. It is the sexless novel that should be distinguished: the sex novel is now normal. But don't think that all Victorian novels were sexless. Ouida scandalized the Victorians.* * *

Grant Allen was boycotted for a couple of years for The Woman Who Did, though it reeked with the Puritanism of his North of Ireland ancestry. George Moore's Mummer's Wife was a Victorian novel. Zola's works, and De Maupassant's were translated and prodigiously discussed in Victoria's reign. They were all considered the limit then. Who fusses about them now?

When they asked me to pay three guineas for Ulysses I said I would not go a penny beyond seven and sixpence. I read scraps of it in The Little Review, not knowing that they all belonged to the history of a single day in Dublin. I was attracted to it by the fact that I was once a young man in Dublin, and also by Joyce's literary power, which is of classic quality. I do not see why there should be any limit to frankness in sex revelation; but Joyce does not raise that question. The question he does raise is whether there should be any limit to the use in literature of blackguardly language. It depends on what people will stand. If Dickens or Thackeray had been told that a respectable author like myself would use the expletive "bloody" in a play, and that an exceptionally fastidious actress of the first rank, associated exclusively with fine parts, would utter it on the stage without turning a hair, he could not have believed it. Yet I am so old-fashioned and squeamish that I was horrified when I first heard a lady describe a man as a rotter.

I could not write the words Mr Joyce uses: my prudish hand would refuse to form the letters; and I can find no interest in his infantile clinical incontinences, or in the flatulations which he thinks worth mentioning. But if they were worth mentioning I should not object to mentioning them, though, as you see, I should dress up his popular locutions in a little Latinity. For all we know they may be peppered freely over the pages of the lady novelists of ten years hence; and Frank Harris's autobiography may be on all the book-stalls.[1] When Linnaeus first wrote on the fertilization of plants, botany was denounced as corrupting to morals. That seems hardly credible now. But in point of genuine frankness there has been no advance upon Rousseau. Mr Harris does not really give himself away as completely as St Augustine or Bunyan.

Is any treatment of sex in the interest of public morals? Most of the people who denounce Ulysses would say no if they would think

1. Shaw was premature on both counts; but a generation after his remarks —rather than a decade—lady novelists were freely using four-letter words, and Frank Harris's *My Life and Loves* was reprinted and widely sold in its unexpurgated version.

out their own position; and that answer would at once reduce them to absurdity. Ulysses is a document, the outcome of a passion for documentation that is as fundamental as the artistic passion—more so, in fact; for the document is the root and stem of which the artistic fancy-works are the flowers. Joyce is driven by his documentary *daimon* to place on record the working of a young man's imagination for a single day in the environment of Dublin. The question is, is the document authentic? If I, having read some scraps of it, reply that I am afraid it is, then you may rise up and demand that Dublin be razed to the ground and its foundations sown with salt. And I may say do so by all means. But that does not invalidate the document.

The Dublin "jackeens" of my day, the medical students, the young bloods about town, were very like that. Their conversation was dirty; and it defiled their sexuality, which might just as easily have been held up to them as poetic and vital. I should like to organize the young men of Dublin into clubs for the purpose of reading Ulysses, so that they should debate the question "Are we like that?" and if the vote were in the affirmative, proceed to the further question: "Shall we remain like that?" which would, I hope, be answered in the negative. You cannot carry out moral sanitation, any more than physical sanitation, without indecent exposures. Get rid of the ribaldry that Joyce describes and dramatizes, and what you object to in Ulysses will have no more interest than a twelfth-century map of the world has to-day. Suppress the book, leaving the ribaldry unexposed; and you are protecting dirt instead of protecting morals. If a man holds up a mirror to your nature and shows you that it needs washing—not whitewashing—it is no use breaking the mirror. Go for soap and water.

From Table Talk of G.B.S. (London and New York, 1925).

VI. GREATNESS IN LITERATURE

Artist-Philosophers

The most famous Shavian statement on the moral basis of great literary art appears in the long preface to Man *and* Superman.

That the author of Everyman was no mere artist, but an artist-philosopher, and that the artist-philosophers are the only sort of artists I take quite seriously, will be no news to you. Even Plato and Boswell, as the dramatists who invented Socrates and Dr Johnson, impress me more deeply than the romantic playwrights. Ever since, as a boy, I first breathed the air of the transcendental regions at a performance of Mozart's Zauberflöte, I have been proof against the garish splendors and alcoholic excitements of the ordinary stage combinations of Tappertitian romance with the police intelligence. Bunyan, Blake, Hogarth, and Turner (these four apart and above all the English classics), Goethe, Shelley, Schopenhauer, Wagner, Ibsen, Morris, Tolstoy, and Nietzsche are among the writers whose peculiar sense of the world I recognize as more or less akin to my own. Mark the word peculiar. I read Dickens and Shakespear without shame or stint; but their pregnant observations and demonstrations of life are not co-ordinated into any philosophy or religion: on the contrary, Dickens's sentimental assumptions are violently contradicted by his observations; and Shakespear's pessimism is only his wounded humanity. Both have the specific genius of the fictionist and the common sympathies of human feeling and thought in pre-eminent degree. They are often saner and shrewder than the philosophers just as Sancho-Panza was often saner and shrewder than Don Quixote. They clear away vast masses of oppressive gravity by their sense of the ridiculous, which is at bottom a combination of sound moral judgment with lighthearted good humor. But they are concerned with the diversities of the world instead of with its unities: they are so irreligious that they exploit popular religion for professional purposes without delicacy or scruple (for example,

Sydney Carton and the ghost in Hamlet!): they are anarchical, and cannot balance their exposures of Angelo and Dogberry, Sir Leicester Dedlock and Mr Tite Barnacle, with any portrait of a prophet or a worthy leader: they have no constructive ideas: they regard those who have them as dangerous fanatics: in all their fictions there is no leading thought or inspiration for which any man could conceivably risk the spoiling of his hat in a shower, much less his life. Both are alike forced to borrow motives for the more strenuous actions of their personages from the common stockpot of melodramatic plots; so that Hamlet has to be stimulated by the prejudices of a policeman and Macbeth by the cupidities of a bush-ranger. Dickens, without the excuse of having to manufacture mo-tives for Hamlets and Macbeths, superfluously punts his crew down the stream of his monthly parts by mechanical devices which I leave you to describe, my own memory being quite baffled by the simplest question as to Monks in Oliver Twist, or the long lost parentage of Smike, or the relations between the Dorrit and Clennam families so inopportunely discovered by Monsieur Rigaud Blandois. The truth is, the world was to Shakespear a great "stage of fools" on which he was utterly bewildered. He could see no sort of sense in living at all; and Dickens saved himself from the despair of the dream in The Chimes by taking the world for granted and busying himself with its details. Neither of them could do anything with a serious positive character: they could place a human figure before you with perfect verisimilitude; but when the moment came for making it live and move, they found, unless it made them laugh, that they had a puppet on their hands, and had to invent some artificial external stimulus to make it work. This is what is the mat-ter with Hamlet all through: he has no will except in his bursts of temper. Foolish Bardolaters make a virtue of this after their fashion: they declare that the play is the tragedy of irresolution; but all Shakespear's projections of the deepest humanity he knew have the same defect: their characters and manners are lifelike; but their actions are forced on them from without, and the external force is grotesquely inappropriate except when it is quite conventional, as in the case of Henry V. Falstaff is more vivid than any of these serious reflective characters, because he is self-acting: his motives are his own appetites and instincts and humors. Richard III, too, is delightful as the whimsical comedian who stops a funeral to make love to the corpse's son's widow; but when, in the next act, he is replaced by a stage villain who smothers babies and offs with people's heads, we are revolted at the imposture and repudiate the changeling. Faulconbridge, Coriolanus, Leontes are admirable descriptions of instinctive temperaments: indeed the play of Coriolanus is the greatest of Shakespear's comedies; but description is not philosophy; and comedy neither compromises the author nor reveals him. He must be judged by those characters into which he puts what he knows of himself, his Hamlets and Macbeths and Lears and Prosperos. If these characters are agonizing in a void about factitious melodramatic murders and revenges and the like, whilst the comic characters walk with their feet on solid ground, vivid and amusing, you know that the author has much to shew and nothing to teach. The comparison between Falstaff and Prospero is like the comparison between Micawber and David Copperfield. At the end of the book you know Micawber, whereas you only know what has happened to David, and are not interested enough in him to wonder what his politics or religion might be if anything so stupendous as a religious or political idea, or a general idea of any sort, were to occur to him. He is tolerable as a child; but he never becomes a man, and might be left out of his own biography altogether but for his usefulness as a stage confidant, a Horatio or "Charles his friend": what they call on the stage a feeder.

Now you cannot say this of the work of the artist-philosophers. You cannot say it, for instance, of The Pilgrim's Progress. Put your Shakespearian hero and coward, Henry V and Pistol or Parolles, beside Mr Valiant and Mr Fearing, and you have a sudden revelation of the abyss that lies between the fashionable author who could see nothing in the world but personal aims and the tragedy of their disappointment or the comedy of their incongruity, and the field preacher who achieved virtue and courage by identifying himself with the purpose of the world as he understood it. The contrast is enormous: Bunyan's coward stirs your blood more than Shakespear's hero, who actually leaves you cold and secretly hostile. You suddenly see that Shakespear, with all his flashes and divinations, never understood virtue and courage, never conceived how any man who was not a fool could, like Bunyan's hero, look back from the brink of the river of death over the strife and labor of his pilgrimage, and say "yet do I not repent me"; or, with the panache of a millionaire, bequeath "my sword to him that shall succeed me in my pilgrimage, and my courage and skill to him that can get it." This is the true joy in life, the being used for a purpose recognized by yourself as a mighty one; the being thoroughly worn out before you are thrown on the scrap heap; the being a force of Nature instead of a feverish selfish little clod of ailments and grievances complaining that the world will not devote itself to making you happy. And also the only real tragedy in life is the being used by personally minded men for purposes which you recognize to be base. All the rest is at worst mere misfortune or mortality: this alone is misery, slavery, hell on earth; and the revolt against it is the only force that offers a man's work to the poor artist, whom our personally minded rich people would so willingly employ as pandar, buffoon, beauty monger, sentimentalizer and the like.

It may seem a long step from Bunyan to Nietzsche; but the difference between their conclusions is merely formal. Bunyan's perception that righteousness is filthy rags, his scorn for Mr Legality in the village of Morality, his defiance of the Church as the supplanter of religion, his insistence on courage as the virtue of virtues, his estimate of the career of the conventionally respectable and sensible Worldly Wiseman as no better at bottom than the life and death of Mr Badman: all this, expressed by Bunyan in the terms of a tinker's theology, is what Nietzsche has expressed in terms of post-Darwin, post-Schopenhauer philosophy; Wagner in terms of polytheistic mythology; and Ibsen in terms of mid-XIX century parisian dramaturgy. Nothing is new in these matters except their novelties: for instance, it is a novelty to call Justification by Faith "Wille," and Justification by Works "Vorstellung." The sole use of the novelty is that you and I buy and read Schopenhauer's treatise on Will and Representation when we should not dream of buy-

ing a set of sermons on Faith versus Works. At bottom the controversy is the same, and the dramatic results are the same. Bunyan
makes no attempt to present his pilgrims as more sensible or better
conducted than Mr Worldly Wiseman. Mr W. W.'s worst enemies,
Mr Embezzler, Mr Never-go-to-Church-on-Sunday, Mr Bad Form,
Mr Murderer, Mr Burglar, Mr Co-respondent, Mr Blackmailer, Mr
Cad, Mr Drunkard, Mr Labor Agitator and so forth, can read the
Pilgrim's Progress without finding a word said against them; whereas
the respectable people who snub them and put them in prison, such
as Mr W. W. himself and his young friend Civility; Formalist and
Hypocrisy; Wildhead, Inconsiderate, and Pragmatick (who were
clearly young university men of good family and high feeding);
that brisk lad Ignorance, Talkative, By-ends of Fairspeech and his
mother-in-law Lady Feigning, and other reputable gentlemen and
citizens, catch it very severely. Even Little Faith, though he gets
to heaven at last, is given to understand that it served him right to
be mobbed by the brothers Faint Heart, Mistrust, and Guilt, all
three recognized members of respectable society and veritable pillars
of the law. The whole allegory is a consistent attack on morality
and respectability, without a word that one can remember against
vice and crime. Exactly what is complained of in Nietzsche and
Ibsen, is it not? And also exactly what would be complained of in
all the literature which is great enough and old enough to have attained canonical rank, officially or unofficially, were it not that
books are admitted to the canon by a compact which confesses their
greatness in consideration of abrogating their meaning; so that the
reverend rector can agree with the prophet Micah as to his inspired
style without being committed to any complicity in Micah's furiously
Radical opinions. Why, even I, as I force myself, pen in hand, into
recognition and civility, find all the force of my onslaught destroyed
by a simple policy of non-resistance. In vain do I redouble the
violence of the language in which I proclaim my heterodoxies. I
rail at the theistic credulity of Voltaire, the amoristic superstition
of Shelley, the revival of tribal soothsaying and idolatrous rites which
Huxley called Science and mistook for an advance on the Pentateuch, no less than at the welter of ecclesiastical and professional

humbug which saves the face of the stupid system of violence and robbery which we call Law and Industry. Even atheists reproach me with infidelity and anarchists with nihilism because I cannot endure their moral tirades. And yet, instead of exclaiming "Send this inconceivable Satanist to the stake," the respectable newspapers pith me by announcing "another book by this brilliant and thoughtful writer." And the ordinary citizen, knowing that an author who is well spoken of by a respectable newspaper must be all right, reads me, as he reads Micah, with undisturbed edification from his own point of view. It is narrated that in the eighteenseventies an old lady, a very devout Methodist, moved from Colchester to a house in the neighborhood of the City Road, in London, where, mistaking the Hall of Science for a chapel, she sat at the feet of Charles Bradlaugh for many years, entranced by his eloquence, without questioning his orthodoxy or moulting a feather of her faith. I fear I shall be defrauded of my just martyrdom in the same way.

However, I am digressing, as a man with a grievance always does. And after all, the main thing in determining the artistic quality of a book is not the opinions it propagates, but the fact that the writer has opinions. The old lady from Colchester was right to sun her simple soul in the energetic radiance of Bradlaugh's genuine beliefs and disbeliefs rather than in the chill of such mere painting of light and heat as elocution and convention can achieve. My contempt for *belles lettres*, and for amateurs who become the heroes of the fanciers of literary virtuosity, is not founded on any illusion of mine as to the permanence of those forms of thought (call them opinions) by which I strive to communicate my bent to my fellows. To younger men they are already outmoded; for though they have no more lost their logic than an eighteenth-century pastel has lost its drawing or its color, yet, like the pastel, they grow indefinably shabby, will grow shabbier until they cease to count at all, when my books will either perish, or, if the world is still poor enough to want them, will have to stand, with Bunyan's, by quite amorphous qualities of temper and energy. With this conviction I cannot be a bellettrist. No doubt I must recognize, as even the Ancient Mariner did, that I must tell my story entertainingly if I am to hold the wedding guest spellbound in spite of the siren sounds of the loud bassoon. But "for art's sake" alone I would not face the toil of writing a single sentence. I know that there are men who, having nothing to say and nothing to write, are nevertheless so in love with oratory and with literature that they delight in repeating as much as they can understand of what others have said or written aforetime. I know that the leisurely tricks which their want of conviction leaves them free to play with the diluted and misapprehended message supply them with a pleasant parlor game which they call style. I can pity their dotage and even sympathize with their fancy. But a true original style is never achieved for its own sake: a man may pay from a shilling to a guinea, according to his means, to see, hear, or read another man's act of genius; but he will not pay with his whole life and soul to become a mere virtuoso in literature, exhibiting an accomplishment which will not even make money for him, like fiddle playing. Effectiveness of assertion is the Alpha and Omega of style. He who has nothing to assert has no style and can have none: he who has something to assert will go as far in power of style as its momentousness and his conviction will carry him. Disprove his assertion after it is made, yet its style remains. Darwin has no more destroyed the style of Job nor of Handel than Martin Luther destroyed the style of Giotto. All the assertions get disproved sooner or later; and so we find the world full of a magnificent débris of artistic fossils, with the matter-of-fact credibility gone clean out of them, but the form still splendid. And that is why the old masters play the deuce with our mere susceptibles. Your Royal Academician thinks he can get the style of Giotto without Giotto's beliefs, and correct his perspective into the bargain. Your man of letters thinks he can get Bunyan's or Shakespear's style without Bunyan's conviction or Shakespear's apprehension, especially if he takes care not to split his infinitives. And so with your Doctors of Music, who, with their collections of discords duly prepared and resolved or retarded or anticipated in the manner of the great composers, think they can learn the art of Palestrina from Cherubini's treatise. All this academic art is far worse than the trade in sham antique furniture; for the man who sells me an oaken chest which he swears was made in the XIII century, though as a matter of fact he made it himself only yesterday, at least does not pretend that there are any modern ideas in it; whereas your academic copier of fossils offers them to you as the latest outpouring of the human spirit, and, worst of all, kidnaps young people as pupils and persuades them that his limitations are rules, his observances dexterities, his timidities good taste, and his emptinesses purities. * * *

From the Preface to *Man and Superman* (London, 1903).

Better than Shakespear?

Few readers remember that the title of this controversial section of a famous Shavian preface concludes with a question mark.

The very name of Cleopatra suggests at once a tragedy of Circe, with the horrible difference that whereas the ancient myth rightly represents Circe as turning heroes into hogs, the modern romantic convention would represent her as turning hogs into heroes. Shakespear's Antony and Cleopatra must needs be as intolerable to the true Puritan as it is vaguely distressing to the ordinary healthy citizen, because, after giving a faithful picture of the soldier broken down by debauchery, and the typical wanton in whose arms such men perish, Shakespear finally strains all his huge command of rhetoric and stage pathos to give a theatrical sublimity to the wretched end of the business, and to persuade foolish spectators that the world was well lost by the twain. Such falsehood is not to be borne except by the real Cleopatras and Antonys (they are to be found in every public house) who would no doubt be glad enough to be transfigured by some poet as immortal lovers. Woe to the poet who stoops to such folly! The lot of the man who sees life truly and thinks about it romantically is Despair. How well we know the cries of that despair! Vanity of vanities, all is vanity! moans the Preacher, when life has at last taught him that Nature will not dance to his moralist-made tunes. Thackeray, scores of centuries later, was still baying the moon in the same terms. Out, out, brief candle! cries Shakespear, in his tragedy of the modern literary man as murderer and witch consulter. Surely the time is past for patience with writers who, having to choose between giving up life in despair and discarding the trumpery moral kitchen scales in which they try to weigh the universe, superstitiously stick to the scales, and spend the rest of the lives they pretend to despise in breaking men's spirits. But even in pessimism there is a choice between intellectual honesty

227

and dishonesty. Hogarth drew the rake and the harlot without glorifying their end. Swift, accepting our system of morals and religion, delivered the inevitable verdict of that system on us through the mouth of the king of Brobdingnag, and described Man as the Yahoo, shocking his superior the horse by his every action. Strindberg, the only genuinely Shakespearean modern dramatist, shews that the female Yahoo, measured by romantic standards, is viler than her male dupe and slave. I respect these resolute tragicomedians: they are logical and faithful: they force you to face the fact that you must either accept their conclusions as valid (in which case it is cowardly to continue living) or admit that their way of judging conduct is absurd. But when your Shakespears and Thackerays huddle up the matter at the end by killing somebody and covering your eyes with the undertaker's handkerchief, duly onioned with some pathetic phrase, as The flight of angels sing thee to thy rest, or Adsum, or the like, I have no respect for them at all: such maudlin tricks may impose on tea-drunkards, not on me.

Besides, I have a technical objection to making sexual infatuation a tragic theme. Experience proves that it is only effective in the comic spirit. We can bear to see Mrs Quickly pawning her plate for love of Falstaff, but not Antony running away from the battle of Actium for love of Cleopatra. Let realism have its demonstration, comedy its criticism, or even bawdry its horselaugh at the expense of sexual infatuation, if it must; but to ask us to subject our souls to its ruinous glamor, to worship it, deify it, and imply that it alone makes our life worth living, is nothing but folly gone mad erotically —a thing compared to which Falstaff's unbeglamored drinking and drabbing is respectable and rightminded. Whoever, then, expects to find Cleopatra a Circe and Caesar a hog in these pages, had better lay down my book and be spared a disappointment.

In Caesar [in *Caesar and Cleopatra*], I have used another character with which Shakespear has been beforehand. But Shakespear, who knew human weaknesses so well, never knew human strength of the Caesarian type. His Caesar is an admitted failure: his Lear is a masterpiece. The tragedy of disillusion and doubt, of the agonized struggle for a foothold on the quicksand made by an acute observation striving to verify its vain attribution of morality and respectability to Nature, of the faithless will and the keen eyes that the faithless will is too weak to blind: all this will give you a Hamlet or a Macbeth, and win you great applause from literary gentlemen; but it will not give you a Julius Caesar. Caesar was not in Shakespear, nor in the epoch, now fast waning, which he inaugurated. It cost Shakespear no pang to write Caesar down for the merely technical purpose of writing Brutus up. And what a Brutus! A perfect Girondin, mirrored in Shakespear's art two hundred years before the real thing came to maturity and talked and stalked and had its head duly cut off by the coarser Antonys and Octaviuses of its time, who at least knew the difference between life and rhetoric.

It will be said that these remarks can bear no other construction than an offer of my Caesar to the public as an improvement on Shakespear's. And in fact, that is their precise purport. But here let me give a friendly warning to those scribes who have so often exclaimed against my criticisms of Shakespear as blasphemies against a hitherto unquestioned Perfection and Infallibility. Such criticisms are no more new than the creed of my Diabolonian Puritan or my revival of the humors of Cool as a Cucumber. Too much surprise at them betrays an acquaintance with Shakespear criticism so limited as not to include even the prefaces of Dr Johnson and the utterances of Napoleon. I have merely repeated in the dialect of my own time and in the light of its philosophy what they said in the dialect and light of theirs. Do not be misled by the Shakespear fanciers who, ever since his own time, have delighted in his plays just as they might have delighted in a particular breed of pigeons if they had never learnt to read. His genuine critics, from Ben Jonson to Mr Frank Harris, have always kept as far on this side idolatry as I.

As to our ordinary uncritical citizens, they have been slowly trudging forward these three centuries to the point which Shakespear reached at a bound in Elizabeth's time. Today most of them have arrived there or thereabouts, with the result that his plays are at last beginning to be performed as he wrote them; and the long line of disgraceful farces, melodramas, and stage pageants which actor-managers, from Garrick and Cibber to our own contemporaries, have hacked out of his plays as peasants have hacked huts out of the Coliseum, are beginning to vanish from the stage. It is a significant fact that the mutilators of Shakespear, who never could be persuaded that Shakespear knew his business better than they, have ever been the most fanatical of his worshippers. The late Augustin Daly thought no price too extravagant for an addition to his collection of Shakespear relics; but in arranging Shakespear's plays for the stage, he proceeded on the assumption that Shakespear was a botcher and he an artist. I am far too good a Shakespearean ever to forgive Henry Irving for producing a version of King Lear so mutilated that the numerous critics who had never read the play could not follow the story of Gloster. Both these idolators of the Bard must have thought Forbes Robertson mad because he restored Fortinbras to the stage and played as much of Hamlet as there was time for instead of as little. And the instant success of the experiment probably altered their minds no further than to make them think the public mad. Mr Benson actually gives the play complete at two sittings, causing the aforesaid numerous critics to remark with naïve surprise that Polonius is a complete and interesting character. It was the age of gross ignorance of Shakespear and incapacity for his works that produced the indiscriminate eulogies with which we are familiar. It was the revival of serious attention to those works that coincided with the movement for giving genuine instead of spurious and silly representations of his plays. So much for Bardolatry!

It does not follow, however, that the right to criticize Shakespear involves the power of writing better plays. And in fact—do not be surprised at my modesty—I do not profess to write better plays. The writing of practicable stage plays does not present an infinite scope to human talent; and the playwrights who magnify its difficulties are humbugs. The summit of their art has been attained again and again. No man will ever write a better tragedy than Lear, a better comedy than Le Festin de Pierre or Peer Gynt, a better opera than Don Giovanni, a better music drama than The Niblung's Ring, or, for the matter of that, better fashionable plays and melodramas than are now being turned out by writers whom nobody dreams of mocking with the word immortal. It is the philosophy, the outlook on life, that changes, not the craft of the playwright. A generation that is thoroughly moralized and patriotized, that conceives virtuous indignation as spiritually nutritious, that murders the murderer and robs the thief, that grovels before all sorts of ideals, social, military, ecclesiastical, royal and divine, may be, from my point of view, steeped in error; but it need not want for as good plays as the hand of man can produce. Only, those plays will be neither written nor relished by men in whose philosophy guilt and innocence, and consequently revenge and idolatry, have no meaning. Such men must rewrite all the old plays in terms of their own philosophy; and that is why, as Stuart-Glennie has pointed out, there can be no new drama without a new philosophy. To which I may add that there can be no Shakespear or Goethe without one either, nor two Shakespears in one philosophic epoch, since, as I have said, the first great comer in that epoch reaps the whole harvest and reduces those who come after to the rank of mere gleaners, or, worse than that, fools who go laboriously through all the motions of the reaper and binder in an empty field. What is the use of writing plays or painting frescoes if you have nothing more to say or shew than was said and shewn by Shakespear, Michael Angelo, and Raphael? If these had not seen things differently, for better or worse, from the dramatic poets of the Townley mysteries, or from Giotto, they could not have produced their works: no, not though their skill of pen and hand had been double what it was. After them there was no need (and *need* alone nerves men to face the persecution in the teeth of which new art is brought to birth) to redo the already done, until in due time, when their philosophy wore itself out, a new race of nineteenth-century poets and critics, from Byron to William Morris, began, first to speak coldly of Shakespear and Raphael, and then to rediscover, in the medieval art which these Renascence masters had superseded, certain forgotten elements which were germinating again for the new harvest. What is more, they began to discover that the technical skill of the masters was by no means superlative. Indeed, I defy anyone to prove that the great epoch makers in fine art have owed their position to their technical skill. It is true that when we search for examples of a prodigious command of language and of graphic line, we can think of nobody better than Shakespear and Michael Angelo. But both of them laid their arts waste for centuries by leading later artists to seek greatness in copying their technique. The technique was acquired, refined on, and elaborated over and over again; but the supremacy of the two great exemplars remained undisputed. As a matter of easily observable fact, every generation produces men of extraordinary special faculty, artistic, mathematical and linguistic, who for lack of new ideas, or indeed of any ideas worth mentioning, achieve no distinction outside music halls and class rooms, although they can do things easily that the great epoch makers did clumsily or not at all. The contempt of the academic pedant for the original artist is often founded on a genuine superiority of technical knowledge and aptitude: he is sometimes a better anatomical draughtsman than Raphael, a better hand at triple counterpoint than Beethoven, a better versifier than Byron. Nay, this is true not merely of pedants, but of men who have produced works of art of some note. If technical facility were the secret of greatness in art, Swinburne would be greater than Browning and Byron rolled into one, Stevenson greater than Scott or Dickens, Mendelssohn than Wagner, Maclise than Madox Brown. Besides, new ideas make their technique as water makes its channel; and the technician without ideas is as useless as the canal constructor without water, though he may do very skilfully what the Mississippi does very rudely. To clinch the argument, you have only to observe that the epoch maker himself has generally begun working professionally before his new ideas have mastered him sufficiently to insist on constant expression by his art. In such cases you are compelled to admit that if he had by chance died earlier, his greatness would have remained unachieved, although his technical qualifications would have been well enough established. The early imitative works of great men are usually conspicuously inferior to the best works of their forerunners. Imagine Wagner dying after composing Rienzi, or Shelley after Zastrozzi! Would any competent critic then have rated Wagner's technical aptitude as high as Rossini's, Spontini's, or Meyerbeer's; or Shelley's as high as Moore's? Turn the problem another way: does anyone suppose that if Shakespear had conceived Goethe's or Ibsen's ideas, he would have expressed them any worse than Goethe or Ibsen? Human faculty being what it is, is it likely that in our time any advance, except in external conditions, will take place in the arts of expression sufficient to enable an author, without making himself ridiculous, to undertake to say what he has to say better than Homer or Shakespear? But the humblest author, and much more a rather arrogant one like myself, may profess to have something to say by this time that neither Homer nor Shakespear said. And the playgoer may reasonably ask to have historical events and persons presented to him in the light of his own time, even though Homer and Shakespear have already shewn them in the light of their time. For example, Homer presented Achilles and Ajax as heroes to the world in the Iliads. In due time came Shakespear, who said, virtually: I really cannot accept this spoilt child and this brawny fool as great men merely because Homer flattered them in playing to the Greek gallery. Consequently we have, in Troilus and Cressida, the verdict of Shakespear's epoch (our own) on the pair. This did not in the least involve any pretence on Shakespear's part to be a greater poet than Homer.

When Shakespear in turn came to deal with Henry V and Julius Caesar, he did so according to his own essentially knightly conception of a great statesman-commander. But in the XIX century comes the German historian Mommsen, who also takes Caesar for his hero, and explains the immense difference in scope between the perfect knight Vercingetorix and his great conqueror Julius Caesar. In this country, Carlyle, with his vein of peasant inspiration, apprehended the sort of greatness that places the true hero of history so far beyond the mere *preux chevalier*, whose fanatical personal honor, gallantry, and self-sacrifice, are founded on a passion for death born of inability to bear the weight of a life that will not grant ideal conditions to the liver. This one ray of perception became Carlyle's whole stock-in-trade; and it sufficed to make a literary master of him. In due time, when Mommsen is an old man, and Carlyle dead, come I, and dramatize the by-this-time familiar distinction in Arms and the Man, with its comedic conflict between the knightly Bulgarian and the Mommsenite Swiss captain. Whereupon a great many playgoers who have not yet read Cervantes, much less Mommsen and Carlyle, raise a shriek of concern for their knightly ideal as if nobody had ever questioned its sufficiency since the middle ages. Let them thank me for educating them so far. And let them allow me to set forth Caesar in the same modern light, taking the platform from Shakespear as he from Homer, and with no thought of pretending to express the Mommsenite view of Caesar any better than Shakespear expressed a view which was not even Plutarchian, and must, I fear, be referred to the tradition in stage conquerors established by Marlowe's Tamerlane as much as to the chivalrous conception of heroism dramatized in Henry V.

From the Preface to *Three Plays for Puritans* (London, 1900).

Postscript: What Is a World Classic?

The request to Shaw, then nearly ninety, that he permit his "meta-biological pentateuch," Back to Methuselah (1921), to be reprinted in the Oxford World's Classics series, and that he supply some additional words to mark the publication, led him to muse about what makes a literary work a world classic.

One of the many summits in the mountain range of human self-conceit is the introduction by an author of his book as a World Classic. He cannot with any decency do it himself. And when he is invited to do so by a publisher whose prestige has been won in serious literature, his gratified compliance must be in the vein of apology and explanation rather than a fanfare of brazen exultation.

Therefore, though I am not addicted to what I have called "the modest cough of the minor poet" I will try to be as apologetic as my nature permits. I have never claimed a greater respect for playmaking than for the commoner crafts; and as every joiner is (or used to be) not only allowed but challenged to produce a masterpiece, I feel no shame in hawking my masterpiece without a cry of stinking fish.

Besides, I do not regard my part in the production of my books and plays as much greater than that of an amanuensis or an organ-blower. An author is an instrument in the grip of Creative Evolution, and may find himself starting a movement to which in his own little person he is intensely opposed. When I am writing a play I never invent a plot: I let the play write itself and shape itself, which it always does even when up to the last moment I do not foresee the way out. Sometimes I do not see what the play was driving at until quite a long time after I have finished it; and even then I may be wrong about it just as any critical third party may.

Take for examples the masterpieces of Dante, of Michael Angelo, and of John Bunyan. The three are beyond all question world

235

classics notwithstanding the legendary fictions and childish superstitions which adapted them to the mental habits of their time,
and still make them intelligible and interesting as stories, but which
also aberrate them again and again into flat absurdity. Dante would
have placed Mahomet in paradise had he realized that his Divine
Comedy, with its ridiculous hell, its Sunday school purgatory, and
its Feminist heaven, was driving at the same world Catholicism as
the Koran. When Michael Angelo painted in the Sistine Chapel the
series of Bible illustrations which culminated in the gigantic fable
of the Last Judgement, he did not know that the series would be
"continued in our next" by Nietzsche in his Thus Spake Zoroaster,
the twain being driven more or less in spite of themselves to shew,
Michael Angelo physically, Nietzsche mentally, not what mankind is
but what it might become. Bunyan, when he was writing The
Pilgrim's Progress, knew very well that he was being moved not by
personal lust to become a Great Writer, but by "grace abounding
to the meanest of sinners." Yet, if when his Holy War was sinking
into the quicksand of sectarian nonsense in which it ends, he had
been shewn a copy of Peer Gynt as an account of what his pilgrim
would come to, or congratulated on having in The Life and Death
of Mr Badman developed to a point not reached by Ibsen until
three hundred years later, he would have been considerably scandalized.

I shall not go on to suggest that Goldsmith's Deserted Village should
be used as a preface to Henry George's Progress and Poverty, and
Keats's Isabella to Marx's Capital; but as a playwright I must not
pass over my predecessor Shakespear. If he could be consulted as
to the inclusion of one of his plays in the present series he would
probably choose his Hamlet because in writing it he definitely
threw over his breadwinning trade of producing potboilers which
he frankly called As You Like It, Much Ado About Nothing, and
What You Will. After a few almost Ibsenish essays in As You Dont
Like It, he took up an old play about the ghost of a murdered
king who haunted his son crying for revenge, with comic relief
provided by the son pretending to be that popular curiosity and
laughing-stock, a village idiot. Shakespear, transfiguring this into a

tragedy on the ancient Athenian level, could not have been quite unconscious of the evolutionary stride he was taking. But he did not see his way clearly enough to save the tons of ink and paper and years of "man's time" that have been wasted, and are still being wasted, on innumerable volumes of nonsense about the meaning of Hamlet, though it is now as clear as daylight. Hamlet as a prehistoric Dane is morally bound to kill his uncle, politically as rightful heir to the usurped throne, and filially as "the son of a dear father murdered" and a mother seduced by an incestuous adulterer. He has no doubt as to his duty in the matter. If he can convince himself that the ghost who has told him all this is really his father's spirit and not a lying devil tempting him to perdition, then, he says, "I know my course."

But when fully convinced he finds to his bewilderment that he cannot kill his uncle deliberately. In a sudden flash of rage he can and does stab at him through the arras, only to find that he has killed poor old Polonius by mistake. In a later transport, when the unlucky uncle poisons not only Hamlet's mother but his own accomplice and Hamlet himself, Hamlet actually does at last kill his enemy on the spur of the moment; but this is no solution of his problem: it cuts the Gordian knot instead of untying it, and makes the egg stand on end only by breaking it. In the soliloquy beginning "Oh what a rogue and peasant slave am I" Shakespear described his moral bewilderment as a fact (he must have learnt it from his own personal development); but he did not explain it, though the explanation was staring him in the face as it stares in mine. What happened to Hamlet was what had happened fifteen hundred years before to Jesus. Born into the vindictive morality of Moses he has evolved into the Christian perception of the futility and wickedness of revenge and punishment, founded on the simple fact that two blacks do not make a white. But he is not philosopher enough to comprehend this as well as apprehend it. When he finds he cannot kill in cold blood he can only ask "Am I a coward?" When he cannot nerve himself to recover his throne he can account for it only by saying "I lack ambition." Had Shakespear plumbed his play to the bottom he would hardly have allowed Hamlet to send Rosencrantz and Guildenstern to their death by a forged death warrant without a moment's scruple.

Two and a half centuries later the same thing occurs to the author of another world classic, Charles Montagu Doughty, who, compared to Shakespear, can be catalogued only as a bigoted simpleton when, undeveloped at the age of 32, he travelled in Arabia. To him the Arabs were dangerous and damned heathens, corrupted by a false religion invented by an imposter named Mahomet who had forged a spurious Bible called the Koran. To defend himself against them he armed himself with a loaded revolver and carried it wherever he went.

The protection seemed very necessary; for the Bedouins were so like himself (or he like them) that they regarded him as a damned infidel; and the fanatically pious among them considered it their religious duty to kill and despoil the Nazarene. Again and again his bags were rifled and the knife was at his throat. Yet with the revolver in his hand and his assailants at his mercy he did not discharge it. Like Hamlet he could not bring himself to judge and kill. Like Shakespear he could not see why: he could only record the simple fact. Yet his travel diary, published long after with the now famous title Arabia Deserta, is a world classic.

This logicless sequel puzzles the student of literature who is trying to find out what qualifies a book to rank as a classic. Doughty, when he began his two years roaming through the Arabian deserts, was what we call an educated English gentleman who had gone through a professional training in medicine. Yet he writes like a child of ten for the most part; and his diary, with scraps of memoranda stuck in anyhow in no order except the order of date, is in no sense a considered work of art. His interests are those of an amateur explorer only; and the comments on Bedouin life, character, and religion, which make his book so readable, change from day to day, from place to place, from meal to meal. On one page all the Bedouins he has known are "a merry crew of squalid wretches, iniquitous, fallacious, and fanatical." Two pages later the Beni Salim are "of gentle and honest manners; and I was never better entertained in nomad menzils." Many of his entertainers were more civilized, tolerant, and sceptical than he. His style is certainly unique; but it suggests the simplicity of a man who had never read a book in his life except the Bible, which he often quotes, less with any artistic appreciation than to shew that its descriptions tally with the facts of eastern life and thought as he found them.

There must have been something majestic or gigantic about the man that made him classic in himself. He was already a poet, for twice in his travel diary he explodes into half a page of prophetic rhapsody; and when he came home he spent the rest of his life in writing immense prophetic epics in blank verse of a Himalayan magnificence and natural eminence that would have made Milton gasp. Small wonder that when the knife was at his throat it got no farther; and when he arrived at the next oasis penniless and in rags, the rulers there clothed him and made those who had robbed him give him back their booty and repay him his stolen money to the last farthing. Englishmen who met him have described him to me as "a mountain of a man"; and extant portraits bear them out as far as portraits can.

It is clear then that in him as in Hamlet-Shakespeare a step in evolution had occurred. * * * What, then, are world classics?

Well, they all try to solve, or at least to formulate, the riddles of creation. In them the Life Force is struggling towards its goal of godhead by incarnating itself in creatures with knowledge and power enough to control nature and circumstances. A classic author has to consider how far he dare go; for though he is writing for the enlightenment of mankind he may not be willing to venture as far as martyrdom for its sake. Descartes burnt one of his books to escape being burnt for having written it. Galileo had to deny what he believed to escape the same fate. The priests forced these alternatives on them not because they did not agree with them, but because they had to govern the people, and the people could be governed only by fictions and miracles, not by the latest steps in science. If the people will not obey their rulers unless they see the blood of St Januarius liquefy, then the priests must work that miracle for them or let them run wild. As long as civilization seems to stand or fall with the belief that God stopped the movement of the sun in its orbit to oblige Joshua as casually as the driver of a tramcar stops his vehicle to pick up a passenger, popes, and emperors must take care that no physicist is allowed to tell the mob that it is the earth that moves round the sun and not the sun round the earth, even when they are entirely convinced that the physicist is right. When I was a municipal councillor I had to connive at bogus miracles, pretending that tubs of soap and water were as magical as the cauldron of Macbeth's witches, because my constituents believed in magic, not in soap and sunshine. It is useless to parrot the old saying that the blood of martyrs is the seed of the Church, and expect scientific heretics to die to advertize their heresies rather than recant to save their lives. Descartes, when he burnt his book, knew that its truths would inevitably be rediscovered and become familiar, and that this would only be retarded by his being burnt for publishing them.

As for me I can write safely on the assumption that Galileo and Descartes knew much more about physics than Moses. But I am not therefore free to publish anything I like. Plays of mine have been banned for many years on grounds injuriously defamatory to myself; and at least one of my books is on the index in Eire, apparently because the heroine does not wear petticoats. The disciples of Pavlov would burn me if they had Torquemada's power. But State intolerance is founded, not now on crude fanaticism, but on the fear that if the people discover that the miracles they believe in are either fables or frauds, and that the scriptures they accept as Divine revelations are questionable in any sentence, they will empty the baby out with the bath water, and defy all religion and all morality. And in fact many of them have done so as far as such defiance is practicable, which is not very far, as disbelief in the Bible story of the ten commandments is no defence against being imprisoned for theft or hanged for murder.

Now it is hardly possible for men engaged daily in the starkly realistic practice of government, which is full of surprises for simpletons, to share the credulities of the crowd. They soon become arch heretics themselves; and as such they persecute heresy only as long as they believe that, as Ibsen put it, society is held together by chain stitched seams which will ravel out if a single stitch is cut. But they find out that this does not in fact happen. When experience taught them that Voltaire could laugh at Habbakuk and call on them to crush the Church as an infamy without immediately bringing down French civilization about their ears they inferred that their own scepticisms could be tolerated safely, and allowed the laws against them to fall into desuetude, without, however, daring to repeal them. It is fairly safe for me personally to fill my books and plays with heresies and even be accepted as a world classic on the strength of them; but it is none the less within quite recent historical memory that the vogue of Voltaire and his fellow-heretic Rousseau's "Get rid of your miracles and the whole world will fall at the feet of Christ" has ended in whole States falling at the feet of Pavlov and Hitler.

The moral of this is that heretical teaching must be made irresistibly attractive by fine art if the heretics are not to starve or burn.

The history of modern thought now teaches us that when we are forced to give up the creeds by their childishness and their conflicts with science we must either embrace Creative Evolution or fall into the bottomless pit of an utterly discouraging pessimism. This happened in dateless antiquity to Ecclesiastes the preacher, and in our own era to Shakespear and Swift. "George Eliot" (Marian Evans) who, incredible as it now seems, was during my boyhood ranked in literature as England's greatest mind, was broken by the fatalism that ensued when she discarded God. In her most famous novel Middlemarch, which I read in my teens and almost venerated, there is not a ray of hope: the characters have no more volition than billiard balls: they are moved only by circumstances and heredity. "As flies to wanton boys are we to the gods: they kill us for their sport" was Shakespear's anticipation of George Eliot. Had Swift seen men as creatures evolving towards godhead he would not have been discouraged into the absurdity of describing them as irredeemable Yahoos enslaved by a government of horses ruling them by sheer moral superiority. Even Ibsen, though his characters, like Shakespear's, reek with volition, perpetrated a tragedy called Ghosts, in which an omnipotent god is discarded for an inevitable syphilis. One of the masters of comedy[1] among my playwright col-

1. St. John Hankin (1860–1909), usually linked with Granville Barker

leagues drowned himself because he thought he was going his father's way like Oswald Alving. Even a mind so keen and powerful as that of Dr Inge has been troubled by the notion that Life cannot survive extremes of temperature, not reach inconceivable heights long after the cooling of the sun makes a good riddance of Yahoo mankind. (The sun, by the way, is getting hotter by the latest guesses.) Discouragement does in fact mean death; and it is better to cling to the hoariest of the savage old creator-idols, however diabolically vindictive than to abandon all hopes in a world of "angry apes," and perish in despair like Shakespear's Timon. Goethe rescued us from this horror with his "Eternal Feminine that draws us forward and upward" which was the first modern manifesto of the mysterious forces in creative evolution. That is what made Faust a world classic.[2] * * *

We are only just discovering that there is such a thing as wishful thinking; but the Creative Evolutionist knows that all thinking is wishful, and that we cannot think until our wishes or fears or cupidities or curiosities create what we call attention. I have known this since my childhood, when somebody shewed me that if I held up my two forefingers in a line from my eyes, I could see two of the nearest when I looked at the farthest, or vice versa, because I had on my two retinas two separate images of everything in sight except the thing I wanted to see. Yet I was conscious of them only when I co-ordinated them. Later on, when I threw over my childish belief in the infallibility of the Bible on discovering that much of it is obsolete or wicked, what struck me most was that the obsolescences and wickednesses had never been hidden from me: they had been staring me in the face all the time. I had simply not thought about them. There must have been an evolutionary growth in my mind which directed my attention to them. Attention is the first symptom of thought. John the Evangelist would have worded it so, had he been born a Victorian.

---

as one of the Edwardian disciples of Shaw.

2. At this point the editor has added, as a concluding paragraph, lines originally published earlier in Shaw's "Postscript."

"Postscript after Twentyfive Years," to the Preface of *Back to Methuselah* (London, 1944).

Index

Moore, George, xii, xvi, xix, 26–29, 41, 103, 213
Moore, Thomas, 136, 233
Morris, William, xii, xvi, xxii, 42, 54–55, 134, 141–42, 157–58, 175, 219, 231
Mozart, Wolfgang Amadeus, 230
Murray, Alma, 124
Mudie, Charles Edward, xv–xvi, 6, 34

Nietzsche, Friedrich Wilhelm, 219, 222, 236
Nordau, Max, xi, xxv
Norris, William Edward, 110–13

Ouida (see Ramée, Mary Louise de la)

Paley, William, 79, 83
Pascal, Blaise, 85
Pater, Walter, xii
Pauli, Charles Paine, 68–69, 71–72
Peele, George, 148
Penrose, Elizabeth (Mrs. Markham), 56
Pinero, Sir Arthur Wing, 203
Plato, 219
Plunkett, Sir Horace, 167
Poe, Edgar Allan, xxiv–xxv, 133, 137–43
Prévost d'Exiles, Antoine François, 105, 213
Priestley, J. B., xxii

Rabelais, François, 104
Raleigh, Sir Walter, 7
Ramée, Mary Louise de la (Ouida), xvi–xvii, 30–32, 33, 38, 213
Raphael, 12, 232
Reeves, Herbert Sims, 124
Rhys, Ernest, 183
Roberts, W., 163
Romanes, George John, 69
Romney, George, 141
Rossetti, Dante Gabriel, 55
Rossini, Gioacchino Antonio, 75, 233
Rousseau, Henri, 73, 241
Rowlandson, Thomas, 141
Rowley, Charles, 190
Ruskin, John, xxii, xxv, xxvii, 40, 42, 47, 55, 140, 175, 189–202

St. Augustine, 214
St. John (the Evangelist), 242
Salisbury, Lord, 31
Salt, Henry S., 125

Sand, George, xii
Savage, Miss Elisa, 68–69, 73–74
Schopenhauer, Arthur, 219, 222
Scott, Sir Walter, xviii, 152, 210, 232
Secker, Martin, 78
Severn, Arthur, 190
Shakespeare, William, x–xi, xii, xiii, xx, xxvi, 7–8, 12, 16, 20, 23–24, 74–75, 85–93, 102, 105, 120, 145, 148–52, 213, 219-22, 225, 227–34, 236–39, 241–42
Shaw, Bernard
    The Admirable Bashville (1902), xxvi, 148–52
    An Unfinished Novel (1887–88; publ. 1958), 3
    Arms and the Man (1894), 234
    Back to Methuselah (1921), 235–42
    Caesar and Cleopatra (1898), xiv, 227–230
    Cashel Byron's Profession (1882), xxvi, 148
    Immaturity (1879; publ. 1930), xix
    Man and Superman (1903), ix, 226
    Major Barbara (1905), xiv, 109
    Mrs. Warren's Profession (1893), xviii, 4
    Pen Portraits and Reviews (1905), ix, xxvii
    Platform and Pulpit (1961), xxvii
    Pygmalion (1912), xvii, xxii
    Saint Joan (1923), xiv
    Table Talk of G.B.S. (1925), 211–15
    Widowers' Houses (1892), xi
Shelley, Mary Godwin, 120
Shelley, Percy Bysshe, xxii–xxiii, 117–26, 132, 219, 223, 232, 233
Smith, Adam, 194
Smollett, Tobias, 54, 139
Sophocles, xxvi
Spontini, Gasparo, 233
Stanfield, Clarkson, 54
Stendhal (see Beyle, Henri)
Sterne, Laurence, 213
Stowe, Harriet Beecher, 119
Strindberg, August, 103, 176
Stevenson, Robert Lewis, 232
Stuart-Glennie, J. S., 231
Swift, Jonathan, 12, 18, 228, 241
Swinburne, Algernon Charles, 136, 232
Synge, John M., xix